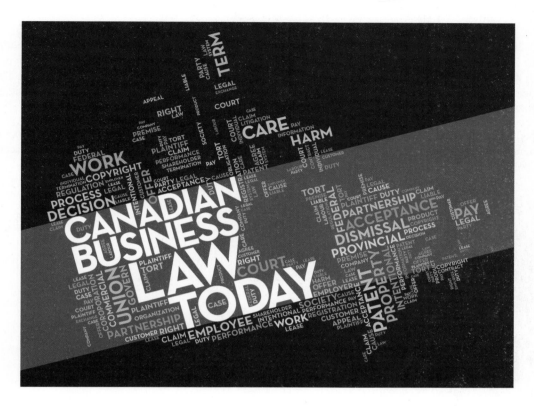

First Edition

Nancy M. Breen
Nova Scotia Community College

Shane A. Ellis
Georgian College

Craig Stephenson
Conestoga College

McGraw Hill Education

Canadian Business Law Today
First Edition

The Internet addresses listed in the text were accurate at the time of publication. The inclusion of a Web site does not indicate an endorsement by the authors or McGraw-Hill Ryerson, and McGraw-Hill Ryerson does not guarantee the accuracy of the information presented at these sites.

ISBN-13: 978-0-07-031006-3
ISBN-10: 0-07-031006-8

1 2 3 4 5 6 7 8 9 10 TCP 1 2 3 4 5 6 0 9 8 7

Care has been taken to trace ownership of copyright material contained in this text; however, the publisher will welcome any information that enables them to rectify any reference or credit for subsequent editions.

Printed and bound in Canada

Portfolio and Program Manager: *Karen Fozard*
Product Manager: *Kevin O'Hearn*
Executive Marketing Manager: *Joy Armitage Taylor*
Product Developer: *Melissa Hudson and Tammy Mavroudi*
Senior Product Team Associate: *Stephanie Giles*
Supervising Editor: *Jeanette McCurdy*
Photo/Permissions Researcher: *Marnie Lamb*
Copy Editor: *Kelli Howey*
Production Coordinator: *Michelle Saddler*
Manufacturing Production Coordinator: *Emily Hickey*
Cover Image and Design: *Dianne Reynolds*
Interior Design: *Dianne Reynolds*
Page Layout: *SPi Global*
Printer: *Transcontinental Printing Group*

ABOUT THE AUTHORS

Nancy Breen

Nancy Breen has been involved in the legal community since her early twenties. After graduating from St. Francis Xavier University (StFX) in 1984, she hit the ground running at a fast-paced law firm as a legal assistant. Over the years, Nancy has worked in numerous law firms as a legal assistant, a consultant, and trainer for lawyers and paralegals and as a senior litigation paralegal. During her tenure as a senior litigation paralegal, she was fortunate to gain courtroom experience by attending a large class-action lawsuit for four months, assisting the lawyers involved in the case. In addition, she has worked on personal injury and large corporate cases over the years. In between positions with law firms, Nancy owned her own business that had several components, primarily as a court reporting service and as a consulting business assisting law firms, small, medium, and large companies, and government organizations.

In 2000, Nancy began teaching at Nova Scotia Community College (NSCC) in Port Hawkesbury, Nova Scotia. Since 2000, Nancy has taught business law in face-to-face, online, and hybrid formats. Her teaching experience in business law and various business courses has led to a passion for the academic editorial process.

Nancy and her husband, Joe, live in Antigonish and Lismore, both located on the Northumberland Strait shoreline of Nova Scotia. Her three children are grown and thriving in their own lives and professional careers, and she has two beautiful little grandchildren. When outside her role at NSCC, Nancy enjoys the company of her family and friends, cottage life, travel, and curling up with a good book.

Shane A. Ellis

Shane Ellis has worked as general counsel, corporate secretary, and VP of legal affairs to various publicly listed and private corporations in the life sciences, aviation, renewable energy, hospitality, manufacturing, construction, and financial sectors. He has had a general law practice and previously taught at Seneca College, Humber College, and Ryerson Polytechnic University. Shane is currently a professor at Georgian College and teaches law courses in Business and Management and in the Automotive Business School of Canada.

Shane's list of academic credentials includes a B.A., J.D., and LL.M., a certificate in mediation, and courses at The Hague Academy of International Law at the International Court of Justice (Netherlands). He is a member of the Bar of Ontario and the Law Society of Upper Canada.

Industry accomplishments include co-authoring a textbook, *Critical Concepts of Canadian Business Law*, and contributing to a legal textbook, *The Rule of Law*. Shane has also presented at conferences on intellectual property and biotechnology.

Craig Stephenson

Craig Stephenson, a recovering lawyer, has a unique blend of formal training and education in various courses in the area of social sciences and law at the university level, as well as practical teaching experience at the college and university level. Craig graduated from McMaster University in 1987 with a B.A. in social science. From 1988 to 1991 he attended University of Toronto Law School, graduating with his LL.B. He was called to the bar in 1992.

From 1993 until 1998, Craig ran a successful sole practitioner legal practice in Brampton, Ontario. He practised in a variety of areas including corporate and small business law, real estate law, estate law, employment law, administrative law, tort law, small claims court law, criminal law, and family law.

In 1998, Craig decided to devote himself to teaching full time and since then has taught law courses at both the college and university level, in conventional classroom formats and blended online hybrids. In addition to Conestoga College, he has taught at Mohawk College, Sheridan College, McMaster University, and the University of Windsor. Craig has also done private corporate training through the Canadian Institute of Traffic and Transportation in the area of transportation law.

Currently, he teaches and oversees the law courses in the Police Foundations and Protection, Security and Investigation programs at Conestoga College in Kitchener, Ontario.

BRIEF CONTENTS

CONTENTS

PREFACE

Business practices constantly evolve and respond to shifts in society, a process that in turn is reflected in the ongoing changes that occur in the laws and rules by which business must operate. The law evolves depending on trends in society, decisions of the courts, and changes in legislation at the federal, provincial/territorial, and municipal levels. To make prudent business decisions, businesspeople must be aware of these changes and the significant implications of the law for their business. As our society changes, it becomes critical for businesspeople to have an idea of what affects them and their business, how to avoid the hazards they may encounter, and the importance of obtaining legal advice when necessary. By having a basic understanding of the fundamental terms and concepts of Canadian business law and the legal issues raised during a transaction, the businessperson will be better prepared to manage risk and participate in the discussions, negotiations, questions, and other events that may transpire.

In this text, students will cover the fundamental topics of Canadian business law. Topics such as the court and legal system, tort law, contract law, employment law, property law, and business organization will be introduced and discussed. The idea behind the topic coverage is to expose students to the areas of law that are commonly encountered, not only by those who are engaged in business activities but by everyone as they negotiate their way through everyday life. The hope is that by exposing students to the specifics of an area of business law as well as to the language and methodology of the law and legal system itself, they will become better able to participate in commercial activities and understand their rights, obligations, and risks. The text has been set at an introductory level for college students, and for many this will be the only law-related course they take. It is hoped that by the end of a course featuring this text a student will have gained the ability to recognize how the law has been applied to a situation, even if they don't agree with the outcome.

To assist students, Learning Objectives are set out at the beginning of each chapter to highlight the primary issues that will be discussed. The relevant Learning Objectives are referenced in the body of the chapter as legal concepts are explained, as well as in the For Review activities at the conclusion of the chapter to support the students' review. Throughout, definitions drawn from the body of the text are provided in the margin to reinforce key issues. Diagrams, tables, illustrations, and links to relevant websites have been included to help make the material more accessible. The Did You Know, Case Study, and Legal Scenario boxes present throughout the chapters provide additional information and illustrate legal issues. The For Review section at the conclusion of each chapter provides questions and activities designed to help students review and reinforce the material covered. This is followed by cases offering an opportunity for students to apply the legal concepts and principles learned in analyzing a fact situation.

FEATURES FOUND IN FIRST CANADIAN EDITION

Feature Boxes

DID YOU KNOW?

The **Did You Know?** feature box provides detailed information about a specific legal matter or topic.

LEGAL SCENARIO

The **Legal Scenario** feature box provides a fact situation illustrating a legal issue.

 ### CASE STUDY

The **Case Study** feature box provides the results of a court's decision that highlights a particular legal issue.

SCENARIO CHALLENGE!

The **Scenario Challenge** feature box provides brief fact situations to assist students in reinforcing the legal issues being examined.

Key Terms are bolded and listed throughout the text and repeated at the end of the text with page references.

End-of-Chapter Material Each chapter includes an extensive selection of assignment material, including Questions, Activities, and Cases for Discussion. Our problem and case material facilitates class discussions.

UNIQUELY CANADIAN PERSPECTIVES AND CONTENT

CHAPTER 1   A look at the Canadian legal system—the areas, sources, and types of law in Canada, how laws are made in Canada, and the Canadian court system.

CHAPTER 2   Designed specifically to examine the resolution of disputes in Canada and how the Canadian civil courts operate.

CHAPTER 3   A view on tort law through Canadian legal cases.

CHAPTER 4   A look at professional liability, product liability and manufacturers, and occupiers' liability through Canadian legal cases and Canadian government regulations.

CHAPTER 5   The necessary elements for the formation of contracts in the Canadian legal context, including the increasingly common electronic contract.

CHAPTER 6   Identifying and dealing with the common problems that arise in contract formation both traditional and online, highlighting how they are dealt with in Canadian common law and public policy.

CHAPTER 7   Examining how the law determining how a contract ends developed from a common law perspective using cases from other common law countries as well as from Canada.

CHAPTER 8   A look at Canada's labour laws and Canadian unions.

CHAPTER 9   Legal issues and terminology relating to owning property in Canada unique to various provinces and territories, including the protection of intellectual property in Canada.

CHAPTER 10   A Canadian perspective on the forms of doing business in the provinces and territories with their various legal requirements and duties, illustrated with decisions from Canadian courts.

CHAPTER 11   An examination of Canadian financial institutions and the control exercised by the different levels of Canadian governments on commercial transactions and Canadian creditors' and debtors' rights.

MARKET LEADING TECHNOLOGY

Learn without Limits

McGraw-Hill Connect® is an award-winning digital teaching and learning platform that gives students the means to better connect with their coursework, with their instructors, and with the important concepts that they will need to know for success now and in the future. With Connect, instructors can take advantage of McGraw-Hill's trusted content to seamlessly deliver assignments, quizzes, and tests online. McGraw-Hill Connect is a learning platform that continually adapts to each student, delivering precisely what they need, when they need it, so class time is more engaging and effective. Connect makes teaching and learning personal, easy, and proven.

Connect Key Features

SmartBook®

As the first and only adaptive reading experience, SmartBook is changing the way students read and learn. SmartBook creates a personalized reading experience by highlighting the most important concepts a student needs to learn at that moment in time. As a student engages with SmartBook, the reading experience continuously adapts by highlighting content based on what each student knows and doesn't know. This ensures that he or she is focused on the content needed to close specific knowledge gaps, while it simultaneously promotes long-term learning.

Connect Insight®

Connect Insight is Connect's new one-of-a-kind visual analytics dashboard—now available for instructors—that provides at-a-glance information regarding student performance, which is immediately actionable. By presenting assignment, assessment, and topical performance results together with a time metric that is easily visible for aggregate or individual results, Connect Insight gives instructors the ability to take a just-in-time approach to teaching and learning, which was never before available. Connect Insight presents data that helps instructors improve class performance in a way that is efficient and effective.

Simple Assignment Management

With Connect, creating assignments is easier than ever, so instructors can spend more time teaching and less time managing.

- Assign SmartBook learning modules.
- Instructors can edit existing questions and create their own questions.
- Draw from a variety of text specific questions, resources, and test bank material to assign online.
- Streamline lesson planning, student progress reporting, and assignment grading to make classroom management more efficient than ever.

Smart Grading

When it comes to studying, time is precious. Connect helps students learn more efficiently by providing feedback and practice material when they need it, where they need it.

- Automatically score assignments, giving students immediate feedback on their work and comparisons with correct answers.
- Access and review each response; manually change grades or leave comments for students to review.
- Track individual student performance—by question, assignment, or in relation to the class overall—with detailed grade reports.
- Reinforce classroom concepts with practice tests and instant quizzes.
- Integrate grade reports easily with Learning Management Systems including Blackboard, D2L, and Moodle.

Instructor Library

The Connect Instructor Library is a repository for additional resources to improve student engagement in and out of the class. It provides all the critical resources instructors need to build their course.

- Access Instructor resources.
- View assignments and resources created for past sections.
- Post your own resources for students to use.

Instructor Resources

- Instructor's Manual [including suggested teaching guide with "flipped classroom" structure]
- Computerized Test Bank
- Microsoft® PowerPoint® Lecture Slides

Superior Learning Solutions and Support

The McGraw-Hill Education team is ready to help instructors assess and integrate any of our products, technology, and services into your course for optimal teaching and learning performance. Whether it's helping your students improve their grades, or putting your entire course online, the McGraw-Hill Education team is here to help you do it. Contact your Learning Solutions Consultant today to learn how to maximize all of McGraw-Hill Education's resources.

For more information, please visit us online: http://www.mheducation.ca/he/solutions

ACKNOWLEDGMENTS

Nancy Breen

I would like to thank my husband, Joe Mendolia, who was a valuable support in his encouragement, inspiration, and review/comments after finishing a chapter. I would also like to thank my daughter, Hillary MacEachern, who provided a lot of encouragement but especially an honest and critical appraisal of the chapters from the perspective of a recent university student. I would also like to thank my daughter Meghan MacEachern and son Daniel MacEachern for all their support in this project.

Shane A. Ellis

I would like to acknowledge the invaluable contribution made by students, whose comments and suggestions over the years have helped to frame the format of this text. As well, I would like to thank the dedicated staff at McGraw-Hill, Melissa Hudson and Kevin O'Hearn, for their encouragement and unflagging support through the various stages of putting the text and instructors' material together. Finally, an enormous thank you to my spouse, Serena, and children, Ariana and Kielan, for their input, and never-ending patience and good humour, that supported me throughout this project.

Craig Stephenson

I would like to acknowledge my wife Mary Jo and son Sam, whose patience with my disappearing into the basement to work on this project knew no bounds. Without their support this text could not have been accomplished.

Reviewers

Bob Bircher	*Camosun College*
Daniel Le Dressay	*Langara College*
Mike Bozzo	*Mohawk College*
Odette Coccola	*Camosun College*
Peter Holden	*Capilano University*
Ronald Morrison	*Kwantlan Polytechnic University*
Frederick Koch	*Sheridan College*
Debbie Roberts	*Georgian College*
Bill Farr	*Red Deer College*
Delano Antoine	*Seneca College*
Daryll Toews	*Red River College*
Lavinia Inbar	*Fleming College*
David Simmonds	*Assiniboine Community College*
Barbara Chapple	*St. Clair College*
Todd Rose	*College of the North Atlantic*
Patti Ann Sullivan	*Centennial College*

CHAPTER 1

BUSINESS LAW

Learning Objectives

After reading this chapter the student will:

LO 1.1	Understand the law's role in society
LO 1.2	Understand how the law plays a part in business
LO 1.3	Understand the importance of protecting a business with risk management
LO 1.4	Identify how ethics plays a role in law and in business
LO 1.5	Identify the types, areas, and sources of law
LO 1.6	Understand how laws are made
LO 1.7	Understand the court system
LO 1.8	Define Alternative Dispute Resolution (ADR) and its benefits

HELP!

As a businessperson, you may experience any of these scenarios:

- HELP! I just started to work in a business and I'm not sure what I need to know about the law.

- HELP! I hear about lawsuits all the time. How do I protect my business? How can I avoid these risks?

- HELP! After hearing about all these business scandals, I'm wondering just how ethical a business really needs to be.

- HELP! My boss said we need to file a claim against a business that hasn't paid its bill. How do I do that? What do I need to know and do?

- HELP! What are government regulations and what do I need to know about them?

LO 1.1   1.1 Law in Today's Society

Laws are made by the people and for the people. Laws exist to help protect society and keep lawlessness from occurring. All types of **laws** provide regulations and rules about how we conduct ourselves and how businesses conduct their business affairs. Additionally, laws help direct our social policy to ensure a fair society. Laws help countries achieve stability, which creates that country's success on many levels—political, social, cultural, and economic.

> **Laws**—the rules of conduct that protect the rights of individuals and businesses.

© Chris Ryan / age fotostock

In a democratic society, laws are made to protect the majority of society. For example, laws under the *Criminal Code of Canada* prevent acts such as assault, impaired driving, kidnapping. or murder. In the world of business, there are many federal, provincial, and municipal laws that protect businesses and the public from harm. The *Personal Information Protection and Electronic Documents Act (PIPEDA)*, for example, protects the information of the public and also provides guidelines for businesses surrounding their legal and ethical responsibilities to the individuals they interact with, like employees and clients.

DID YOU KNOW?

What Is PIPEDA?

PIPEDA (Personal Information Protection and Electronic Documents Act) applies to the collection, use, or disclosure of personal information in the course of a commercial activity. Organizations covered by the Act must obtain an individual's consent when they collect, use, or disclose the individual's personal information. The individual has a right to access personal information held by an organization and to challenge its accuracy, if need be. Personal information can be used only for the purposes for which it was collected. If an organization is going to use it for another purpose, consent must be obtained again. Individuals should also be assured that their information will be protected by appropriate safeguards.

Under *PIPEDA,* the definition of organization includes an association, partnership, person, or trade union.

A **Privacy Tool Kit for Businesses and Organizations** can be found at https://www.priv.gc.ca/information/pub/guide_org_e.asp (accessed November 2015).

Source: Office of the Privacy Commissioner of Canada.

It is important to develop a **privacy plan (or policy)** for your business, to make your employees aware of their privacy rights and those of your customers and to communicate this information to reduce the risk of a breach of private information. The site in the link above provides resources you can use to create a business that takes its information security seriously.

Privacy Plan or Policy—a list of rules of conduct for employees relating to the creation, usage, control, and maintenance of information.

DID YOU KNOW?

The items a business should put in their company's privacy policy

A business dealing with another business or an individual dealing with a business will feel more secure if they know that their information will be kept private. You may be the person tasked with drawing up a company privacy policy, perhaps in a draft form before it is sent on to the company's lawyer. What do you think might go into a company privacy policy? Would you consider these items?

- A pledge to protect the privacy of the customer/client;
- What data/information is collected and how it is collected;
- Type of information collected automatically (via cookies on a website, for example);
- Notification if your data/information will be provided to a third party and, if so, why;
- Explanation for the sharing of information with "trusted partners" for certain purposes, such as your address for a delivery or courier service, or the sharing of information because it is required by law (e.g., a subpoena);
- Assurances and details on how your information is being kept secure;
- An "opt-out" provision so customers and clients can unsubscribe to your company or its website;
- Multiple contacts for the contact information—telephone number(s), email, and postal address; and
- Date the policy becomes effective.
- Don't forget when writing a company policy for the public to:
  - Be clear and concise—don't use jargon or industry-specific language;
  - Focus on keeping the language simple and direct;
  - Make the policy easy to find;

- ◦ Research standard practices of similar companies; and
- ◦ Obtain a privacy trust seal from a well-recognized trust service provider such as TRUSTe or Trust Guard to build client confidence.

Source: Virginia "Ginny" Edwards, Esq.

CASE STUDY

Randall v. Nubodys Fitness Centres (2010 FC 681)

Randall, an employee of a not-for-profit organization, had taken advantage of a co-pay program at Nubodys Fitness Centre. Randall's employer, Feed Nova Scotia, would pay for 50 percent of his membership. Well into his fitness membership and while at a staff meeting, Randall's supervisor talked to the employees about the corporate gym membership and employee participation. During the course of this meeting, the supervisor indicated the number of times various employees had used the fitness centre. Although Randall did not mention his discomfort at this disclosure about his fitness participation, he did contact a representative of Nubodys via email. He was later called into his supervisor's office and was advised that the employer required the frequency of visits to Nubodys and had Randall, under duress, sign a release form to disclose this information to his employer.

Later, Randall left Feed Nova Scotia and continued to inquire at Nubodys about their privacy rules and procedures. He finally made a complaint to the Privacy Commissioner of Canada under *PIPEDA*, alleging the failure of Nubodys to protect his privacy. The Privacy Commissioner ruled that the respondent, Nubodys Fitness Centre, disclosed information to Mr. Randall's employer and that there was a breach of *PIPEDA* as Nubodys did not have a consent form and should not have released the frequency of Mr. Randall's attendance at the gym and that Mr. Randall's complaint was well-founded. The Commissioner then provided recommendations to Nubodys regarding the release of personal information and changes to their internal policy.

The matter then went to the Federal Court of Canada, which found that there was a breach of privacy but that no losses were incurred by Mr. Randall and that Nubodys had properly remedied the issue by changing their internal policies.

LO 1.2 **1.2** Law and the World of Business

As you know from your other business courses, the world of business is complex. There are rules, regulations, processes, and procedures that a person needs to know in order to be successful in their field of business. As a businessperson, it is very important to know about the law and the different areas of the law in order to minimize the risks that can occur. For example, if someone slips and falls outside your business, how should you handle it? Should you call your lawyer? Do you even have a lawyer?

Business law is just one area of law; it has various aspects, and many are even intertwined. In this textbook we will be looking at the components of the law that a businessperson should have some reasonable idea of so they can make informed decisions and know when they might be in trouble and require legal advice.

Business Law—all the laws that are created in order to form and run a business.

From the moment a businessperson (or -persons) forms a business, throughout the life of the business and possibly to the completion of the business, laws are in place to protect the business, the owner, and the public. Laws also guide the businessperson in the proper way to conduct the business, such as sending the GST or HST that is collected from sales to the government in a timely manner.

DID YOU KNOW?

That documentation is EVERYTHING in protecting you and/or your business

Many lawsuits fall flat on their face when required to produce evidence or documentation to back up their claim. In fact, most cases never see a courtroom but, instead, will "settle out of court." This often means that one side in the case will be advised or will realize that their claim is not as strong as they had first thought or hoped. In fact, they might be at risk of having a more expensive situation on their hands if they continue down the slippery slope of the lawsuit.

Let's consider some instances where a business would not have critical documentation to protect their interest to the point they could lose a lawsuit or have to settle out of court and pay considerable money. These instances might include not documenting the following:

- The circumstances around a slip and fall—weather conditions, what was done to the property prior to the accident, photographs, witnesses, a detailed account of any conversation with the injured person.
- The circumstances and attempts to help an employee who has exhibited psychological issues that would require them to be removed from their job. How many attempts? What did they consist of? Copies of letters to the employee outlining the issues and consequences.
- The circumstances of an altercation between a student and a teacher. What happened in the period of time prior to the altercation? Was there any previous misconduct? Was there counselling? If so, when?
- Expenditures, payroll information, income, registration of the business, and other items that would be required by the federal or provincial governments.

As you can see, the law can be a great help to society and to businesses to protect their rights and ability to do business. However, it is the responsibility of each business to understand its obligations to the public, its customers/clients, employees, and society in general, and when in doubt to obtain the services of a lawyer.

In order to conduct a business properly, a business owner must understand the importance of risk management and how a businessperson can protect their business, employees, and customers from actions that could damage them.

LO 1.3   # 1.3 Law and Risk Management

James Steidl / Shutterstock.com

One reason why businesspeople take a business law class is to understand how they can stay out of trouble. Let's take this idea outside the business world for a moment. In our personal lives, we know that we should never drink and drive. This rule is set by law and there are repercussions if we do drink and drive and are caught, which may include a fine, the loss of our licence, jail time, or other penalties based on a number of factors.

In the world of business, the same rules apply; the law is set and a business must follow the law in order to avoid risk and harm to itself or others. If, for example, a business doesn't manage hazardous materials properly, there may be ramifications based on a hazardous materials law (set out by each province) and the business may be penalized in a number of ways including but not limited to a financial fine or penalty, procedural changes, or a mandated business closure, depending on the extent of the damage caused by the hazardous materials. A business may take the risk of not getting caught by dumping hazardous materials anyway; however, strong business management means knowing and understanding the risks and managing them legally and ethically.

Risk management focuses on the actions of a business and the knowledge of the law so that it will avoid consequences that affect the welfare of the business. Let's look at an example of a situation where risky actions hurt a business to the point that it went bankrupt.

Risk Management—a positive business management practice that realizes and assesses the risks associated with the activities of the business.

LEGAL SCENARIO

One decision and it all went up in...snow!

Robert Miller sat in his office at Fluffy Snow Resort and looked at the phone cradled in his hand. He could not believe that everything he worked for would be gone. His lawyer had just called and informed him that the decision of the provincial Supreme Court had been given.

Miller recalls the day he made the decision to not listen to his manager of operations when he was advised that his parking area near a potential avalanche area should be closed and a new area created in a safer location. The cost of constructing a new parking area was significant and Miller thought they could do the construction the following summer and not interrupt the resort during its busy season.

Unfortunately for Fluffy Snow Resort and for Rob Miller, his shareholders, and his employees, an avalanche occurred injuring 27 people and destroying over 50 cars. The lawsuits began and Fluffy Snow Resort's insurance company paid millions of dollars to the injured. Soon all of the financial reserves of the company were depleted.

Miller had to inform his shareholders of the Court's decision and lay off all the employees of the resort. It was a disaster and Miller wished he had managed this risk better. Fluffy Snow Resort, a small ski resort, had to declare bankruptcy because of the decision of its owner.

LO 1.4   1.4   Business Ethics and the Law

Merriam-Webster's Online Dictionary defines *ethics* as "...rules of behavior based on ideas about what is morally good and bad..."

Source: By permission. From Merriam-Webster's Collegiate® Dictionary, 11th Edition © 2016 by Merriam-Webster, Inc. (www.Merriam-Webster.com).

Business ethics involves the way a business behaves, and encompasses the moral decisions made by its **stakeholders**. More and more we hear about unethical practices, behaviour, and decisions by owners, officers, employees, officials, and other stakeholders of a business. The law is very involved in the ethical decisions of a business, and decisions made that are harmful to customers, employees, or society can end the reputation and welfare of any business.

> **Business Ethics**—the way a business behaves; moral decisions made by the stakeholders of a business.

> **Stakeholders**—people and groups that are directly and indirectly involved in the business such as employees, shareholders, suppliers, and charitable organizations.

Business decisions must take into account what is good for those affected by the business, such as employees, shareholders, suppliers, customers, and society in general. If a company makes an unethical decision, it can affect the lives of everyone involved in the business if the repercussions are severe. Decision makers at Enron, for example, a large conglomerate, made numerous unethical decisions that destroyed the company and, in turn, left their employees unemployed and their shareholders with significant financial losses. Even smaller businesses face decisions on ethical dilemmas, sometimes on a daily basis. What would some of those decisions be? Let's take a look:

DID YOU KNOW?

Some ethical decisions that a business may have to make in the business world:

- How to handle a sexual harassment complaint by an employee in a way that does not hurt the business yet ensures the employee is cared for.
- How to submit information to Canada Revenue Agency regarding its taxes to maximize financial profits while at the same time following tax rules.
- How to present information provided to shareholders in the annual report in a way that allows the numbers to reflect the significant work of the business but that does not skew the data.
- How to present inaccurate information regarding the safety of a product that was just uncovered in testing in a way that ensures the public is safe yet at the same time does not jeopardize upcoming shareholder meetings.
- How to manage a conflict of interest when a new applicant for a manager job happens to be a best friend.
- How to listen to instructions from a chief executive officer when the instructions are unethical.

Knowing and managing risk when making decisions by understanding the guidelines, rules, regulations, and laws of an industry will help in the success of a business. Being a business owner is a huge responsibility and it is important that the business owner be aware of the ethical and legal ramifications of each decision. However scary that may be, there is always a support team surrounding a business, including legal counsel, management, human resources, and other in-house or external resources to help guide those at the helm who are propelling the business forward.

LO 1.5   1.5   Types, Areas, and Sources of Law in Canada

One of the more confusing parts of studying or having knowledge of the law is the types of law, the areas of law, and where law comes from. It is important to understand in what area you may require legal assistance when you are or potentially could be involved in a legal issue. Because there are two types of law, several areas of law, and two major sources of law, it can make the entire concept of law a bit tricky. Let's look first at the two types of law.

Two Types of Law

Public Law

When a businessperson considers an issue, a dispute, or a rule regarding the relationship between themselves and society, they must think about public law. **Public law** includes areas of law such as criminal law, administrative law, and constitutional law. We'll look at these areas of law later in this chapter.

Public Law—sets the rules for the relationship between the person(s)/organization and society.

Private Law

When a businessperson is engaged in **private law**, this refers to the relationship between the individual and another individual, organization/business, or individuals. This is where you would find lawsuits. These rules of engagement could involve a dispute, a harm done to someone or their property, or a breach of an agreement between individuals or organizations/businesses. In the upcoming chapters, we will be examining in detail private law and how it impacts individuals and businesses. It is the area that most businesses seek legal advice on.

> **Private Law**—sets the rules of engagement between individuals. Also called *civil law*.

Areas of Public Law

Public law is divided into four distinct areas: criminal law, constitutional law, administrative law, and tax law. Municipal, provincial/territorial, and federal governments have laws that specifically govern their jurisdiction, so when issues or disputes arise between an individual or organization and the government, they are required to resolve the dispute.

For businesses and organizations, public law dictates what the business or individual can do, what they cannot do, the governing body that makes those decisions, and the process that happens when there is a dispute. For a businessperson, the key to success in an organization embroiled in a legal dispute is to know what the legislation allows or prohibits your business to do—and, further, when you have a question to know when it is best to obtain legal advice.

Now, let's take a brief look at the four areas of public law.

Criminal Law

When an individual or an organization breaks a law, there are serious implications. Simply put, **criminal law** deals with a set of rules such as the *Criminal Code of Canada* that individuals and organizations must obey. If they do not, then there is a dispute between that individual or organization and the organization that will prosecute (i.e., the Crown prosecutor). Criminal law is designed to protect society from crimes such as assault, battery, theft, identity theft, fraud, and murder.

> **Criminal Law**—the area of law where a defendant is charged with a crime and the lawyer who prosecutes the accused (the Crown prosecutor) brings the defendant to trial. The Crown prosecutor must prove beyond a reasonable doubt that the defendant is guilty of the crime(s).

While businesses and organizations don't routinely deal with disputes concerning some of the above examples of crimes, they must be very aware of corporate crimes against their organization and within their organization.

© Design Pics/PunchStock

DID YOU KNOW?

White-Collar Crimes Today

There are many types of white-collar crimes—criminal acts that affect individuals and organizations and that are caused by individuals or organizations. Let's look at some examples:

Ponzi and pyramid schemes—the old adage "if it sounds too good to be true, it probably is" sums up Ponzi schemes. A Ponzi scheme happens when a high-return investment is promised but can't be realistically met on an ongoing basis although the perpetrator(s) manipulates the funds so that it looks like it can. Initially, high dividends are paid to the first group of investors (so they can spread the word) but the deal falls apart when the con artist leaves with the money of the investors or runs out of targets.

Money laundering is the process by which criminals conceal or disguise the proceeds of their crimes or convert those proceeds into goods and services. It allows criminals to infuse their illegal money into the stream of commerce, thus corrupting financial institutions and the money supply, thereby giving criminals unwarranted economic power.

Tax evasion is when individuals or organizations do not pay their just taxes.

Identity theft is when an individual or organization's financial integrity is compromised because their financial information has been stolen. The RCMP website has interesting information on identity theft: http://www.rcmp-grc.gc.ca/scams-fraudes/id-theft-vol-eng.htm.

Kickbacks and bribery occur when an improper payment (cash and/or a favour) is made to an influential or decision-making person in return for help.

Bankruptcy fraud is when an individual or organization attempts to not pay their debts (but may have the financial ability to do so) by claiming bankruptcy.

Source: Adapted from U.S. Department of Justice, "White-Collar Crime," http://www.fbi.gov/about-us/investigate/white_collar.

SCENARIO CHALLENGE!

Which activities would constitute a criminal activity?

- A paper products salesperson takes a purchasing manager on an all-expenses-paid golfing weekend.
- A business or individual transfers land and equipment to another related person before declaring bankruptcy.
- A business or individual declares property that they do not own in a fire insurance claim.
- A business owner intentionally "forgets" to tell their accountant about selling a piece of equipment.
- An employee tells a friend about an undisclosed upcoming merger of their company with a larger company resulting in the shares becoming more valuable.

Constitutional Law

Constitutional law involves issues between our *Charter of Rights and Freedoms* or the *Constitution Act* and individuals or organizations. This is a specialized area of law where cases, if deemed to be important to the citizens of Canada, often appear before the Supreme Court of Canada.

It also limits the exercise of governmental power over individuals through the protection of human rights and fundamental freedoms. An example of this would be the right to wear religious symbols in the workplace.

 CASE STUDY

Saskatchewan (Human Rights Commission) v. Whatcott (2013 SCC 11, [2013] 1 SCR 467)

In the case of *Saskatchewan v. Whatcott*, the *Charter of Rights and Freedoms*, in particular freedom of religion and freedom of expression, was examined.

In 2001 and 2002, Whatcott distributed flyers in the mailboxes of homes in Saskatoon containing homophobic messages. The Saskatchewan Human Rights Tribunal found these flyers constituted hate speech and were contrary to Saskatchewan's human rights legislation. Saskatchewan Court of Queen's Bench upheld this finding. The case was appealed to the Saskatchewan Court of Appeal, and this court found that the flyers could not be considered hate publications because the issues contained in the flyers were controversial and any speech regarding controversial issues should be protected regardless of its content. The Saskatchewan Human Rights Commission appealed to the Supreme Court of Canada. Whatcott argued that it was unconstitutional and breached his right to freedom of religion and freedom of expression and that the provincial provision was unjustified.

The Supreme Court of Canada found that the hate speech provision was constitutional and justified. In its unanimous decision, the Court looked at hate speech as harmful to society and that the provisions provided reasonable limits.

Administrative Law

As our society becomes more complex, more regulations are required. For example, in today's global economy the shipment of goods from one country to another has many legal regulations. As a result, countries must use regulators such as Transport Canada, which regulates the companies transporting goods (and people) over air, land, and sea.

Administrative law is important for businesses because each business belongs to an industry that has a group of laws and regulations—municipally, provincially, federally, and perhaps internationally—that must be adhered to.

Each organization below creates rules to maintain and regulate any businesses or organizations that are part of their specific industry. For example, the Canadian Radio-television and Telecommunications Commission governs radio stations, television stations, and any other business or organization that is involved in the radio or television industry.

Here are some examples of regulators, tribunals, and boards that would impact organizations across Canada:

- Alcohol and gaming commissions (provincial)
- Securities Commission (provincial and federal)
- Canadian Radio-television and Telecommunications Commission (federal)
- Environmental review boards (provincial and federal)
- Human rights tribunals (provincial and federal)
- Energy boards (federal and provincial)
- Farm loan boards (provincial)
- Labour relations boards (provincial)
- Zoning commissions (municipal)
- Postsecondary institutions (provincial)

LEGAL SCENARIO

Infractions and Repercussions

When the Ontario Liquor Inspector entered the premises of Ye Olde Tavern at 11:00 p.m. on a Friday, he knew he would be writing some fines. As he looked around the local college's watering hole, he could see immediately the following infractions:

- Overcrowding
- Removal of alcohol from the premises
- Unauthorized persons behind the bar
- Encouraged immoderate consumption
- Underage patrons.

Because the Ontario Alcohol and Gaming Commission is a regulator and is bound by a set of administrative rules, the Inspector has to go through a process in order to fine the establishment with the list of what they have done wrong and the penalty. In this case, the Ontario Alcohol and Gaming Commission could shut Ye Olde Tavern for 21 days or the fine can be appealed to the Ontario Alcohol and Gaming Commission Appeal Board.

As you can see, there are several groups that might have a direct impact on a business or organization. In Chapter 8, you will see the importance of human rights commissions/boards/tribunals in the area of employment law.

So what happens when a business is dealing in the area of administrative law and has an issue? Each commission/board/tribunal would have a process that the organization would follow in order to have its issue resolved.

Tax Law

The Tax Court of Canada is a superior court in which individuals and companies may litigate with the Government of Canada on matters arising under legislation over which the Court has exclusive original jurisdiction. The bulk of the appeals to the Court relate to income tax, goods and services tax, and employment insurance.

Source: http://cas-ncr-nter03.cas-satj.gc.ca/portal/page/portal/tcc-cci_Eng/About.

When an individual or organization has an issue with their federal income tax and, in particular, a decision of the CRA (Canada Revenue Agency), for example, it can be decided before the tax court. The Tax Court of Canada hears and determines appeals and references from the following:

- *Income Tax Act*
- *Employment Insurance Act* (formerly the *Unemployment Insurance Act*)
- Part IX of the *Excise Tax Act* (GST)
- *Canada Pension Plan*
- *Old Age Security Act*
- *Petroleum and Gas Revenue Tax Act*
- *Cultural Property Export and Import Act*
- *Customs Act* (Part V.1)
- *Air Travellers Security Charge Act*
- *Excise Act, 2001*
- *Softwood Lumber Products Export Charge Act, 2006*
- *War Veterans Allowance Act*
- *Civilian War-related Benefits Act*
- Section 33 of the *Veterans Review and Appeal Board Act*

Source: *Tax Court of Canada Act*, Section 12, http://laws-lois.justice.gc.ca/eng/acts/T-2/page-2.html#h-5.

Individuals and organizations can represent themselves. However, in complex tax issues it is always prudent to obtain the advice—and, if necessary, representation—of a tax lawyer.

Civil Law

Private (civil) law deals with disputes between individuals where one party has been harmed or injured and is seeking compensation. An example of this would be a slip and fall outside of a business. Civil or private law is also called tort law. Civil/private/tort law has to do with an injury that a person, persons, or organization commits on another person, persons, or organization. The person/persons/organization who is injured is called the *plaintiff*, and they sue the person who injured them. The person/persons/organization who is being sued is called the *defendant*. Cases involving civil/private/tort law are held in the superior court of the province.

Source: http://www.justice.gc.ca/eng/csj-sjc/just/02.html, accessed November 2015.

In some situations, someone engages in criminal activity under public law and then is sued because of damage that is done because of that activity to another person under private law. For example, a person can be charged and convicted of fraud, an offence under the *Criminal Code of Canada* (public law) and later that person can be sued for breach of contract (breaking a contract and causing damage as a result). Figure 1.1 contrasts criminal law and civil law.

Figure 1.1: **Criminal Law vs. Civil Law**

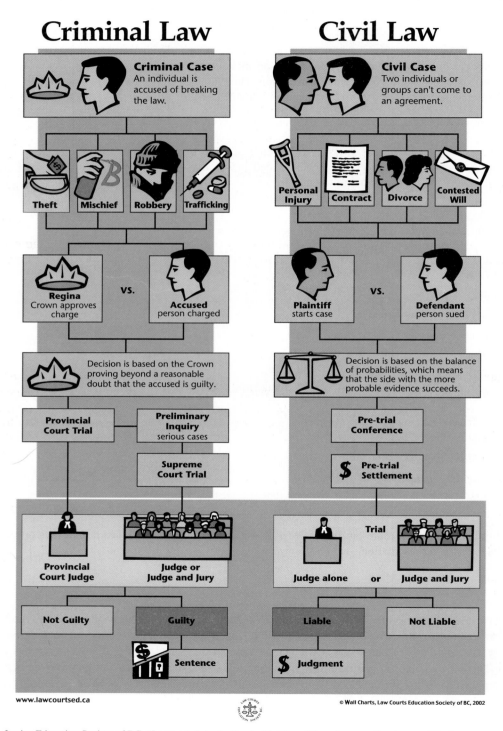

Justice Education Society of BC, "Lesson 1: Introduction to Civil Law," *Law Lessons: Teachers and Students,* http://www.lawlessons.ca/lesson-plans/3.1.comparing-criminal-and-civil-law. Courtesy of Justice Education Society of BC.

Sources of Law

Canadian law as we know it came from Britain, as Canada was once a dominion of Britain and, as a result, Canada followed the laws of its "mother" country—British Common Law. As of 1759, when the country fell under British rule, Canada has used British Common Law (with the exception of Quebec, which uses the laws from France). Our laws are a combination of statute (civil) law and common law. These two sources of law allow our country to deal with disputes, illegal actions, disagreements, and the breaking of regulations and rules. They also give us a guide to the consequences when a person, persons, organization, business, or other party harms or injures another.

Statute Law

The first place a person may look when wondering whether they or their business is doing something wrong would be the "rule book." In Canada, we have various rule books that help us understand what wrong is, and what happens when we do something wrong. For example, if we break into a house and steal the homeowner's wallet, the *Criminal Code of Canada* states that that is a wrongdoing and that the person who did the wrongdoing can be punished if found guilty. From a business perspective, a simple example would be the rules and regulations about a business claiming expenses on its corporate income tax. The *Income Tax Act* outlines what a business can and cannot claim regarding its corporate expenses and what the penalty may be if the business is not following the Act. These codes, rules, and regulations are known as **statute law**.

> **Statute Law**—a set of codes, rules, and regulations that are created by the government or an administrative body (e.g., *Criminal Code of Canada, Income Tax Act, Copyright Act, Matrimonial Property Act, Family Law Act*).

Common Law

Common law comes from the doctrine of **stare decisis**. Other names for common law include case law and precedent law. The concept is that judges will hand down decisions and those decisions are used in similar cases. Common law provides consistency to the world of law in that what has happened or decided in one case, we can potentially expect in a case that has similar elements. In some cases, a judge or judges may create a precedent when a matter is different from anything in the past. For example, since the inception of the Internet there have been a host of new cases that have come before the court where the issues involved never existed before, such as online bullying or the act of clicking "I accept" on a website.

> **Common Law**—based on decisions handed down from case to case that is not criminal law; decisions of previous and similar cases are used as a basis for a court decision.

> **Stare Decisis**—a doctrine where lower courts, in similar matters, use the decisions of higher courts.

CASE STUDY

R. v. Nedelcu (2012 SCC 59, [2012] 3 SCR 311)

In the case of *R. v Nedelcu*, Nedelcu was the owner and driver of a motorcycle that was in an accident. Nedelcu was not seriously injured but his passenger was. Nedelcu was charged with dangerous driving causing bodily harm and impaired driving causing bodily harm. The victim's family also sued Nedelcu for negligence in a civil action.

In the civil case before the Ontario Supreme Court, Nedelcu testified in a discovery (a procedure prior to trial) that he had no memory of the accident. In his criminal trial, held later, he gave a very detailed testimony of the accident. However, on cross-examination based on his testimony during discovery, Nedelcu was found to be unreliable and he was found guilty of dangerous driving causing bodily harm.

Nedelcu appealed his criminal case and the decision of the trial judge was overturned. His conviction was set aside and a new trial was ordered. The case was then appealed to the Supreme Court of Canada, which held that an appeal should not be allowed, the guilty verdict was to be restored, and there would not be a new trial.

SCENARIO CHALLENGE!

Consider the situations below and indicate which area of law should be contacted for each.

- Unhappy with the rejection of his immigration application, Jacques wanted to take the matter further so he searched for a lawyer who specializes in _____.
- After receiving a document indicating that her retail store had been sued for wrongful dismissal, Rebecca sought a lawyer who specializes in _____.
- Josh, a bouncer at a bar, had been in a bar fight while trying to have a patron leave the establishment. The police arrived and now Josh is in jail. Who should he call?
- Confused about the regulations for the disposal of industrial material used in the creation of their product, Cassie and James decided to contact what kind of lawyer?

There are several areas of law, and within each area there are further divisions. For example, in civil law you would find contract law, property law, and family law. Any dispute between individuals that requires a solution or a remedy is considered a civil law matter. In administrative law, municipal, provincial, and federal laws, agencies, and other law-making institutions would be a party against an individual seeking resolution of a dispute. In criminal law, most cases would occur under the *Criminal Code of Canada* but some cases may be found under a provincial law, such as Ontario's *Highway Traffic Act*, or under a municipal law such as a noise bylaw.

When a business is involved in a legal dispute, it must determine the best strategy for the circumstances. This may require the expertise of a lawyer in that particular area of law. For example, where a business is involved in a case where it is suing or being sued it may want a litigation lawyer, a specialist in the area of civil law. In the case of a criminal case, naturally, a criminal lawyer may be the best strategy. Consulting a constitutional specialist would be a very solid business decision in a legal matter that involves the *Canadian Charter of Rights and Freedoms*. Because businesses are constantly involved in regulations, rules, and laws pertaining to their particular industry, a lawyer with experience in administrative law might be the best bet.

Table 1.1 shows four different cases where a business is involved in the four areas of law.

Table 1.1: Four Different Cases

Administrative Law: *Wijesinghe v. Canada (Minister of Citizenship and Immigration), 2010 FC 54*

In this case, the Department of Citizenship and Immigration denied Wijesinghe's work permit application because he was deemed overqualified by a visa officer. He had obtained the job but he could not work without a work visa.

This matter was heard in the Federal Court and the matter was sent back for redetermination by another visa officer.

Criminal Law: *R. v. Glubis, 2015 SKPC 143*

This is a case in Saskatchewan where a farmer and his wife had two businesses that had grown significantly over the years. Unfortunately, their bookkeeping skills had not demonstrated standard accounting practice when dealing with two businesses. Glubis was charged with 17 counts of illegal business practices concerning their business tax reporting.

The defendant was found guilty of many of the charges, such as evading taxes, unreported income, underreporting income, and collecting but failing to report GST.

Civil Law: *R. (Ont.) v. Ron Engineering & Construction (Eastern) Ltd., [1979] 24 OR (2d) 332 (ONCA), revd [1981] 1 S.C.R. 111*

An interesting case of a mistake in the tendering of a bid. A contractor tendered a bid that was significantly lower than it should have been. He wanted to withdraw his bid, once he realized the error, without penalties.

The contractor sued the company for the return of the deposit, which was held as a penalty for the withdrawal of the bid. The company counter-claimed.

The trial judge ruled that the company should keep the deposit and the Court of Appeal reversed the trial judgment. The Supreme Court of Canada ruled that the appeal of the contractor would be allowed and overturned the decision of the Ontario Court of Appeal.

Constitutional Law: *R v. Latimer, 2001 SCC 1*

In this constitutional case, a man was charged with murdering his disabled daughter in Saskatchewan. The case sparked the controversial argument of mercy killing.

Tracy Latimer was 12 years old with cerebral palsy, was a quadriplegic, could not speak, and had the mental capacity of an infant. Even with all these medical problems, none were life threatening. Doctors had suggested a feeding tube would help her health. Tracy had numerous surgeries and her parents felt that another surgery would be cruel. Mr. Latimer poisoned his daughter with carbon monoxide.

Latimer was convicted of second degree murder but it was overturned because of the Crown's improper instructions to the jury. In the second trial, he was again convicted of second degree murder but only sentenced to one year rather than the minimum 10 years because the circumstances were viewed as cruel and unusual. The Court of Appeal later increased the sentence to 10 years. Latimer appealed to the Supreme Court of Canada, which held that the 10-year minimum sentence in this case did not amount to cruel and unusual punishment under the *Canadian Charter of Rights and Freedoms* and that the fairness of the trial was not compromised by the lateness of the decision on whether the jury could consider the defence of necessity.

Figure 1.2 shows the two primary sources of law in Canada—case law and legislative law—and their origins. It is from these two sources that our legal system is developed.

Figure 1.2: **Sources of Law**

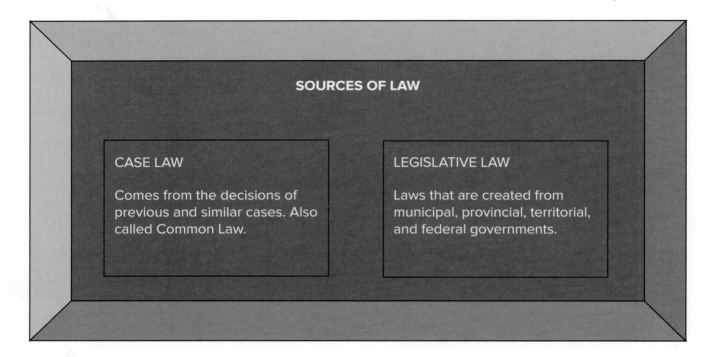

As you can see in the figure, there are two streams for where our law comes from. Businesses must understand all the relevant legislative laws, rules, and regulations that pertain to their business. These would be municipal laws (planning, zoning, waste management), provincial/territorial laws (a law regarding forestry), and federal laws (human rights). In some cases, laws are created by more than one level of government. In those cases, the federal government supercedes (wins over) lower levels of government, like the province.

Historically, the Canadian legal system comes from both the English and French systems. In fact, the province of Quebec still retains civil law where the rest of Canada follows common law (case law) and legislative law.

Common law is the law of precedent. This means that judges will apply similar and previous cases in a legal case. And, as noted previously in this section, another term of the law of precedent is *stare decisis*. So in other words, if there is a case before the Court the judge will look at cases where the issue is similar and use those cases to assist in his or her decision. The judge will generally look at cases that have appeared in higher courts because decisions in higher courts will overrule those in lower courts.

LO 1.6   1.6 How Laws Are Made in Canada

The Canadian Government website has a comprehensive section that discusses how Canada's laws are made or changed. The Canadian Parliament creates laws that pertain to Canada from a federal perspective, while each province or territory makes laws in the areas it is responsible for. The *Constitution Act* (1867 to 1982) is the supreme law in Canada and outlines the responsibilities of the federal government and provincial governments.

Source: http://www.justice.gc.ca/eng/csj-sjc/just/05.html, accessed November 2015.

The consolidation of constitutional documents can be found on the Canadian Government's Department of Justice website. These documents, the ***Constitution Act*** 1867 to 1982 and the ***Charter of Rights and Freedoms***, as mentioned above, are the foundation of our justice system and, indeed, our society. It is always a good idea for a businessperson to understand the essence of these constitutional documents so that they will be the stewards of fairness and legality in their business operations.

Source: http://laws-lois.justice.gc.ca/eng/Const/Const_index.html, accessed September 2015.

Constitution Act 1867—outlines the executive and legislative powers of federal and provincial governments.

Constitution Act 1982—entrenches the *Canadian Charter of Rights and Freedoms* as well as other rights such as Aboriginal rights.

Charter of Rights and Freedoms—included in the *Constitution Act 1982*; protects Canadians' fundamental freedoms such as freedom of religion, our mobility, legal and democratic rights, to name a few. (See http://laws-lois.justice.gc.ca/eng/const/page-15.html.)

CASE STUDY

R. v. Smith, 2015 SCC 34, [2015] 2 S.C.R. 602

This is a case that went to the Supreme Court of Canada regarding the constitutional and Charter right of Smith, who was charged with possession and possession for the purpose of trafficking cannabis under the *Controlled Drugs and Substances Act*.

The trial judge of the B.C. Supreme Court found that the prohibition on non-dried forms of cannabis—in Smith's case it was topical and edible forms of cannabis—unjustifiably infringed on his rights under the *Canadian Charter of Rights and Freedoms* and Smith was acquitted.

The case was appealed by the Crown (prosecution) and the B.C. Court of Appeal dismissed the appeal and affirmed the acquittal. The case was then appealed to the Supreme Court of Canada, which found that Smith had standing in terms of his constitutional rights and affirmed his acquittal.

Once a **statute** (or a legislation or an Act) is enacted, it is then that a judge will uphold the law. Statutes supercede any judge-made ruling. Once Parliament or a provincial/territorial legislature creates an Act by way of statute, it becomes the law by which judges will rule. If you look at the laws of each province, territory, and municipality as well as the federal laws, you will see a host of "rules" that must be followed. Those rules are either Acts or they are **regulations**, both of which guide society in their actions.

Statute—a law enacted at the municipal, provincial, or federal level.

Regulations—laws developed by departments and other organizations in specific areas.

In fact, the Canadian Government's Department of Justice has provided a consolidated list of Acts and regulations. At http://laws-lois.justice.gc.ca/eng/acts/ you will find an alphabetical listing of the official Acts and the official regulations for the federal government.

Table 1.2 shows some common statutes (Acts and regulations) of which a businessperson should have some knowledge.

Table 1.2: Common Statutes a Businessperson Should Know

Federal	*Canada Labour Code* *Competition Act* *Income Tax Act* Canada Occupational Health and Safety Regulations Food and Drug Regulations
Provincial/territorial—each province or territory has its own set of statutes	Property Employment Standards Provincial Court Public Health
Municipal—each municipality has its own set of statutes (bylaws)	Property Tax Commercial Property Noise

Regulations help society by clarifying rules that govern specific areas. For example, banking regulations outline what can be done by banking institutions under the federal government's *Bank Act*. By providing government departments and other institutions with the power to make regulations, the government is more efficient and effective.

LO 1.7

1.7 The Court System

Kaspars Grinvalds / Shutterstock.com

Canada has a multi-level court system. Because there are provinces, territories, and municipalities in Canada, there are various avenues for resolving disputes. From the point of view of strategic decision making, it can be important for the businessperson to understand the various courts they may be dealing with and the legislation that falls under the different jurisdictions. Most importantly, a business should seek legal advice when a matter has come to a head and has proceeded to the court.

Courts in Canada help people resolve disputes fairly—whether they are between individuals, or between individuals and the state. At the same time, courts interpret and pronounce law, set standards, and decide questions that affect all aspects of Canadian society.

Canada's **judiciary** is one branch of our system of government, the others being the legislative and the executive. Whereas the judiciary resolves disputes according to law—including disputes about how legislative and executive powers are exercised—the legislature (Parliament) has the power to make, alter and repeal laws. The executive branch (in particular, the prime minister and ministers, the public service, as well as a variety of agencies, boards, and commissions) is responsible for administering and enforcing the laws.

The courts interpret and apply the Constitution, as well as legislation passed by both levels of government. They also develop and apply the common law.

Source: Canada's Court System, page 1, http://www.justice.gc.ca/eng/csj-sjc/just/img/courten.pdf. Department of Justice Canada 2015. Reproduced with the permission of the Department of Justice Canada, 2016.

Role of the Courts

The justice system is the mechanism that upholds the rule of law. Our courts provide a forum to resolve disputes and to test and enforce laws in a fair and rational manner. The courts are an impartial forum, and judges are free to apply the law without regard to the government's wishes or the weight of public opinion. Court decisions are based on what the law says and what the evidence proves; there is no place in the courts for suspicion, bias or favouritism. This is why justice is often symbolized as a blindfolded figure balancing a set of scales, oblivious to anything that could detract from the pursuit of an outcome that is just and fair.

Source: "The Role of the Courts," *Canadian Superior Courts Judges Association,* http://www.cscja-acjcs.ca/ role_of_courts-en.asp?l=4.

The Courts' Organization

As stated above, the Canadian court system is multi-layered, with each province and territory having its own judicial system. Federally, there is another court system. There also are administrative boards and tribunals that deal with less formal disputes. Figure 1.3 provides an overview of the hierarchy of the Canadian civil courts.

Figure 1.3: Hierarchy of Canadian Civil Courts

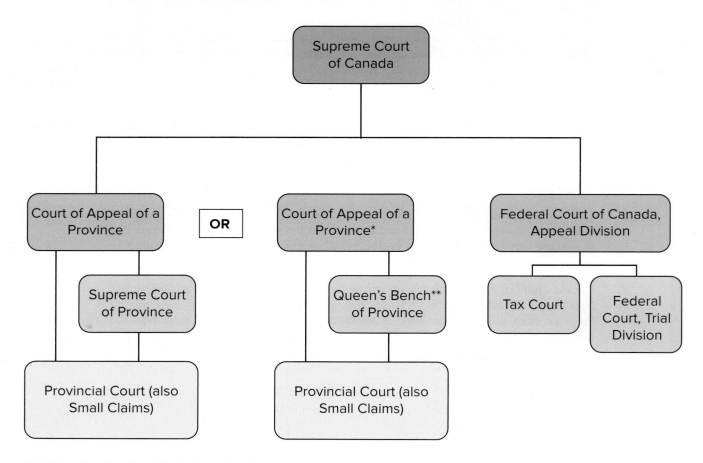

*   In Newfoundland and Labrador it is referred to as Supreme Court, Court of Appeal and in P.E.I. as Supreme Court, Appeal Division

** In Quebec it is referred to as Superior Court; in Nunavut it is referred to as Court of Justice

More information regarding the court system in Canada is presented in Chapter 2.

SCENARIO CHALLENGE!

Consider the situations below and find similar case law that would provide a solution:

- A trespasser on private property gets injured when she slips on a newly painted deck.
- A person invited to an event who purchased a ticket becomes intoxicated and drives home.
- A cottage owner allows a family friend to use the cottage for the weekend and their child becomes injured in the hot tub on the deck.

LO 1.8   # 1.8 Alternative Dispute Resolution (ADR)

One thing is true—legal work has a cost. A lawyer who prepares documents so that the company is in good standing with the various departments and in accordance with the various regulations and laws is beneficial to the company. In other areas, such as civil litigation, where one person(s) is suing another, participants will require a lawyer to appear with them in court, prepare their documentation, and negotiate on their behalf. All in all, this costs businesses money and can dip into their profitability.

As the name suggests, **Alternative Dispute Resolution (ADR)** is another way for disputes between persons and/or companies to be solved. Several benefits exist for both sides in using ADR:

- Saves money—no costly court fees
- Saves time—no lengthy trial process
- Creates goodwill—preserves diplomatic relationship between the parties because they work together toward a solution both sides can live with
- Increases compliance—parties are more likely to comply with a mutual decision
- Maintains privacy—sessions are not open to the public
- Reduces stress—because of reasons listed above!

Alternative Dispute Resolution (ADR)—different ways to solve a dispute that do not involve the formality of a court or civil litigation such as mediation and arbitration.

There are several forms of ADR—such as mediation and arbitration, to name just two—and these will be explored in more detail in Chapter 2, Resolution of Disputes.

FOR REVIEW

Questions

1. What is the importance of understanding law to a business today? (LO 1.1)
2. What is common law? What is legislative law? Are there other names for these laws? (LO 1.5)
3. Define the areas of law. What is the difference between them? (LO 1.5)
4. How would you compare a criminal case to a civil case? (LO 1.5)
5. Why would the parties in a civil case want to pursue Alternative Dispute Resolution? (LO 1.8)
6. Why is it important for a business to develop a privacy plan? (LO 1.1)
7. What is meant by the term "risk management"? (LO 1.3)
8. Vandals have destroyed a bench in a park owned by the town. Is this a matter of public or private law? (LO 1.5)
9. Explain whether the enforcement of the following organizations' rules would involve administrative law: (LO 1.5)
   (a) The Liquor Control Board
   (b) The Tropical Fish Breeders Association
   (c) The Institute of Law Clerks
   (d) The Canadian Radio-television and Telecommunications Commission

Activities

1. Interview a manager of a local small or medium business to understand how they deal with legal issues. What issues do they see a lawyer about? What should a businessperson know about government acts and regulations? (LO 1.1)
2. Go to the Government of Canada website and explore the *Constitution Acts* of 1867 and 1982, which includes the *Canadian Charter of Rights and Freedoms*. Familiarize yourself with the Acts. Create a table that outlines the parameters of both acts. (LO 1.6)
3. Individually, or in a small group, create a hypothetical case where:
   a. A businessperson is charged under the *Criminal Code of Canada*
   b. A business is sued under the *Canadian Charter of Rights and Freedoms*
   c. A business is sued in a civil litigation matter
   In each of the above, outline the facts of the case and how it would proceed. (LO 1.6)
4. Research the Federal Court of Canada and discuss what it is and the types of cases it hears. (LO 1.7)
5. Look in local, regional, and national newspapers to find an article about a case of significance to that area or the country. Discuss this with your classmates. (LO 1.7)
6. Research the various situations where two parties might decide on ADR. (LO 1.8)
7. Describe the purpose behind a company developing a privacy policy and list five key elements that you believe should be included in that policy. (LO 1.1)
8. Your company's chief financial officer, to whom you report, has asked you to revise the production numbers for the past month so the financial statements will look better for the shareholders' meeting. You recently bought a house and don't want to lose your job, but you are not comfortable falsifying the numbers. What are the steps you might take in dealing with this situation? (LO 1.4)

CASES FOR DISCUSSION

Case #1

Monty and Karen are opening a natural food store in the upcoming year. They are currently working through their business plan but now must decide what steps they need to take regarding their legal responsibilities in opening such a business in Saskatoon, Saskatchewan. You have just been hired by Monty and Karen and, because you have taken a business law course, they are looking to you to provide some information and research on what steps should be taken before seeking legal advice, hoping to save some dollars.

What does it mean to you when Monty and Karen use the term "legal responsibilities"? What kind of research should you do to help them? How would you divide up the different areas of law that they should consider? Are there any specific statutes that they need to know about? In the training of their staff, are there any regulations that need to be addressed? (LO 1.5)

Case #2

Elaine operated a business selling body lotions and creams. She would often display her products on tables set up on the sidewalk immediately in front of her store. To make her products more visible, she had strong floodlights attached to the top of the storefront, which automatically came on when it began to get dark and were used to illuminate the tables on the sidewalk. On a Tuesday afternoon it began suddenly to get dark and rain lightly, but Elaine was busy inside the store and did not have an opportunity to get out and cover the tables on the sidewalk.

Unknown to Elaine, a bottle of lotion had fallen onto the sidewalk and the contents had leaked onto the walkway in front of the table. As a pedestrian crossed in front of her store the floodlights came on suddenly and the pedestrian, briefly blinded by the lights, slipped on the spilled lotion. Elaine came running out of the store as a man helped the woman who had fallen back to her feet. Elaine heard the woman tell the man she was okay, only a bit shaken, and that it was her own fault for not looking where she was going. The rain had spread the lotion even further on the sidewalk so Elaine quickly got a mop and cleaned up the mess. Meanwhile, the woman who had fallen limped off muttering about the bright spots floating in her eyesight.

If you were responsible for advising Elaine at the time of this accident, what risk management actions would you recommend she take? (LO 1.3)

CHAPTER 2

RESOLUTION OF DISPUTES

Learning Objectives

After reading this chapter the student will:

LO 2.1   Understand the civil court systems in Canada

LO 2.2   Understand the hierarchy of the Canadian civil courts

LO 2.3   Understand the litigation process and civil court proceedings

LO 2.4   Explain Alternative Dispute Resolution

LO 2.5   Explain risk management and how lawyers help to resolve disputes

HELP!

As a businessperson, you may experience any of these scenarios:

- HELP! I have just received a legal notice with my company's name on it but I'm not sure what it is.

- HELP! A company owes my organization money but I'm not sure how to collect it.

- HELP! A former employee is suing my business for unjust dismissal. Can he do that?

- HELP! My lawyer is using words like "discovery" and "interlocutory" in the lawsuit against my company and I'm very confused.

- HELP! I don't like the result of my lawsuit in court. What can be done?

- HELP! I don't want to go through an expensive lawsuit in the court system. What are my alternatives?

- HELP! I need to ensure my organization won't get into any legal trouble; when should I be talking to a lawyer?

LO 2.1   2.1 The Civil Court Systems in Canada

To understand and be able to use the legal process, a businessperson needs to be familiar with the court systems, provincially and federally.

The two courts that a businessperson generally interacts with are civil courts and criminal courts. Criminal court deals with matters that involve one party causing damage to another party. The act causing the damage has violated a statute or law, making it illegal. We will examine criminal law in a few instances where it applies to business. However, our main focus is on the civil law and the civil courts, as these are the courts where most matters concerning businesses are dealt with.

Because of books, TV, and movies, most people understand the criminal system in its basic form. For example, many people are aware that when a person is caught committing a crime, he or she generally goes to court (or pleads guilty). However, the litigation system is more complex. **Litigation** means resolving a legal dispute in the civil court system. In basic terms, one side is the **plaintiff** (the person who sues) and the other side is the **defendant** (the person who is sued). There can be more than one plaintiff and more than one defendant in a **lawsuit**.

Litigation—a complex process to resolve a legal dispute in the civil court system based on the evidence presented by those involved in the dispute.

Plaintiff—a person(s) or organization that sues another person or organization.

Defendant—a person(s) or organization that is being sued.

Lawsuit—a dispute between two or more parties brought before a civil court for a decision.

Plaintiffs and defendants can be any of the following:

- Individuals
- Corporations
- Not-for-profit organizations
- Governments

A civil court matter can be settled at any time or it may proceed to **trial**. At the end of a trial, there is a "winner" and a "loser." However, as you will soon see, it is far more complicated than that!

Trial—the formal hearing of a court case before a judge (or jury or both).

Civil litigation can be called any of the following:

- An action
- A matter
- A lawsuit
- A proceeding
- A case
- An application

Source: http://www.lawhelpontario.org/lawsuits-disputes/superior-court/how-to-guides-superior/overview-superior-court/

It is important to note that only a small percentage of civil cases ever go to trial. Many steps and procedures, sometimes taking years to go through, have to happen before the case gets to trial. Both plaintiff(s) and defendant(s) come to realize—or will be told by their lawyers—that this process is very expensive. As stated above, it is possible that at any time in this process the plaintiff and defendant may decide on a settlement. A **settlement** is a resolution of the dispute that is acceptable to both sides, resulting in the matter reaching a conclusion without going through the full court process. Settlements can happen before a matter goes to court or at any time during the trial.

> **Settlement**—resolution of the dispute that is acceptable to both sides bringing the matter to its final disposition.

Civil law, as you read in Chapter 1, goes back hundreds of years and is based on precedent and the common law. The parties go through a well-defined process in order to bring the matter to a resolution. The plaintiff must prove her/his case on the **balance of probabilities**. In litigation, the outcome or verdict of a case is decided upon, or based on, similar cases in the past. We look at a few examples in the following Case Study features.

> **Civil Law**—the area of law that deals with parties that have a dispute. The parties go through a well-defined process in order to bring the matter to a resolution. The plaintiff must prove her/his case on the balance of probabilities.

> **Balance of Probabilities**—in a civil matter, the standard of proof requiring that something be proven to have more likely occurred than not occurred.

 CASE STUDY

Childs v. Desormeaux (2006 SCC 18)

The case of *Childs v. Desormeaux* is a case of duty of care involving a guest who brought his own alcohol to a BYOB (bring your own booze) house party hosted by Zimmerman and Courier in 1999. Desormeaux, who had a history of impaired driving, was invited to a house party, brought his own alcohol, and became intoxicated. He left the party and went to his car after his hosts asked him if he was "okay." Desormeaux then drove into oncoming traffic and hit another car in a head-on collision, killing one and injuring three other passengers. Childs, a teenager at the time, was seriously injured with a severed spine and subsequently was paralyzed from the waist down.

Desormeaux was found guilty in criminal court and received a 10-year sentence. A civil action was commenced by Childs against Zimmerman and Courier in the Supreme Court of Ontario where the trial judge found that the hosts, as reasonable people, should have foreseen that Desormeaux could have caused an accident and that they had a duty of care. However, the judge dismissed the action because of legislation and policy.

The case was appealed to the Court of Appeal for Ontario, which upheld the decision of the Ontario Supreme Court (dismissed the case) because the hosts did not have control over the supply and service of alcohol and were not a commercial business.

Childs appealed to the Supreme Court of Canada in 2006 and the appeal was dismissed (previous courts' decisions were upheld) because a duty of care on the part of the hosts could not be found.

Many cases do not go to the Supreme Court of Canada. They may stop at the superior/supreme court of the province, or they may stop at the appeal court stage. An example is the case of *Tilden Rent-A-Car Co. v. Clendenning*.

 CASE STUDY

Tilden Rent-A-Car Co. v. Clendenning (1978, 83 DLR (3d) 400

Clendenning rented cars from Tilden Rent-A-Car, at the airport, when on a business trip in Vancouver. He requested the $2/day full non-deductible coverage. He did not read nor was he told of the exclusion clause that denied coverage with the consumption of alcohol.

Clendenning consumed alcohol and drove into a pole, writing off the vehicle. He was later convicted for impaired driving and sued Tilden when they would not cover the damages of the accident because he didn't read the rental contract and indicated that he wouldn't have gotten the coverage if he had known of the exclusion clause.

The Ontario Supreme Court decided that Clendenning could collect the insurance as he quickly signed the contract and was not told about the exclusion clause and that Tilden should have taken reasonable measures to ensure he understood the clause(s). The case was dismissed.

Tilden then appealed the decision of the Supreme Court of Ontario. The appeal was dismissed. Tilden did not pursue an appeal to the Supreme Court of Canada and the matter ended.

As you can see from the *Desormeaux* and *Clendenning* cases, trial matters can go from a criminal case and then to a civil case. The criminal trial is held first, and after the outcome of that trial some cases will go to a civil court. Keep in mind that this does not happen in all criminal matters.

The court system in Canada for civil cases exists both on a provincial and federal level. In civil law there are various courts—trial courts, appeal courts, and the Supreme Court of Canada. Different names for each court system are also given, depending on the province. For example, in British Columbia the court that would hear a civil matter would be the Supreme Court of British Columbia, while in New Brunswick it would be called Queen's Bench. Not only do courts have different names, but they tend to have different procedures and maximums for a monetary **claim**. For example, a civil case can be heard in the Supreme Court of Manitoba for a monetary value of $10,000, but in Nova Scotia the value has to exceed $25,000.

© Vintagemedstock | Dreamstime.com

Claim—the plaintiff's legal assertion or demand for a loss; the defendant can respond to this claim.

LO 2.2   2.2 Hierarchy of the Canadian Civil Courts

We mentioned three courts above, but there are other courts that a businessperson should be aware of. The hierarchy of the Canadian court system is explained in more detail in this section.

Supreme Court of Canada

Art Babych / Shutterstock.com

The Supreme Court of Canada is the highest court in Canada and is the highest **appeal** court. This high court hears only cases that may affect Canadian society as a whole, and the fabric of our country now and/or in the future. A decision that is made in the Supreme Court of Canada cannot be appealed—it is the final stage for any court matter.

> **Appeal**—when the losing party in any court case disagrees with the decision of the court, it will wish to have a higher court look at the case and come to a decision.

A case is generally heard at the provincial level in a superior court. If the plaintiff(s) or defendant(s) are not happy with the decision, they can appeal the decision to the provincial Court of Appeal. The result of this appeal may be appealed to the Supreme Court of Canada but only under certain conditions. If "**leave to appeal**" is given (that is, permission by three Supreme Court Justices), the case may be brought before the Supreme Court of Canada because of its importance to the public.

> **Leave to Appeal**—permission for a case to be heard in the Supreme Court of Canada.

DID YOU KNOW?

Facts about the Supreme Court of Canada

- Deals with criminal, civil, administrative, and constitutional cases;
- When addressing a Supreme Court judge/justice use Justice plus their last name: Mr. Justice or Madam Justice. In writing, The Honorable Madam or Mr. Justice;
- The head of all of the judges is the Chief Justice or The Right Honourable Justice (last name);
- There are nine Supreme Court of Canada justices; three members must be from Quebec;
- The Supreme Court of Canada is located in Ottawa;
- Court hearings are open to the public;
- There can be a minimum of five justices hearing a case to the maximum of nine; a minimum of three justices write the decision;
- Only cases that the Supreme Court of Canada deems of public importance will be heard (there are some exceptions);
- A request for a leave to appeal (permission to have the Supreme Court of Canada hear the case) must be provided to the Court. It is either accepted or denied.

Source: Adapted from "Frequently Asked Questions," *Supreme Court of Canada*, May 2, 2016, http://www.scc-csc.gc.ca/contact/faq/qa-qr-eng.aspx.

LEGAL SCENARIO

An Upward Battle

James, from Nova Scotia, had just purchased a new electric car but wasn't happy with the sound system. He took his car and purchased a top of the line car stereo system from Snazzy Electronics for $2,500. After two months, the car stereo began to have problems and James kept returning it to Snazzy. The manager and owner of Snazzy Electronics explained that it was his electric car's component that was the problem and not the stereo system and that he shouldn't have had it done after the purchase but had the car company do the installation.

After three months, James had a mechanical breakdown with his car and he returned it to the dealership. He quickly found out from the mechanic that the sound system had been improperly installed and that the mechanical breakdown was the result of the Snazzy Electronics install. Because the sound system was not part of the car's warranty nor was the damage to the internal components of the car because of the installation, the cost to James to repair his car was $6,200 and he also no longer had a sound system.

James believed that Snazzy Electronics was responsible for the mechanical breakdown. Snazzy Electronics' owner didn't agree and refused to pay the costs for repairs.

James went to small claims court because the damage to his car and the resulting claim against Snazzy Electronics was less than $25,000. James was successful in his small claims court action; however, Snazzy Electronics was not happy with this outcome and appealed it to the Supreme Court of Nova Scotia. Again James was successful, and again Snazzy Electronics took the matter to the Appeal Court of Nova Scotia, where the Court of Appeal affirmed (agreed) with the findings of the trial court and dismissed the case.

(Provincial) Court of Appeal

In the Legal Scenario example, had Snazzy Electronics wanted to continue to spend money on its case, this company could apply for leave to appeal to the SCC. Please note that in order to appeal a case, it must be because the trial judge made an error in some way. For example, when a judge errs because of an application of law or because some evidence was overlooked, then the unsuccessful party can lodge an appeal. Three judges hear an appeal case. Often there are time limitations for a party to appeal a decision. These rules and procedures can be found on each province's website.

(Provincial) Supreme Court or Queen's Bench (Superior Courts)

The highest trial court in a province or territory is called either the Supreme Court or Queen's Bench, depending on the province. Nunavut and Quebec have different names for this level of court. (Refer to Figure 1.3 for the court's proper name for each province and territory.) For ease, we will refer to this trial court as the Superior Court. Because of the procedural complexities, parties whose cases are before this court are generally represented by lawyers.

The Superior Court is for matters with a financial claim of over $25,000 (in most provinces). For serious crimes, the Superior Court hears the cases. The judges are appointed to their positions by the federal government.

Provincial Court

Provincial court is generally not a court for business law. Provincial court judges are appointed by the province and hear criminal matters for less serious crimes. Provincial courts deal with criminal matters that generally fall under the *Criminal Code of Canada*. This is not a court that deals with disputes, but rather with crimes. As stated previously, a criminal matter may appear in a provincial (or supreme) court first and then go to a civil court.

Small Claims Court

Businesses today often appear in small claims court if the monetary amount of a claim is less than $25,000 (this may be lower or higher depending on the province). An adjudicator (who is also a lawyer) presides over this court and parties are generally not represented by a lawyer.

CASE STUDY

Honda Canada v. Keays, 2008 SCC 39, [2008] 2 SCR 362

In the case of *Honda Canada v. Keays*, Mr. Keays, an employee of Honda Canada, was diagnosed with chronic fatigue syndrome. Once diagnosed, Honda asked Mr. Keays to meet with an occupational therapist in order to be assessed and accommodated. Soon after, Keays retained lawyers in order to come to an agreement with Honda.

Honda then asked Keays directly to meet with their doctor without responding to Keays's lawyers' letter. Upon advice of counsel, Keays refused and Honda warned him again that he must visit a doctor. Keays refused again and so he was fired from Honda. The case went to the Supreme Court of Ontario where Keays, the plaintiff, was awarded 15 months' (later extended to 24 months') pay in lieu of notice and $500,000 in punitive damages against Honda.

Honda appealed the decision but the Ontario Court of Appeal upheld the decision yet reduced the damages against Honda to $100,000.

The case was then appealed to the Supreme Court of Canada where the Court upheld the initial decision of the Ontario Supreme Court of 15 months' pay in lieu of notice but set aside the punitive damages.

CASE STUDY

Dr. Henry Morgentaler—Changing Canadian Society

In 1988, the Supreme Court of Canada decided that the current cumbersome administrative practices that women in Canada had to endure in order to procure an abortion were unconstitutional. This landmark decision made abortions in Canada legal by ending criminal restrictions and finding Section 251 of the *Criminal Code* to be unconstitutional. It all began with a doctor in Quebec named Dr. Henry Morgentaler.

In the 1970s, Dr. Henry Morgentaler was acquitted (found not guilty) on three occasions for performing abortions in Quebec. Dr. Morgentaler raised the defence of necessity (the duty to safeguard and protect women). The Province of Quebec appealed the acquittal because they thought Dr. Morgentaler was guilty. The Quebec Court of Appeal overturned the acquittal, meaning they no longer found him not guilty. Dr. Morgentaler then appealed his conviction to the Supreme Court of Canada, where his conviction was upheld and so he went to prison for 18 months.

Throughout the mid 1970s, Dr. Morgentaler was embroiled in legal battles that included acquittals, new trials, and controversial news media in Quebec and, indeed, throughout Canada. By 1976 Quebec realized that it could not enforce the abortion law because a jury acquittal could not be appealed (called the *Morgentaler Amendment to the Criminal Code of Canada*), so since then Quebec has allowed abortion clinics.

Morgentaler went on to challenge and hoped to overturn the abortion laws in Canada by stating a claim against the federal government in *Morgentaler v. The Queen* but was unsuccessful. He continued his crusade throughout the 1980s and once again was before the court, but in this case in Ontario where he and two colleagues were charged and acquitted by a jury. The case was appealed by the Attorney General for Ontario and the decision of the Supreme Court of Ontario was reversed and a verdict was substituted with a conviction. Dr. Morgentaler then appealed to the Supreme Court of Canada and, in 1988 in a landmark decision, the court ruled 5–2 in favour of Dr. Morgentaler.

© The Canadian Press/Blaise Edwards

As you can see in the *Morgentaler* case, the Supreme Court was the final stage of the matter and, as a result, the entire abortion issue changed Canadian society. The Supreme Court of Canada will continue to make landmark decisions that you may or may not agree with. Ultimately, the decisions of the Supreme Court of Canada present the core of what a democratic society requires to settle differences that affect the people of this country.

The following case study examines a case that came before the Federal Court of Canada. The **Federal Court of Canada** consists of two divisions, the trial division and an appeal division. Information and decisions of this court can be found at http://cas-cdc-www02.cas-satj.gc.ca/fct-cf/.

Federal Court of Canada—deals with cases between individuals or organizations and the federal government, such as income tax disputes; also deals with patents, customs, immigration, and maritime law.

CASE STUDY

Ahmed v. Canada (Public Safety and Emergency Preparedness), 2016 FC 197

A case that came before the Federal Court of Canada involved the applicant, a business manager of Cheech Glass Ltd., Faraz Ahmed, who sought to hire a temporary foreign worker (TFW) and provided the Department of Employment and Social Development with an application to hire this worker. The case worker on Mr. Ahmed's file refused to issue a positive Labour Marketing Impact Assessment that would have been required for the business. Mr. Ahmed managed to hire the temporary foreign worker under the Temporary Foreign Worker Program (TFWP).

Mr. Ahmed and his representative, over a period of months, made applications to the TFWP and they were declined because of insufficient information. In the Department's final decision, they stated that the Applicant had not sufficiently demonstrated that they looked to hire a suitable Canadian in the stated occupation and that their recruitment effort was also not sufficient to hire a Canadian, particularly where there was no evidence of a labour shortage.

The applicant argued that the case worker did not provide information in a timely manner, changed instructions and guidelines and a host of other errors. The applicant wished for the Federal Court to provide a judicial review of the process because of the breach of procedural fairness. The Federal Court dismissed the request for judicial review.

LO 2.3 — 2.3 Understanding Civil Litigation Processes and Proceedings

Businesses hope that they will never be embroiled in a legal **action**, but at some point it might happen. It is important for a businessperson to be aware of the legal implications that may be taken against an individual, organization, or government as a result of carrying on business. In particular, with the exception of the incorporation and annual reporting of an organization, the average businessperson doesn't think about the costs (monetary and time) involved in commencing a legal action (suing or being sued).

> **Action**—a litigation term where one party sues another.

Each province has a set of processes and rules (civil procedure rules) so that an action can begin or be defended and the case brought to its conclusion. This roadmap is very specific and often has time limitations. Failure to meet a timeline may have consequences.

There are three specific parts to civil court proceedings:

1. The **filing** and serving of pleadings
2. The questioning of each party and witnesses
3. The trial

Filing—presenting your documents: claim, defence, or counter-claim, for example, to the court and the opposing parties.

CASE STUDY

Actions Commenced by Notice of Civil Claim in British Columbia

1. **The Plaintiff (and their lawyer)** decide whether to bring an action in Small Claims Court or the Supreme Court.
2. **Plaintiff** starts the action by filing and serving a notice of civil claim or a statement of claim (different terms may be used in each province). Documents would be filed with the Prothonotary (clerk of the Court).
3. **Defendant may** file and serve a response or a **defence**.
4. **Defendant may** file and deliver a **counter-claim**, a **cross-claim**, or a third party claim, if applicable.
5. If required, **plaintiff** files and delivers a response to the counter-claim.
6. If required, **third party** files and serves a response.
7. **Plaintiff or defendant** decides whether to proceed by fast track (moving the case along fast through case management) litigation. **Pleadings** are closed.
8. **Plaintiff and defendant** start **discovery** process (discovery of documents; examinations for discovery; **interrogatories**).
9. Plaintiff and defendant may need to make **pre-trial applications** in **chambers** to obtain directions or assistance from the court.
10. **Plaintiff and defendant** consider resolving case (mediation/settlement) without going to trial. A settlement may occur at any point in the litigation.
11. **Plaintiff and defendant** prepare for trial by setting trial date; considering expert opinions; preparing documents and witnesses for trial.
12. **Plaintiff and defendant** attend the trial and receive **judgment** and award of **costs**.
13. **Plaintiff or defendant** (winning party) prepares and files documents with the court
14. **Plaintiff or defendant** enforces judgment, which would be a separate proceeding.

Source: Adapted from Justice Education Society of BC, *Overview of the Civil Litigation Process,* http://www.supremecourtbc.ca/sites/default/files/web/Overview-of-the-Civil-Litigation-Process.pdf. Courtesy of Justice Education Society of BC.

Defence—the response by the defendant to the claims/demands made by the plaintiff.

Counter-Claim—a claim made by the defendant against the plaintiff in the same matter.

Cross-Claim—a claim against a co-defendant.

Pleadings—written legal documents that start and defend a claim/allegation (e.g., statement of claim, defence, cross-claim, counter-claim, etc.).

Discovery—a meeting where questions and answers are asked of the parties and their witnesses, held under oath, prior to trial to obtain further information and evidence.

Interrogatories—written questions provided by one party to the other that are answered in writing and signed under oath.

Pre-trial Applications—motions made before the court and made in chambers (less formal) where the judge decides on small matters connected with the case.

Chambers—where judge and lawyers present motions that affect the case for a decision by the judge (in some provinces, e.g., Nova Scotia).

Judgment—the remedy given to the successful party by the court.

Costs—the judgment may include a portion of the costs (legal fees, filing fees, etc.) the successful party incurred during the course of the case and paid by the unsuccessful party.

LEGAL SCENARIO

The Case of the Missing Documents

Sandra, a paralegal, looked at the lead lawyer with fear in her eyes. She nodded but with uncertainty when he asked "Are you *sure* these documents were not disclosed?" It was just this morning that she saw documents that were scanned and stored on a separate server at their law firm years ago when the case had just begun and before her employment at the firm.

Sandra and her group of litigators were the lawyers for the plaintiffs in a large class action lawsuit. The lawsuit began before Sandra's time at the firm. Thousands of documents were produced by all of the plaintiffs, 15 in total, as well as the defendant, a large construction company. Each side (plaintiffs and defendant) provided a photocopy of all documents that were relevant to the case, such as letters, memos, contracts, financial statements, expenses incurred, income tax statements, subcontractors' documents, maps, and many other documents. Once each side had compiled the documents, they were indexed (each document had a number and was included in a Table of Contents) and exchanged. Each volume of these documents was roughly 4 cm thick. Additionally, these volumes of documents were also provided electronically on an external hard drive. In total, each side had over 80 volumes of documents.

Once the documents had been exchanged, the examinations for discovery had begun. The case was well into its second month of discovery when Sandra realized that some documents that had been stored on a section of the server they didn't generally use had not been provided to opposing counsel. She understood that this was a real no-no! It was imperative that all relevant documents had to be provided to opposing counsel or the non-disclosure could cause a major headache for her litigators.

Sandra set a meeting with her litigators after realizing they had potential undisclosed documents and told them about this issue. She provided a possible solution to them and they agreed that they would inform opposing counsel as well as the judge in the case that there potentially could be more documents that were discovered.

Sandra spent the next two days going through each and every document and cross-referencing them against the documents they had disclosed. With over 300 documents to review, she found that only four had not been disclosed and were of minor relevance. Fortunately, there was no "smoking gun" (a document or detail that was hidden and could be detrimental) in the bunch.

Figure 2.1: **Basic Litigation Process**

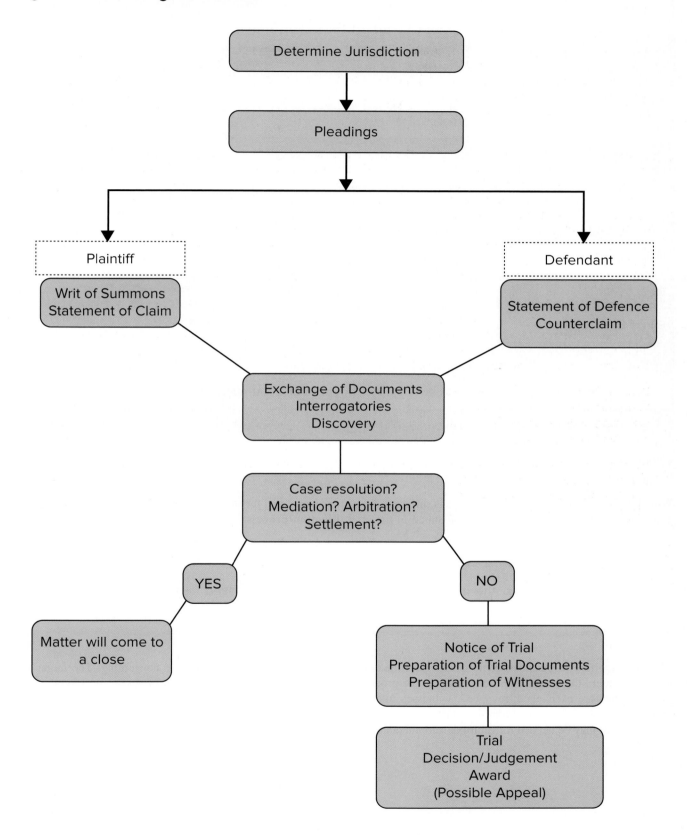

As you can see in Figure 2.1, the roadmap for a case to go from beginning to end involves quite a journey. You can also find the litigation process or the civil procedure rules for a civil case for each province at the following sites:

Ontario	www.attorneygeneral.jus.gov.on.ca/english/courts/civil/ suing_and_being_sued_7.asp
Alberta	https://albertacourts.ca/provincial-court/civil-small-claims-court/civil-claim-process
Saskatchewan	www.sasklawcourts.ca/index.php/home/court-of-queen-s-bench/civil
Manitoba	web2.gov.mb.ca/laws/rules/qbr1e.php
Quebec	www.justice.gouv.qc.ca/english/publications/generale/proc-civ-a.htm
New Brunswick	www.gnb.ca/0062/regs/Rule/rule_list.htm
Nova Scotia	www.courts.ns.ca/Civil_Procedure_Rules/cpr_home.htm
Prince Edward Island	www.courts.pe.ca/supreme/index.php?number=1003816
Newfoundland/Labrador	www.court.nl.ca/supreme/general/faqs.html#civfaq
Northwest Territories	https://www.justice.gov.nt.ca/en/court-rules/
Yukon	www.yukoncourts.ca/courts/supreme/ykrulesforms.html
Nunavut	http://www.nunavutcourts.ca/court-policies-nucj/rules

While the litigation process for civil cases is different for each province and territory, there is only a slight variance. Most provinces and territories use the roadmap stated in the **civil litigation process** chart in Figure 2.1 and also use the same terminology.

Civil Litigation Process—the process that the party suing or being sued must go through from the beginning to the final disposition.

What is important to businesspeople is that the litigation process is both expensive and time consuming. The larger the monetary claim, the longer and more involved the process is. A business may be embroiled in litigation for several years, as documents are exchanged, reviewed, witnesses interviewed, and settlements accepted or rejected. This investment in time—especially management time—and money can distract an organization from its primary function while it also absorbs resources that may be needed for future development and daily operations.

LEGAL SCENARIO

When litigation is happening, keep this in mind!

In the litigation process, your lawyer will ensure that all legal aspects are followed. However, it is important to keep some important details in mind:

- All documents pertaining to a case MUST be disclosed;
- Any information in a document or record that is not relevant can be redacted (blacked out);
- All records (letters, reports, emails, voicemails, videos, maps, drawings, spreadsheets, bank records, tax returns, doodles on a document, handwritten notes, etc.) that are in your possession or control are subject to disclosure to the other party in the legal action;
- You may be required to provide additional documents or answer questions that the opposing counsel may request.
- There are three instances where you do not need to disclose documentation.
  1. Solicitor–client privilege: records between you and your lawyer
  2. Litigation privilege: records between you and a third party involved in the case as you prepare for trial
  3. On a "without prejudice basis": records dealing with negotiations to settle the dispute.

LO 2.4

2.4 Alternative Dispute Resolution

© Wavebreakmedia Ltd | Dreamstime.com

When an action arises against your business or your business begins an action against a person, organization, or government, it is crucial that you and your organization retain the services of a lawyer unless the claim is small, and even a small claim might require the services of a lawyer. However, there are alternative ways to resolve disputes between parties that don't require litigation.

As introduced in Chapter 1, Alternative Dispute Resolution (ADR) is becoming a common occurrence because compared to litigation it offers the following advantages:

- Is less costly
- Provides speedy results
- Allows parties to resolve their difficulties in a more friendly manner
- Allows parties to have more involvement in the resolution of their dispute

For example, if John and Henry have a land dispute that has not been resolved and they do not wish to incur costs that might add up to more than the land is worth, they may contact a **mediator** who will help them come to a mutually agreed resolution. Mediators can be found online, or through provincial or countrywide organizations such as Family Mediation Canada (www.fmc.ca) or the ADR Institute of Ontario (www.adrontario.ca).

> **Mediator**—a trained and certified third party who will assist the parties with their dispute through negotiation.

Several formats exist for ADR, but the most common or popular are mediation and arbitration.

Mediation is a popular type of ADR. Because mediation encourages the parties to go through their issues and come to an agreement through a process, the final result is up to the parties and not the mediator. At any time, the parties may agree to disagree and return to the litigation process.

> **Mediation**—parties come together and solve their issue(s) with the assistance of a trained mediator.

LEGAL SCENARIO

Sheep Grazing or Property Selling?

Archie and Duncan are stepbrothers who have just been given a parcel of property in the Last Will and Testament of their deceased father. The land is adjacent to Archie's property and Archie has used the land for a grazing space for his sheep for the last 10 years. Duncan is in need of money and wishes to sell the property to a prospective purchaser who has been inquiring about the property. Archie doesn't want to sell the property and also has no interest in purchasing the property.

Archie and Duncan have never been close and communications between them have never been warm. In fact, they rarely communicate or get together for family events except for their father's birthday once a year.

Neither Archie or Duncan want to incur the costs and the hard feelings that a court battle could produce, so they turn to a local mediator to help them out since they couldn't agree on how to proceed after meeting a few times after the reading of their father's will.

Archie and Duncan meet with the mediator, who is trained in negotiation, and they tell her their reasons for either selling or retaining the property. At the end of their session, Archie and Duncan have agreed to subdivide the property in half where Archie can use the property for his sheep and Duncan can sell his property to the prospective purchaser and split the cost of the subdivision.

Another possibility for a business when mediation might either not work or be too informal is **arbitration**, in which parties come together in a process that is more formal than mediation but less formal than a court setting to resolve their issues with the assistance of a selected **arbitrator**. Arbitrators are found on government websites and are generally governed by law in most provinces and territories. See http://www.amic.org/ for more information on arbitrators and arbitration.

Arbitration—parties come together in a process that is more formal than mediation but less formal than a court setting to resolve their issues with the assistance of a selected arbitrator.

Arbitrator—parties come together to solve their issue(s) with the assistance of an arbitrator who is trained in the more formal arbitration process and is prepared to make a decision on the issue that is final and binding.

Arbitration is traditionally found in union/management disputes. However, organizations are using binding and unbinding arbitration as a means to resolve more complex disputes in a cheaper and faster manner than litigation. A person or panel will listen to all the facts and evidence and then come to a decision. It is up to the two parties to decide if the arbitration will be binding or not in advance of the arbitration process.

The Government of Canada has a handy pamphlet (http://www.justice.gc.ca/eng/rp-pr/csj-sjc/dprs-sprd/dr-rd/index.html) that outlines the different ways to handle disputes without going to court and should be reviewed so that businesspeople today are current with the latest ADR information.

LO 2.5   2.5 Risk Management and How Lawyers Help Resolve Disputes

At the end of the day, businesspeople must make decisions on whether a dispute can be easily dealt with or whether a lawyer must get involved. It is always the logical approach to obtain legal advice for a contentious issue before moving forward. It is critical to move progressively on that first step—perhaps it is to go through a mediation process first and see how that goes. If the issue goes sideways then arbitration may be used—and then, as a final possibility, the litigation route.

As a businessperson, you must evaluate the situation and the risk that the situation will escalate because of your words or actions. Businesses may have problems with management, employees, contractors, suppliers, governments, and others, but it is critical for businesses and individuals to recognize when to obtain legal advice, and also to seek the best method of resolution for the dispute.

FOR REVIEW

Questions

1. What is the difference between a plaintiff and a defendant? Can you have more than one plaintiff or defendant? Explain. (LO 2.1)
2. Find three cases from three different courts. Who are the parties in each case? (LO 2.1, 2.2)
3. Explain what is involved in a "settlement" of a civil litigation matter, and what benefits or problems it may present. (LO 2.3)
4. What is the difference between the balance of probabilities and beyond a reasonable doubt? (LO 2.1)
5. List other titles/expressions for civil litigation. (LO 2.3)
6. Why does it take so long for some cases to be resolved? (LO 2.3)
7. What does it mean to "appeal" a case? (LO 2.2))
8. Why is having a small claims court important? (LO 2.2)

9. What are civil procedure rules? (LO 2.3)

10. What is ADR? What are the types of ADR? Why is it valuable for a business to seek ADR? (LO 2.4)

Activities

1. Browse newspapers, magazines, or websites and other periodicals for a recent civil case. Explain the background of the case, outline the issues of the case, and provide the outcome. (LO 2.1)

2. Interview a lawyer or look online for an interview of a Canadian lawyer who talks about the legal system in Canada or a case they were involved with. (LO 2.1)

3. Find a case in each level of court (Supreme, Appeal, and Supreme Court of Canada) and explain the case and its final outcome. (LO 2.2)

4. Create your own civil case and explain the issues, the parties, and the court in which it will be heard. Indicate the steps that your plaintiff or defendant will have to go through. (LO 2.2, 2.3)

5. Choose a province and explain the hierarchy of its court system. (LO 2.2)

6. Choose a province other than British Columbia: research and outline the litigation process for that province. (LO 2.3)

7. Briefly explain the differences between mediation and arbitration and provide examples of circumstances in which one of these forms of ADR might be more effective than the other in resolving a dispute. (LO 2.4)

8. Discuss individually or in small groups the various risks that businesses might experience. Provide a list of five risks; find a case that represents those risks and discuss the outcome. (LO 2.5)

CASES FOR DISCUSSION

Case #1

Fred runs a small business selling customized signs and banners. Dennila ordered 15 custom-designed and printed banners from Fred for an event she was planning. The order cost $26,500. Unfortunately, the event was a disaster: only one-third of the people Dennila had hoped to attract bought tickets and showed up. As a result, Dennila defaulted on her payment to Fred for the order he delivered.

Fred, needless to say, is very angry and cannot afford to write off the money owed to him. Knowing you took an excellent course on business law at your college and still have your textbook, *Canadian Business Law Today,* for reference, he has come to you to ask advice as to what his options are in these circumstances. You know that the monetary limit for a claim in small claims court in the province where Fred operates his business is $25,000.

Outline for Fred the different methods available to him in trying to collect his outstanding account against Dennila. Explain the benefits and problems that each approach may present. (LO 2.1)

Case #2

The Sinclairs, a young couple, had purchased their dream home on a lovely street in their home town. It was in a newly developed neighbourhood with a great price of $250,000. The young couple decided that they would get funding from a bank through a mortgage but required a down payment. It was decided that they would get their down payment from the Millers, close friends who had come into some money when they sold their business a few years ago. The down payment of $30,000 was given to the Sinclairs with a verbal agreement to pay it back over five years.

As the years went on, the Sinclairs made their mortgage payments but they had not paid back one cent on the down payment they borrowed from their friends the Millers. The Millers had made numerous requests to the Sinclairs, after two years of non-payment, for their $30,000 or even a payment schedule. The Sinclairs ignored all requests.

The Millers really weren't sure what to do. This process put a serious strain on their friendship. At this point, they knew they couldn't go to small claims court because of the amount they were claiming. Also, they were at a point in their lives where they had children in sports and also had purchased some assets and didn't have the money to get involved in a lawsuit. What would you suggest the Millers should do and why? (LO 2.4)

CHAPTER 3

TORT LAW

Learning Objectives

After reading this chapter the student will:

LO 3.1 Define the concept of tort law

LO 3.2 Differentiate between intentional torts and unintentional torts

LO 3.3 Identify the types of intentional torts

LO 3.4 Consider the defences to unintentional torts

LO 3.5 Discuss the application of risk management when dealing with torts

HELP!

As a businessperson, you may experience any of these scenarios:

- HELP! A former client has been posting inaccurate information about your business on their Facebook page.

- HELP! An employee is sharing confidential information with a competitor.

- HELP! A bouncer at a tavern you manage has forcefully evicted an inebriated customer and injured her.

- HELP! Your delivery driver, while talking on his cell phone, has hit a pedestrian at an intersection.

- HELP! You have just caught a shoplifter in your grocery store.

What do you do?

Unfortunate events do occur in the course of doing business and sometimes they are related to legal issues. If a legal situation like one of the scenarios above happens, successful businesspeople need to understand the legal implications of the situation and when they need to contact a lawyer.

However, you can minimize the risk for you and your business before something goes wrong by:

- Understanding your duty and the care that must be taken toward others (e.g., employees, customers, the public).
- Knowing what a "reasonable person" would do.
- Recognizing if and when you need to contact a lawyer.
- Understanding the implications of your failure to act.
- Comprehending the statutes involved in your jurisdiction.
- Realizing that you may have to compensate the injured party.

LO 3.1   3.1 What Is Tort Law?

Simply stated, tort law is an area of the law that holds an individual or business accountable for either intentional or unintentional harm caused to another person or business.

When you hear about the concept of tort law, it may be in the context of something that happens because a person or business does something wrong that causes harm or loss to another person or business. So, tort law is law related to wrongdoing, and it can affect a business's everyday activities and strategic planning. By understanding this concept, a businessperson can analyze their business activities and identify and manage the risks that may occur whether they meant to do something wrong or not. Additionally, tort law provides us with guidelines of the repercussions of a wrongdoing. Keep in mind that a **tort** does not involve a contract between parties.

Tort—an action committed by an individual or business that causes harm, intentionally or unintentionally.

Tort law is a matter of common law, decided by judges in a civil trial. However, it can also be statute-based, as in the case of assault and battery and the *Criminal Code of Canada*. A person committing a tort is called a **tortfeasor**.

Tortfeasor—the person committing a tort.

LO 3.2   3.2 Intentional and Unintentional Torts

A tort is an important concept to the world of business. There may be times when a businessperson is unaware that their actions or behaviour are harmful. Tort law has two distinctive parts: intentional and unintentional torts.

An **intentional tort** occurs when a person or business consciously and deliberately causes harm to another individual or business. Various intentional torts include assault and battery, false imprisonment, slander, and libel.

Intentional Tort—deliberate harm.

On the other hand, an **unintentional tort** occurs when a person or business has caused harm to another person or business, not deliberately but because the tortfeasor(s) is careless in their action.

© Bowie15 | Dreamstime.com

Unintentional Tort—not deliberate harm.

Intentional and unintentional torts will be discussed in more depth later in this chapter. But first, can you identify which scenarios below are intentional torts and which are unintentional torts?

SCENARIO CHALLENGE!

Identify which scenarios are intentional torts and which are unintentional torts

- A bouncer at your establishment evicts, with aggressive force, a drunk patron who falls and suffers a serious concussion. The patron also has a very thin skull and the result of the fall is permanent brain damage.
- Your employee accesses information about a client without a valid reason.
- A hockey player on your company-sponsored hockey team cross-checks an opposing player causing the opposing player a back and neck injury. The injured hockey player is unable to finish the season.
- A business has a staff party at which drinks are served in large amounts. When the party comes to a close, a staff member goes to a local casino and gambles away thousands of dollars, putting her in a dire financial situation that results in her defaulting on her mortgage and losing her house.

So, when faced with a wrongdoing or a situation like those in the Scenario Challenge, the first question a businessperson must ask is: What exactly happened?

Businesspeople need to be knowledgeable about tort law in order to protect the business, themselves, their employees, and their stakeholders from legal wrongdoing. A critical consideration is that a businessperson needs to be aware of the business's exposure; **business exposure** involves recognizing what is a wrong action or activity and how to minimize or eliminate that exposure. It is important to decrease the probability of a loss for a business in terms of time, human resources, and money.

Business Exposure—actions that make a business vulnerable.

- Has the situation been documented?
- Was it an employee or a contractor who is at fault?
- Was it deliberate or not deliberate?
- Was anyone injured?
- Were there financial damages? If so, in what amount?

The legal principle of **vicarious liability** makes an employer personally responsible to pay for the damages or injuries caused to another individual or business by an employee who was acting in the course of their employment when the harm was done. The law has gone so far as to decide that, as well as an employee's negligent actions, an employer may even be held responsible for an employee's criminal acts.

Vicarious Liability—an employer is responsible for injuries caused by an employee while acting in the course of their employment.

LO 3.3 ## 3.3 Types of Intentional Torts

Sometimes bad things happen to good people, it's been said. Sometimes, it can be even intentional—or deliberate. When an intentional wrongdoing, injury, or harm occurs and the injured party pursues the issue in court, it is a tort—where one person sues another in order to be compensated for their loss. When we use the word "compensated," we don't mean just money. Compensation can be various other ways to remedy the situation and attempt to return the injured party to as close as possible to their original state. For example, if the person who commits the injury is found to be at fault, the court may ask the person to return stolen property or repair the damages. The court often will award the injured a monetary **remedy** for loss of work, pain and suffering, and other damages such as the costs associated with the lawsuit.

Remedy—the compensation, financial or other, when a person(s) is successful in a lawsuit. Also called damages.

A court will look at three elements that must occur in a deliberate wrongdoing:

1. Did the person who committed the alleged harm (defendant) do it on purpose?
2. Did the actions of the defendant result in the injury?
3. Is there a monetary and measurable damage that occurred?

Often, intentional torts will not be the first instance where the person who committed the harm appears in court. Because intentional torts such as battery and assault are against the law, the defendant will appear in court for a criminal case first and then later in a civil court.

First, we will examine two common intentional torts that come from actual or threatened harm to a person: *battery* and *assault*.

One may not think of **battery** in the context of the operation of a business, but it can happen. One of the most common areas is where bouncers are involved in the security of a business. If a bouncer intentionally harms a patron, the establishment may be facing a lawsuit. Another example would be where a medical doctor gives medical treatment without consent resulting in harm to the patient. The bottom line for the intentional tort of battery is that there is unconsented, physical harm.

> **Battery**—the physical intentional and unconsented contact that causes harm; is an unlawful offence and a tort.

Another intentional tort is **assault**. Unlike battery, assault is the threat of harm. Physical harm doesn't have to occur for the tort of assault. For example, if a person threatens to punch another person, the person threatened can bring a lawsuit using the tort of assault.

> **Assault**—the intention or threat of unwanted physical contact that causes harm.

Categories of intentional torts include but are not limited to:

- Torts involving customers
- Torts involving other businesses
- Torts involving business property
- Torts from words
- Torts relating to privacy

Intentional Torts Involving Customers

Training of personnel in retail, food service, or any type of business that serves customers is critical for a business to avoid a lawsuit involving an intentional tort. **False imprisonment** is an example of a situation where a business needs to know their rights and the rights of their customers.

> **False Imprisonment**—intentionally confining an unwilling person within a specified area.

The intentional tort of false imprisonment as it relates to the customer is an important category to a business. An example of this would be where a store security person holds someone suspected of shoplifting until the police arrive. Several factors would need to be examined by the court in this case. For instance, the court will ask: Did the security person actually see the person shoplift the item? Did the customer ask to leave?

False imprisonment does not mean that a person suffers physical injury. Simply the idea of being imprisoned is enough of a threat. The person who imprisons the customer for shoplifting, for example, must have reasonable cause to ask the customer to accompany them until the police arrive. The bottom line is that personnel dealing with customers must get training to know what the *Criminal Code of Canada* says about false imprisonment.

" A STRAIGHT LEFT AGAINST A SLOGGING RUFFIAN. "

Intentional Torts Involving Other Businesses

It is common for businesses to interact with other businesses. Generally, when there is a breach of an agreement (contract), this breach falls under litigation and contract law. In the case where it is an intentional tort, there are three main types: *passing off*, *inducing breach of contract*, and *interference with economic relations*.

Have you ever purchased a product that you thought was a designer product? Did you wonder why the price was so low? This would be an example of **passing off**, and it occurs when a company represents to the public a product or service as their own when, in fact, the product or service concept belongs to another company.

Passing Off—falsely representing to the public another company's product or service as your own.

DID YOU KNOW?

What the *Criminal Code of Canada* says:

ARREST WITHOUT WARRANT AND RELEASE FROM CUSTODY

Arrest without warrant by any person

494. (1) Any one may arrest without warrant

(a) a person whom he finds committing an indictable offence; or

(b) a person who, on reasonable grounds, he believes
   i. has committed a criminal offence, and
   ii. is escaping from and freshly pursued by persons who have lawful authority to arrest that person.

Arrest by owner, etc., of property

(2) The owner or a person in lawful possession of property, or a person authorized by the owner or by a person in lawful possession of property, may arrest a person without a warrant if they find them committing a criminal offence on or in relation to that property and
   (a) they make the arrest at that time; or
   (b) they make the arrest within a reasonable time after the offence is committed and they believe on reasonable grounds that it is not feasible in the circumstances for a peace officer to make the arrest.

http://laws-lois.justice.gc.ca/eng/acts/c-46/FullText.html

 CASE STUDY

Ciba-Geigy Canada Ltd. v. Apotex Inc., [1992] 3 SCR 120

The case of *Ciba-Geigy Canada Ltd. v. Apotex Inc.* illustrates the tort of passing off.

Facts: Ciba-Geigy brought passing off actions against its competitor, Apotex, alleging that its metoprolol tablets, a hypertension drug, are unique and known by reason of their size, shape, and colour. Ciba-Geigy had sold such tablets for some time. Apotex started to produce metoprolol tablets, which it was licensed to do. However, its tablets were the same size, shape, and colour as those of Ciba-Geigy's.

Decision: Ciba-Geigy was successful. The Ciba-Geigy product was well known and similarities in the product manufactured by Apotex were likely to cause confusion with members of the public who would be taking the drug.

As you will read in Chapter 5 in this textbook, a contract is an agreement enforceable through the law and agreed upon by two or more parties, with benefits for all. In the tort of **inducing breach of contract**, the defendant would knowingly and deliberately cause a breach in a contract between two parties. For example, this would occur if a business were seeking a particular person for a job opening and deliberately went after a competitor's employee to hire them away, thereby breaching the employment contract between the employee and his or her employer. Inducing breach of contract is an economic tort where the plaintiff suffered a loss because the defendant convinced a third party to break the contract.

Inducing Breach of Contract—an economic tort where a person or person convinces a third party to breach his/her contract with the plaintiff.

Another economic intentional tort is that of **interference with economic relations**. Similar to inducing breach of contract in that there is an interference with the parties in a contract, this tort involves illegal actions that harm the plaintiff's business. A common example of this would be when an employee steals confidential or intellectual information and gives it to a competitor, causing the plaintiff to lose money and/or profit share. Other business-to-business torts are listed in Table 3.1.

Interference with Economic Relations—deliberate illegal interference with the interests of a third party.

CASE STUDY

A.I. Enterprises Ltd. v. Bram Enterprises Ltd., 2014 SCC 12

Four brothers owned an apartment building in Moncton, New Brunswick. Three brothers wanted to sell the apartment building and one brother did not. The brother and his company that did not want to sell the building (A.I. Enterprises Ltd.) had the opportunity to purchase the building from the other three brothers, he did want to purchase it at the appraised value at or before the contractual deadline.

Over time, other purchasers were interested in the building over the appraised value but these sales never closed. The plaintiffs, the three brothers, said that A.I. Enterprises hindered the sales by not allowing potential purchasers to easily view the property and filing documents against the title of the property. Later, A.I. Enterprises did purchase the property at the appraised value. The three brothers sued A.I. Enterprises for the amount they could have received from potential purchasers and the amount A.I. Enterprises purchased it for because A.I. interfered with economic relations.

The case went to the Supreme Court of Canada where the Court had to decide what was meant by "unlawful means." The Court concluded that there was not interference with economic relations as the conduct complained about was not one of civil liability to the third party. The Court did find, however, that the brother (A.I. Enterprises) was an officer of the plaintiffs' company and had a fiduciary responsibility to their company. By obstructing the sale of the apartment building, he breached his fiduciary duty but did not unlawfully interfere with his brothers' economic success.

Table 3.1: Other Business-to-Business Torts

Tort	Action	Loss or Harm	Example
Intimidation	Threat of unlawful act against plaintiff	Coerces plaintiff to act in a manner that causes plaintiff loss	Using the threat of physical harm to force a competitor to cease operations
Deceit	Misleading the plaintiff using a false statement	Reliance on false statement causes plaintiff harm	Greatly exaggerating the features and value of a product being sold
Conspiracy	Two or more defendants act together to cause harm	Combined action causes plaintiff financial loss	Two parties working together to sell a product into another seller's exclusive territory

Intentional Torts Involving Business Property

Many businesses own the land and buildings where they conduct business, or they may lease or rent out land and buildings. Another type of property is chattels—which is an item that has ownership but is not a fixture and can be moved. An example of a chattel would be a mobile home. Business property and the law will be looked at in more depth in Chapter 9 in this textbook.

Businesspeople should be aware of the following instances that involve business property: *trespass to land, trespass to chattels,* and *nuisance.*

Trespass to land can take place by someone going on a property intentionally, or it can also be unintentional. In either case, it means that the defendant has not obtained permission to enter or occupy the land.

amygdala_imagery/Getty Images

Trespass to Land—entering and/or occupying land or property not owned and without permission or restricting the enjoyment of the property by its owners.

Permission to enter onto someone's land can be either expressed or implied. For example, a person can enter onto a property because they are expressly invited—as in the case of a retail store sending an invitation to their premium customers to shop during a special after-hours event during the holiday season. Implied permission or consent happens when a store hangs an "OPEN" sign indicating it is open for business during the stated hours.

When trouble hits, it is generally when someone will not leave a property when they have been asked to leave. Once a person or persons is asked to leave the property, the implied or expressed permission is now gone. For example, if a person continually takes a shortcut through a store to get to another business without making a purchase, the business owner can ask that person to stop. Once they are asked to stop coming onto the property, they must do so or they are trespassing on the property after that.

Businesses, from offices to manufacturers to farmers and fishers and every type of business in between, often have to deal with trespassers. It can be as simple as people who "dumpster dive"— going into dumpsters to find food, clothing, or other "treasures" a business may throw out—or people who build a campfire in a field that a campground owns but they have not paid for a campsite.

In terms of a **trespass to chattels**, an example would be where a construction site trailer office is damaged by vandals who go on the construction site. Another situation may be where a bulldozer is taken from a construction site and driven several kilometres away and destroyed. Both of these cases involve intentional actions of a person or persons.

Trespass to Chattels—causing damage, destroying, using, or removing a plaintiff's chattels.

Sergey Mironov / Shutterstock.com

A term we hear more often is the intentional tort of **nuisance**. Nuisance generally takes the form of noise and odours, but can also be other types of interference such as vibrations. Students are often aware of the noise bylaws in many towns and cities. These bylaws are created to allow the owners or renters of the property to enjoy the property within reason. That is why there is usually a "quiet" bylaw that states the time when loud music and other noises must be lowered.

Nuisance—the interference in the right to enjoy real property.

Intentional Torts from Words

"Upon my tongues continual slanders ride, The which in every language I pronounce,
Stuffing the ears of men with false reports."—William Shakespeare, *Henry IV, Part 2*

Oh yes, words can be an intentional tort. A person or business's reputation is a valuable part of their being. Any intentional harm to that reputation can give rise to a lawsuit. A harm or wrong by words, either written/printed or spoken, (1) must be false, (2) must harm a person's reputation, and (3) must be heard by someone. The three terms for an intentional tort from words are *defamation, slander,* and *libel.*

The tort of **defamation** will arise from either a spoken comment or gesture, which is known as **slander**, or through something of a more permanent form such as a written letter, a magazine article, a report, or perhaps a television broadcast, in which case it is referred to as **libel**. If an injured party can prove libel, damages are presumed and an award of money is made to compensate for the injury to the party's reputation. On the other hand, if the tort of defamation is based on slander, there is no presumption of injury to reputation and the plaintiff is required to prove they suffered damages as a result of the comment. With the increasing use of online communications, which have the capability to reach a far wider audience and the seeming anonymity provided by user names, the tort of defamation is experiencing a legal overhaul through court challenges.

Defamation—a false statement that must harm a person's or business's reputation.

Slander—oral defamation.

Libel—written defamation.

DID YOU KNOW?

In Nova Scotia, a 15-year-old girl discovered a fake Facebook profile that included her picture, a slightly modified version of her name, and identifying other particulars. The page also included unflattering commentary about the girl's appearance and sexually explicit adverse comments.[1] The individual who posted the Facebook page might well have committed the tort of defamation.

[1] Facts of *A.B. v. Bragg Communications Inc.,* 2012 SCC 46, [2012] 2 SCR 567.

Another area of intentional torts from words that businesses are particularly vulnerable to is **injurious falsehood**.

> **Injurious Falsehood**—when a reputation is lost because of false statements about a product or service. Also called slander of goods.

Take, for example, when a competitor of a product or service makes statements about its competition that are false and misleading. If these statements harm the business the competitor can be sued for injurious falsehood, and if evidence reveals the statements to be false that business would likely have to pay damages. Again, businesses must be aware of what their representatives and employees say about the competition and other businesses. If what you say injures a person or business, you could find yourself embroiled in an expensive lawsuit.

As mentioned above, if the statement that is made is true, then the lawsuit will fail. Additionally, if the defence of "fair comment" is given where the statement was made for the public good, is based on evidence, and made without malice, the lawsuit may not go forward.

The defences for those who find themselves as defendants in a defamation lawsuit are:
* Truth—the statement was true with evidence to prove it.
* Absolute privilege—areas where you can speak freely, e.g., Parliament, giving evidence in court, or in a regulatory manner where someone is investigating a complaint.
* Qualified privilege—where statements may be defamatory but not malicious and are used for a specific reason, such as a job reference.
* Fair comment—statements that are opinions and are not malicious.
* For the public good—urgent or necessary statements that serve the public interest.

Intentional Torts Relating to Privacy

You have no doubt heard the phrase "You are invading my privacy"! Well, that is exactly what the intentional tort relating to privacy is—an **invasion of privacy**. Privacy is critical to both individuals and businesses, and we all expect that our business will stay our business unless we want to divulge any information.

> **Invasion of Privacy**—private information that is disclosed to unauthorized people.

New to the tort scene in Canadian courts is the tort of **intrusion upon seclusion**, which has been the focus of a number of court cases recently. This tort occurs when the plaintiff suffers from the defendant intruding upon their privacy and where they suffer harm from the actions of the defendant's intrusion. Most likely these cases will be dealing with situations where is theft of personal information for fraudulent activities or humiliation of the plaintiff.

> **Intrusion upon Seclusion**—where one intrudes upon the seclusion or privacy of another.

© Andres Rodriguez | Dreamstime.com

 CASE STUDY

Jones v. Tsige, 2012 ONCA 32 (CanLII)

Facts: the defendant, an employee of the bank used by the plaintiff, had accessed the plaintiff's banking records at least 174 times over a period of four years. It is to be noted that the defendant was in a common-law relationship with the plaintiff's ex-husband at the time. The plaintiff sued the defendant for damages for invasion of privacy.

Decision: The Ontario Court of Appeal overturned the Ontario Supreme Court decision and granted a summary judgment. The court ruled that the law should recognize the need to protect people from unreasonable intrusion into their private affairs. The Court awarded $10,000 damages to the plaintiff.

LO 3.4   **3.4** Unintentional Torts and Their Defences

Lisa and Jenn and the Bumblebee Remains

Setting: Office of the manager of the bottling line in building #2 of a beverage manufacturer late on a Thursday afternoon in early April. The telephone rings and the frustrated manager picks up the phone.

Caller: Boss, there's a problem with the inspection light for the bottle line. We need to replace the bulb.

Boss: How long will that take? We have to get the delivery out by 5:00 this afternoon to make the quota for the month.

Caller: Ten minutes should do it.

Boss: Okay, just keep the line filling and get it done as fast as you can or you can kiss your bonus goodbye.

Caller: You got it!

Two months later on a hot, sunny afternoon, two friends are relaxing by the side of a pool:

Jenn: Lisa, are you going to drink the rest of that bottle so we can head to the club?

Lisa: Sure, there's not much left.

Jenn watches as Lisa pours the rest of the bottle into her glass. They both notice the liquid get thicker and slower as it drains out of the bottle until finally, a slimy, filmy lump slops out of the bottle and into Lisa's glass. Jenn's eyes grow wide as she recognizes the tiny wings and colouring and the remains of a decomposing bumblebee. With the taste of the drink still on her tongue, Lisa realizes what it is, and what she's done. Her stomach rumbles as she tries to hold down her lunch. Jenn rushes Lisa to the nearest hospital, where Lisa's stomach is pumped out. In the rush of taking Lisa to the hospital, Jenn damages her car when she enters a parking space too quickly and bumps a light standard in the hospital parking lot.

An investigation indicates the bottle was filled on a Thursday afternoon in early April of that year at building #2 of the beverage manufacturer.

Lisa now has an irrational fear of bottled beverages and has to give up her dream job as a landscape gardener after developing a morbid fear of bees. Jenn is annoyed at the repair bill for her front bumper.

When the manager of the beverage company received the news that Lisa had filed a lawsuit against the company for physical, financial, and emotional injuries, she shook her head and muttered: What was I thinking?

The law related to unintentional torts is full of those "What was I thinking?" moments. Consider the following Legal Scenario:

LEGAL SCENARIO

What Was I Thinking?

What was I thinking when I left that pipe on the sidewalk in front of the restaurant door while I ran to get my screwdriver from the truck?

What was I thinking when I posted that metal sign over the customer line at the cash register with low-tack tape?

What was I thinking when I didn't bother to put out the "slippery when wet" sign after the floor was cleaned?

What was I thinking when I talked to a patient in the grocery store about their medical condition?

What was I thinking when I left confidential folders on the picnic table at the park?

At the core of unintentional torts, and the most common reason for a legal action based on tort law, is **negligence**—careless actions that unintentionally cause physical or financial harm to another individual and/or their property.

Negligence—a failure to exercise the degree of care toward another individual expected of a reasonable person in the circumstances.

The situations to which negligence may apply are limited only by the human imagination: a dentist with a heavy cold who sneezes while drilling a patient's tooth; an experienced soccer player who slide tackles an opponent on a concrete gym floor; a server at a bar who does not want to refuse an attractive customer.

Negligence is a question of risk. In managing the risks associated with business operations, decisions are made that may have unintentional results of physical, emotional, or financial injury to another person that require financial compensation under certain circumstances. In the case of Jenn and Lisa, was the plant manager careless about the safety of the beverage consumer when she made the decision to keep the filling line going? How reasonable were her actions in the circumstances? Did she fully assess the risks involved in making her decision?

In determining whether the tort of negligence is present, there are key elements that must be established:

* Was there a duty not to cause harm owed by one individual to another?
* What level/standard of care was applicable if there was a duty?
* Did the individual's actions fail to meet that standard of care?
* Was the other person's injury caused by that failure?

The plaintiff must prove on a balance of probabilities that…

* The defendant owed a duty of care
* The defendant breached the standard of care
* The breach of care caused the damage

Duty of Care

The first indicator in establishing responsibility for the tort of negligence is the presence of a duty of care. A **duty of care** means not to cause injury, and is owed by one individual or business to another. As individuals, we are required to exercise care toward people or businesses that we can reasonably predict might be harmed by our actions or failure to act. At the core of establishing duty of care, the court must determine whether the person causing harm could reasonably foresee or predict that his or her action(s) would cause injury to another.

> **Duty of Care**—not to cause injury; is owed by one individual or business to another.

The scope of the duty was considered in the case of *Donoghue v. Stevenson.*

CASE STUDY

Donoghue v. Stevenson [1932] AC 562

Facts: The plaintiff, Donoghue, was served a ginger beer manufactured by Stevenson, in a dark coloured bottle as part of a meal paid for by her friend. At the bottom of the bottle, Donoghue found a decomposed snail and later became seriously ill from drinking the ginger beer. Donoghue sued Stevenson claiming negligence on the part of the manufacturer for not having a proper system for inspecting the bottles and that the company owed a duty of care to her as a potential consumer of the ginger beer.

Decision: The court decided the manufacturer owed a duty to Donaghue and had failed to meet a reasonable standard of care. Lord Atkin wrote: "A person who engages in the manufacture of articles of food and drink intended for consumption by the public has a duty of care to those whom he intends to consume his products...."

The duty of care has been extended to hold commercial hosts, such as bar owners, responsible for allowing customers to drink too much and then sending them off to walk along a country road where they are hit by a careless motorist, and for accidents caused by customers who have had too much to drink and subsequently cause motor vehicle accidents.

CASE STUDY

Stewart v. Pettie, [1995] 1 S.C.R. 131

The Supreme Court of Canada considered the extension of the duty of care to commercial hosts in the case of *Stewart v. Pettie*.

Facts: The Mayfield Dinner Theatre Inn in Edmonton, Alberta served several double rum and cokes to Stewart's brother, Stuart Pettie, over the course of the evening at a company party. The theatre was aware that Stewart and her party had arrived by car and that Stewart and her sister-in-law did not drink that evening. When the group left the restaurant, his sister and the others in the party permitted Stuart Pettie to drive. The car struck a light post and Stewart sustained head injuries.

Decision: At the Supreme Court of Canada, it was held that a commercial host owes a duty of care to people who foreseeably could be injured by their drunken customers, but since some of the party were not drinking, the theatre was entitled to assume that a non-drinker would be driving and the commercial host, in this situation, was not responsible for the accident.

The Court held that a vendor of alcohol owes a duty of care and must take reasonable steps to meet that duty and prevent the risk of harm to the public.

Standard of Care and Breach of Duty

The concept of a duty implies there is a certain level, or standard, of behaviour that is expected from the person who is responsible for performing the duty. For example, a customer would expect that a skilled mechanic would properly put back all the parts to the car after the repair. The tort of negligence determines what the standard behaviour is for a person based on the standard behaviour of a reasonable person. If the defendant's actions were similar to the actions of a reasonable person in the same situation, then his or her actions are not negligent. However, if the defendant's actions have fallen below the reasonable level expected by society, the defendant may be found negligent.

In determining whether someone's behaviour has fallen below the level expected, the courts have used the standard of the ordinary, **reasonable person** and asked: What would a reasonable person have done under similar circumstances? The standard applied is not that of a perfect person but an ordinary person, someone who would give careful thought to the probable results of their actions before taking the first step in performing them.

Reasonable Person—an ordinary person, someone who would give careful thought to the probable results of their actions before taking the first step in performing them.

CASE STUDY

Crocker v. Sundance Northwest Resorts Ltd., [1988] 1 S.C.R. 1186

The Supreme Court of Canada considered this issue in the case of *Crocker v. Sundance Northwest Resorts Ltd.*

Facts: The plaintiff, Crocker, took part in an annual "tube race" involving inner tubes from large earth-moving machines. A few days before the race, Crocker had paid a $15.00 registration fee and signed an application form, unaware that it contained a disclaimer releasing the defendant, Sundance Resorts, from "all claims and demands of any nature."

At the race Crocker appeared very intoxicated and bought more drinks at the bar operated by Sundance Resort at the top of the hill. Crocker's drunken state was obvious to those around him and the starter warned Crocker he should not take part in the race. However, the starter did not try to stop him. Crocker broke his neck when he was thrown from the tube going down the hill and was left paralyzed and a quadriplegic as a result.

Decision: The Supreme Court of Canada found Sundance Resort negligent in allowing an obviously incapacitated person to take part in a dangerous activity, as the Resort owed the plaintiff a duty of care to take all reasonable steps to prevent him, an intoxicated participant, from taking part in the race and not just warning him.

Further, it was held the disclaimer on the application form did not protect the resort because Crocker was not made aware of it. Further, even if Crocker had known he was signing a disclaimer, it was Crocker's mental state at the time the injury happened that made the disclaimer void.

See Section 4.3 for another view on this landmark case.

Considering the example at the beginning of this section, could the bottling plant manager reasonably foresee that in deciding to continue filling bottles while the inspection light was repaired, a consumer could be injured? If so, then a duty of care not to injure the ultimate consumer of the beverage sold by the company to the public would exist, and the standard to apply for that duty would be what a reasonable person would have done under similar circumstances.

Causation

Once the duty has been established and the level of care is identified, the question becomes whether there is a connection between the plaintiff's physical, emotional, or financial damage and the action taken by the defendant. There has to be a link between the act and the harm. A common question is "but for"—*but for* the actions of the defendant, would the plaintiff be injured? Let's look at a case regarding this concept, *Clements v. Clements*.

 CASE STUDY

Clements v. Clements, 2012 SCC 32

The plaintiff and defendant were husband and wife at the time of a motorcycle accident. The couple were on a motorcycle that was heavily overloaded by approximately 100 pounds. The plaintiff, who was sitting in the passenger's seat of the motorcycle, suffered a traumatic brain injury as a result of being thrown from the bike. The defendant was unaware that there was a nail in the tire, and when he went to pass a car the nail fell out and the tire deflated causing the motorcycle to wobble and then crash.

The plaintiff sued the defendant for causing her injury because of this negligence in driving a motorcycle too fast when it was overloaded.

The trial judge found that the defendant's negligence did contribute to his wife's injury but for the plaintiff's inability to prove scientifically (*but for* his actions nor non-action, she would not have been injured) that he was negligent, the trial judge had to use the material contribution test (a test used when there is more than one possible reason for injury). The trial judge found the defendant liable.

The case was appealed to the British Columbia Court of Appeal, which set aside the judgment and dismissed the case by finding that the "but for" causation and the material contribution test did not apply.

The case was further appealed and the Supreme Court of Canada allowed the appeal and ordered a new trial.

Negligence is conduct falling below the standard of care expected from a reasonable person in similar circumstances. If someone has carelessly injured another person, it is expected that the injured party should be compensated in money for that injury.

Nonetheless, the courts have not found liability on the part of the defendant in situations where the consequences could not have been foreseen.

From the example at the beginning of this section, it could be argued that Lisa's physical and mental injuries occurred as a result of the bottling manager's failure to meet the standard of care. The damage to Jenn's car, however, might not meet that test as it could not be foreseen as resulting from the manager's decision to continue the filling line during repairs.

Although the damage caused must be of a type that could be reasonably foreseen, the courts have determined that the tortfeasor takes the victim as they find him or her and will be fully liable if the victim suffers greater than foreseeable injuries because of a pre-existing condition. For example, if a person has a pre-existing medical condition such as brittle bones, that pre-existing condition will be included by the court in determining the amount of compensation to be paid by the tortfeasor.

Defences for Unintentional Torts

Remoteness of Damage

The **remoteness of damage** defence is used when there appears to be no reasonable connection between the actions of the defendant and the harm caused to the plaintiff. The courts have accepted the defence that the injuries were caused by some other act that entered the chain of events outside of the defendant's negligent actions. This separate and distinct act is seen as an intervening action by some third party that enters into the chain of events between the initial action and the ultimate injury to the plaintiff.

Remoteness of Damage—no reasonable connection exists between the actions of the defendant and the harm caused to the plaintiff.

LEGAL SCENARIO

Definitely NOT Time to Play in the Sand!

A car on the highway, operated by a distracted driver texting his friend, ran into the rear of the car in front of it at high speed, causing the struck car to ram the back of a very large truck carrying an enormous amount of fine sand. The truck had been stopped due to traffic. In hitting the truck, the poorly maintained gears controlling the dumping mechanism engaged, and tonnes of sand were dumped on the middle car, resulting in the driver suffocating before he could be dug out.

In hitting the car at high speed, the initial driver would have been able to reasonably foresee serious injuries to the driver and damage to the car, but not death by suffocation.

Contributory Negligence

The plaintiff's claim in an action based on negligence may fail or be reduced if the injured party's own conduct contributed to, or caused, the damage complained of, known as **contributory negligence**. In thosce provinces with legislation dealing with negligence in civil actions, this would be a statutory defence requiring the court to apportion damages between the plaintiff and the defendant according to their respective degrees of responsibility for the injuries suffered.

Contributory Negligence—plaintiff's own conduct contributed or caused the damage.

Watch Where You Run!

A jogger goes out at night for a run along an unlit country road, dressed in a dark jogging outfit with no reflective tape or headlamp. The driver of an approaching car travelling slightly above the speed limit does not see the jogger until the last minute, and in swerving to miss him catches the jogger with the back of the car, knocking him down and breaking his left leg and arm.

In a case such as this, the court might determine the jogger was partly at fault as a result of his decision to wear a dark suit at night with no reflective tape while jogging on an unlit road—perhaps 40 percent. The driver of the car may be responsible for 60 percent of the jogger's injuries due to speed and not paying attention while driving.

Assumption of Risk

The defence of *volenti non fit injuria*, referred to as **voluntary assumption of risk**, is available if the injured party, the plaintiff, was aware of the risk associated with the activity and consented to assume that risk. However, the risk assumed must be recognizable to the individual agreeing to take part, as well as normal for the activity being considered. For example, an individual might consent to assume the risk associated with skydiving. However, if the parachute is a new design being tested for the first time and the person jumping is unaware of that, the risk assumed is not recognizable and the defendant's use of the defence of *volenti non fit injuria* would likely not be successful.

Voluntary Assumption of Risk—the plaintiff is aware of the risk associated with the activity and has consented to assume that risk.

LO 3.5   3.5 Risk Management Regarding Torts

Unintentional torts arise from situations based on negligence which, as we have seen, involves risk and risk management. Being able to anticipate and/or assess the legal risks involved with any action being contemplated by a business means you, as a businessperson, can add value to the organization. Your ability to respond to the action of another individual that has caused physical or financial damage to your organization is a powerful skill. Additionally, knowing how to avoid a "What was I thinking?" moment by increasing a business's understanding of the potential legal problems associated with a course of action is a skill that is invaluable to carrying on a business.

It is interesting to see the numbers of associations and organizations that produce website information for their members and the public regarding risk management so they can avoid a lawsuit. Associations from various provinces such as construction, forestry, producers, health, and manufacturers, to name a few, create and distribute information that can assist in lowering risk. Another element in managing risk involves understanding when legal advice should be obtained before starting a new activity and how to speak with the legal service provider to obtain the information required.

- Tort law may be in the context of "something that happens because a person or business/organization harms another person, business, or organization."
- As a businessperson, you should understand and minimize the risk of various activities.
- A tortfeasor is the person or business committing the tort.
- Torts are intentional or unintentional.
- Intentional torts are deliberate; unintentional torts are not deliberate.

- Intentional torts fall into several categories that involve customers, other businesses, business property, words, and privacy.
- Duty of care and standard of care are important in the concept of unintentional torts.
- Negligence is at the core of unintentional torts.
- The reasonable person is important in understanding unintentional torts.
- There are several defences to negligence.
- Businesses must train their employees and be prepared to manage their risk to avoid lawsuits.

FOR REVIEW

Questions

1. What is tort law and why is it important in the management of a business? (LO 3.1)
2. What is the difference between intentional torts and unintentional torts? (LO 3.2)
3. When a business has been exposed to a situation where there is a tort, what does this mean? How can it be minimized? (LO 3.1)
4. What is a "remedy"? List and discuss the types of remedies that are common. (LO 3.3)
5. What is passing off? What is inducing breach of contract? Discuss examples of these two concepts. (LO 3.3)
6. What are the differences among intimidation, deceit, and conspiracy? Give examples. (LO 3.3)
7. Explain and provide examples for the five defences to a defamation lawsuit. (LO 3.3)
8. What is negligence? What are the key elements of negligence? (LO 3.4)
9. What is duty of care and why is it important? (LO 3.4)
10. Why do courts consider the "reasonable person"? Who is the reasonable person? (LO 3.4)
11. Explain "but for" as it relates to causation. Provide an example. (LO 3.4)
12. Discuss contributory negligence and provide an example for this term. (LO 3.4)
13. Explain how a business can reduce its risk of involvement in a tort. Provide an example. (LO 3.5)

Activities

1. In a group, discuss, outline, and explain what you would do to decrease your risk for the tort of false imprisonment for your retail convenience store. (LO 3.2)
2. Provide a two- to three-line scenario and decide whether it is an intentional or unintentional tort. (LO 3.2)
3. Provide a criminal wrongdoing and explain which tort applies (e.g., I called the police in the middle of the night because teenagers jumped into my pool and wouldn't leave when asked). (LO 3.3)
4. Briefly explain the concept of duty of care in terms of establishing liability for unintentional torts. (LO 3.4)
5. Briefly explain the concept of the reasonable person in the context of a tort based on negligence. (LO 3.4)
6. In *Crocker v. Sundance Northwest Resorts Ltd.*, would it have made any difference to the decision of the court if the starter in charge of the race had: (LO 3.4)
   a. told Crocker he was disqualified from the race but Crocker went anyway?
   b. disqualified Crocker and sent him to the chalet but Crocker sneaked back to the tube and took part in the race?
   c. disqualified Crocker and refunded him the $15.00 entry fee before Crocker went down the hill in the tube?
   d. refused to allow Crocker to race and had another employee of the resort escort Crocker to the sidelines?

CASES FOR DISCUSSION

Case #1

Haley is an inventor who developed a new product that could cool the temperature of liquids very rapidly. She named it "ICY HOT." The product was a thick ceramic plate that used electricity and a beyond-micro compressor. The temperature of the liquid in a glass placed on the plate could be lowered by 15 degrees Celsius in a matter of minutes.

Haley wanted to promote her new product and arranged with a local retail store to allow her to demonstrate ICY HOT in the store on a Saturday morning. She set up her demonstration booth and was amazing the customers with her sales banter and the effect her product had in producing iced coffees from hot coffee, which she was offering to passersby. The ceramic plate Haley used to chill the drinks was on a table in front of her, along with three other display plates that were not being used. Haley had put up a small, handwritten sign on the table indicating the plate could become so cold that it would burn skin if not handled properly.

During a quiet period at the booth, Hector, a store customer, wandered by just as Haley had turned her back and bent down to get more clean coffee glasses for the demonstrations. You know where this is going. Curious, Hector picked up a plate to examine it, not realizing it was the demonstration plate. Haley turned around just in time to see Hector scream loudly in pain and pass out on the floor, with the plate stuck to his hand. Haley, acting quickly, unplugged the plate and screamed for management to call for an ambulance. The manager, rushing up, began to pry the plate off Hector's hand, tearing the skin, before Haley stopped him and told him to leave it to the paramedics.

Hector came to while the paramedics were removing the plate from his hand as they were on route to the hospital. Hector sustained significant damage to his right hand that was made worse by the manager's actions. Hector won't be able to work as a violinist with the city's orchestra again. Haley has decided to move from applied research and product development to pure research. The manager is on a first aid course.

Analyze and discuss the tort liability of the various parties involved in this fact situation.

Case #2

Hillary, owner of SpiritAway Spa and Salon, arrived at her desk at 10:30 in the morning. She smiled at the thought of her successful business that was launched only two years ago. SpiritAway Spa was a thriving business in a growing industry. Because of her business's reputation, she employed 15 hair stylists and aestheticians. SpiritAway was clearly contributing to the local economy.

Hillary had just received her financial analysis from her accountant that morning. By providing a quiet, high-end haven and top-notch customer service, SpiritAway had seen a 20 percent increase in sales from the previous year. It was an exciting time indeed!

Hillary's attention was suddenly drawn to a dreadful noise coming from outside her tranquil establishment. The sound of dogs barking reverberated throughout the spa, even though the windows were shut and the ventilation system was on. Hillary had never heard dogs barking before anywhere near her building.

She soon heard a series of knocks on her office door. Several of her staff entered with concerned faces and indicated that the dogs had been barking since early morning. They could see the three junkyard-type dogs in a fenced-in area next door to the spa.

Hillary contacted the owner of the building. The owner indicated that his tenant, owner of a new recording studio, kept the dogs for added security in his newly renovated building with noise-cancelling walls.

Hillary voiced her complaint that the dogs' barking continuously through the work day was driving her clients away. The owner of the building said he didn't have to comply with Hillary's request as there were no municipal bylaws in that area of town regarding noise.

What is the tort in this case? What would you advise Hillary to do?

CHAPTER 4

SPECIFIC ISSUES IN TORT LAW

Learning Objectives

After reading this chapter the student will:

LO 4.1 Understand professional liability and how it relates to the tort of negligence

LO 4.2 Understand the implications of product liability for manufacturers

LO 4.3 Understand occupiers' liability as a tort

HELP!
As a businessperson, you may experience any of these scenarios:

- HELP! I sought professional advice for my business but have found that the advice was in error. What can I do?

- HELP! As a working professional, I know I have responsibilities. What are those responsibilities?

- HELP! I have to develop an organizational manual with a focus on product safety. What do I need to know?

- HELP! What is occupiers' liability? I am wondering if I should be concerned for those patrons entering my business premises.

LO 4.1   ## 4.1 What Is Professional Liability?

Merriam-Webster's Online Dictionary defines *professional* as "...relating to a job that requires special education, training, or skill..."

Source: By permission. From Merriam-Webster's Collegiate® Dictionary, 11th Edition ©2016 by Merriam-Webster, Inc. (www.Merriam-Webster.com).

Professional liability is a tort of negligence for professionals that protects them from economic loss in the event that their client suffers from injury due to the service(s) they have provided. Professionals such as lawyers, doctors, accountants, insurance brokers, and engineers, to name a few, are held to a high standard and have a **fiduciary duty** to their clients.

> **Professional Liability**—a tort of negligence for professionals that protects them from economic loss in the event that their client suffers from injury due to the service(s) they have provided.

> **Fiduciary Duty**—a standard by which professionals have a legal responsibility to their client to provide a service or advice in the best interest of their client without personal gain.

Engineer
Accountant
Officer **Doctor**
Director
Lawyer
Architect

Words and concepts such as trust, loyalty, responsibility, honesty, and good faith represent the term fiduciary duty. It is a relationship where a patient, client, or beneficiary expects their interests to be protected by the professional. For relationships such as patient–doctor, lawyer–client, director/officer–corporation, architect–client, fiduciary duty holds a high standard of care and is often used as a guideline that provides the framework for the relationship.

If an issue occurs between the client and the professional where the client suffers economic loss or injury, the client can sue the professional for negligence. As you saw in Chapter 3, concepts such as duty of care and reasonable foreseeability are key in the tort of negligence. In addition, the relationship between proximity of the loss to the relationship of the parties is critical.

It is increasingly important in today's complex modern business world that professionals have guidelines that are developed for their profession and by their profession. In light of cases such as Enron, the responsibilities of those who were to protect the best interests of their shareholders and employees were not provided and this has shed more light on the vulnerability of these professional relationships. In most professions, there are associations and societies that serve as regulators for the profession and, in turn, provide the rules, guidelines, restrictions, and disciplinary action if a professional breaches their duty. As you can imagine, most professionals carry liability insurance in the event of a court case and, in most cases, the insurance costs are high.

CASE STUDY

The Rise and Fall of Enron: A Brief History

CBC News Posted: May 25, 2006 12:21 PM ET

Enron's origins date back to 1985 when it began life as an interstate pipeline company through the merger of Houston Natural Gas and Omaha-based InterNorth. Kenneth Lay, the former chief executive officer of Houston Natural Gas, became CEO, and the next year won the post of chairman.

From the pipeline sector, Enron began moving into new fields. In 1999, the company launched its broadband services unit and Enron Online, the company's website for trading commodities, which soon became the largest business site in the world. About 90 per cent of its income eventually came from trades over Enron Online.

Growth for Enron was rapid. In 2000, the company's annual revenue reached $100 billion US. It ranked as the seventh-largest company on the Fortune 500 and the sixth-largest energy company in the world. The company's stock price peaked at $90 US.

However, cracks began to appear in 2001. In August of that year, Jeffrey Skilling, a driving force in Enron's revamp and the company's CEO of six months, announced his departure, and Lay resumed the post of CEO. In October 2001, Enron reported a loss of $618 million—its first quarterly loss in four years.

Chief financial officer Andrew Fastow was replaced, and the U.S. Securities and Exchange commission launched an investigation into investment partnerships led by Fastow. That investigation would later show that a complex web of partnerships was designed to hide Enron's debt. By late November, the company's stock was down to less than $1 US. Investors had lost billions of dollars.

On Dec. 2, 2001, Enron filed for bankruptcy protection in the biggest case of bankruptcy in the United States up to that point. (WorldCom's collapse would later steal that dubious honour.) Roughly 5,600 Enron employees subsequently lost their jobs.

The next month, the U.S. Justice Department opened its investigation of the company's dealings, and Ken Lay quit as chairman and CEO.

In January 2004, Fastow agreed to a plea bargain and a 10-year sentence. He pleaded guilty to one count of conspiracy to commit wire fraud and one count of conspiracy to commit securities fraud. He also agreed to cooperate with federal prosecutors.

In February, Skilling entered a plea of not guilty to 40 charges, including wire fraud, securities fraud, conspiracy, insider trading and making false statements on financial reports.

Lay was charged with fraud and making misleading statements in July. He pleaded not guilty to the 11 charges.

Lay, Skilling go on trial

The trial of Lay and Skilling began in January 2006. Lay and Skilling both testified for more than a week in their own defence. Some of the charges against them were dropped.

Prosecutors alleged that Lay and Skilling used "accounting tricks, fiction, hocus-pocus, trickery, misleading statements, half-truths, omissions and outright lies" to commit their crimes.

Lawyers for the two accused said their clients may be guilty of bad business judgment at Enron, but they never broke the law. "The company failed, but it did not fail because of a fraud," Lay's lawyer, Bruce Collins, told the jury in the case.

Defence lawyers also argued that former Enron executives who took plea deals and testified against Lay and Skilling accepted responsibility for crimes they didn't commit.

Testimony wrapped up, with the jury beginning deliberations on May 17 and presenting the verdict on May 25.

Source: CBC LICENSING.

CASE STUDY

Galambos v. Perez, 2009 SCC 48, [2009] 3 S.C.R. 247

Perez, a part-time bookkeeper and later office manager at a law firm, sued her employer, Galambos, for negligence, breach of contract, and breach of fiduciary duty. Perez had used her personal credit card and money for the firm's bank account to help the firm during difficult financial times to the tune of $200,000. Galambos did not ask Perez to use her money, and later when he became aware of these loans he asked her to reimburse herself with interest. Perez only reimbursed herself $15,000. During this time, the firm had provided legal services to Perez for two mortgages and a last will and testament for her and her husband. The firm did not pay nor expect to be paid for these services. The firm eventually went into receivership, Galambos went bankrupt, and Perez became an unsecured creditor.

The Supreme Court of British Columbia (B.C.) dismissed Perez's claims and the case was appealed to the B.C. Court of Appeal, which set aside the original decision of the Supreme Court of B.C. and granted Perez $200,000. The Court of Appeal found that there was a power-dependency relationship between Perez and Galambos and that Perez was entitled to protection because of Galambos's fiduciary duty as the employer. The Supreme Court of Canada allowed the appeal and restored the decision of the trial judge.

Fiduciary Duty and the Tort of Negligence

DILBERT © 2005 Scott Adams. Used By permission of UNIVERSAL UCLICK. All rights reserved.

In terms of fiduciary duty and the tort of negligence, there are times where the relationship between the professional and their client will not work out. In these cases, the client (or patient, corporation, etc.) finds that the professional did not have the duty of care and had neglected the trust placed in them. Society and the law take the client–professional relationship very seriously and place it at a higher level of duty because the client is viewed as being in a vulnerable position because they depend on the professional's knowledge, experience, and training.

It is important for the businessperson also to understand that there are time limitations on when you can commence a lawsuit against a professional. Again, once you realize there is a breach of their professional duty, you would want to hire a lawyer to represent your interests.

In order to establish professional liability, meaning negligence in a fiduciary relationship, several factors must exist:

1. One individual within the relationship is a professional, meaning they hold a duty of care
2. The professional is in a position of power or trust and the client/patient, etc. relies on the professional
3. There is a breach of that duty of care where the client/patient, etc. suffered a loss because the professional did not meet or fell below the standard duty of care set by the profession
4. The professional did not reasonably foresee the loss suffered by the client/patient, etc. because of the professional's conduct

What would some of these situations look like where a professional is deemed negligent in their fiduciary duty? Examples might include the following:

*   A physician who does not have secure protection of patient records
*   An architect who has overcharged and went over the quoted price
*   A lawyer who represents both sides of a property transaction without disclosing that he or she is doing so
*   A director of a company who makes secret deals and profits from the deals at a loss for the company
*   An engineer who does not check specifications for the construction of a bridge

So, what does that mean to a businessperson? Businesspeople need to be aware of the relationship between them and the professional. They need to understand the conditions of the association. For example, when you retain a lawyer, you will be asked to review and sign a representation agreement outlining the specific legal services that will be provided along with the fees and costs of the case. In the case of a business hiring an architect to design a new office building, a contract will be signed outlining the services and fees that will be rendered and the costs involved, if any. These contracts also involve items such as timelines, contractors, and various other things that might be involved in the project. For a sample of an architect's standard agreement visit www.raic.org, which provides information about the architectural profession and resources. As mentioned above, most professions have an organization they belong to and these may be provincial, national, or international. As a businessperson, you may want to familiarize yourself with the standards of a profession when you are tendering work or before you sign any contract for services.

LEGAL SCENARIO

Chloe, the Young Gallery Entrepreneur

Chloe was a young entrepreneur who had been in business for three years, since graduating from university. She made the conscious decision to leap into the world of owning her own business after several internships with various art galleries in the city. Her business had grown considerably in the past three years with the addition of new and exciting artists who were gaining national and international recognition.

Chloe recognized the need to expand her present gallery in order to serve both her customers and her artists. In her current location she was "landlocked"—both sides of her present gallery had businesses that had no intention of moving in the near future. After several months she found the perfect location, an abandoned warehouse in an area of the city that was experiencing rejuvenation. After contacting the owner, she agreed to lease one-quarter of the warehouse with exposure to the busier side of a renovated area of the city block. Now, she had to find an architect and a contractor to do the work. After contacting several companies and firms, she had made her decision. She felt good about her decision because she had contracts in place and knew the direction and speed at which she was going, not to mention her bank account would be able to handle it and her bank manager was pleased with the contracts.

How did Chloe make her decision? What types of questions did she ask? What type of research did she do?

In a nutshell, there are many professions that outline what the professional within each profession can and cannot do for their clients or in the interests of their clients. In most professions, liability insurance is required in order to perform duties for clients/patients, etc.

4.2 Product Liability and Manufacturers

Africa Studio / Shutterstock.com

Have you ever used or consumed something that was broken, tainted, dangerous, or improperly prepared or manufactured? If you have, you have the right to contact the business or the manufacturer and let them know about the issue you have encountered. A manufacturer has the highest responsibility to the public.

Over the years, thousands of products have been "recalled" because of a manufacturer's defect. Think of the number of cars, baby cribs, medications, and foods that have "gone viral" or where warnings were broadcast in every medium possible. Why was it important for the manufacturer to get the message out? Again, manufacturers have a major responsibility to the public to ensure that their products are safe in design and manufacturing, and if they are not they have the duty to warn the public.

More here than anywhere, the manufacturers and companies that provide goods and services to the public must protect the public. A plaintiff in any case of product liability and manufacturer's liability, negligence (rather than strict liability) is the focus. This means that:

(a) The company had a duty of care

(b) The company breached the duty of care

(c) The plaintiff suffered harm because of that breach

One of the most known and discussed cases regarding **product liability** is the case of *Mustapha v. Culligan*. Let's take a look.

Product Liability—the responsibility of the manufacturer to create safe products.

CASE STUDY

Mustapha v. Culligan of Canada Ltd., 2006 CanLII 41807 (ON CA)

This case is the quintessential case of a product containing a very displeasing object, enough that the plaintiff, Mustapha, suffered psychiatric harm such as the inability to shower, drink, or have sex.

The plaintiff, Mustapha, and his wife were replacing a bottled Culligan brand water onto the dispensing machine at home when they saw a dead fly and a piece of another fly in the fresh, new bottle. As a result, the plaintiff became obsessed with the idea that the water he had consumed in the past from this company was not purified. Mustapha claimed that he suffered from a major depressive disorder because of this experience and sued Culligan Water. Mustapha won the case and was awarded $341,775 plus pre-judgment interest.

Culligan Water then appealed the decision of the Ontario court, which overturned the decision. The case was then appealed to the Supreme Court of Canada, which found that the plaintiff established three of the four requirements to be successful in a negligence case. The four requirements are duty owed, a breach of the standard of care, resulting damage, causation and sufficient proximity. The fourth requirement had to do with the proximity of the injury and damage. The Court found that the damage was too remote for the injury, Mr. Mustapha's psychiatric disorders. The appeal was dismissed.

Every product that you purchase for personal or corporate consumption has a very high duty of care by the manufacturer. For example, if you purchase a toy for a child and the toy has a defect that causes an injury or death, the manufacturer may be responsible. The safety of products is so important that the federal government has strict laws dealing with **consumer product** safety. The Act is called the *Canada Consumer Product Safety Act* (CCPSA). Many regulations have been developed under this Act, which provides strict rules about the manufacturing of such items as children's jewellery, strollers, hockey face protectors, candles, and so on.

> **Consumer Product**—means a product, including its components, parts, or accessories, that may reasonably be expected to be obtained by an individual to be used for non-commercial purposes, including for domestic, recreational, and sports purposes, and includes its packaging.

The Act also interprets consumer safety as it relates to the labelling and documentation of a product. Warning signs, advertising, storage, transporting, and instructions are just some of the areas that are strictly regulated. Simply, the Act regulates a product from the moment it is manufactured until consumer consumption.

The protection of consumer products is not just an important part of the manufacturer's duty of care but also of its distributors, resellers, and representatives.

The CCPSA defines *danger to human health or safety* as:

> any unreasonable hazard—existing or potential—that is posed by a consumer product during or as a result of its normal or foreseeable use and that may reasonably be expected to cause the death of an individual exposed to it or have an adverse effect on that individual's health—including an injury—whether or not the death or adverse effect occurs immediately after the exposure to the hazard, and includes any exposure to a consumer product that may reasonably be expected to have a chronic adverse effect on human health.

For a business, it is crucial to know and understand the regulations surrounding consumer products. Some questions to ask include:

- Is the product safe?
- Has it been tested?
- Has it been approved to be manufactured?
- Does the packaging and labelling follow the regulations?
- Does your business have policies in place for product recalls?

There are many questions to ask before you sell a consumer product, and it is important to understand the legal responsibilities at hand.

Let's take a look at a case that deals with product defects.

CASE STUDY

Hollis v. Dow Corning Corp., [1995] 4 S.C.R. 634

In 1983, Hollis had breast implants manufactured by Down Corning Corporation to correct a deformity as recommended by her physician. She was not warned by her physician, Dr. Birch, of any risks post-surgery or the possibility that the implants might rupture. A year after the surgery, after an examination by Dr. Birch, she began a baker's course which involved rigorous upper body movements. The following year, she noticed a lump and began to have pain in her right breast. She consulted another physician, Dr. Quayle, who removed the implants. After the removal, Hollis's medical condition worsened. This resulted in a mastectomy performed by a third physician who opted for a different type of implant.

Hollis sued Dow Corning Corporation, its Canadian agent, Dr. Birch, and Dr. Quayle for the negligent manufacturing of the implant. She was successful in the British Columbia Supreme Court against Dow Corning and the action against the agent and doctors was dismissed. She was awarded damages and costs. Dow tried to appeal the case in the British Columbia Court of Appeal but it was dismissed because they found that Dow had failed to warn Hollis about the post-surgery risks. The Court of Appeal also allowed a new trial for Hollis against Dr. Birch.

The Supreme Court of Canada also dismissed Dow's appeal against Hollis and Birch because they found that Dow was negligent in not informing Dr. Birch about the possible post-surgical complications, something the company had known as early as 1979. In the Supreme Court decision, it stated:

> A manufacturer of a product has a duty in tort to warn consumers of dangers it knows or ought to know are inherent in the product 's use. This duty is a continuing one, requiring manufacturers to warn not only of dangers known at the time of sale, but also of dangers discovered after the product has been sold and delivered. All warnings must be reasonably communicated, and must clearly describe any specific dangers that arise from the ordinary use of the product. The duty to warn serves to correct the knowledge imbalance between manufacturers and consumers by alerting consumers to any dangers and allowing them to make informed decisions concerning the safe use of the product. The nature and scope of this duty varies with the level of danger entailed by the ordinary use of the product. In the case of medical products, the standard of care to be met by manufacturers in ensuring that consumers are properly warned is necessarily high.

DID YOU KNOW?

Manufacturers should be aware of the four categories for a product liability claim to proceed:

1. Manufacturers have a duty of care to consumers to ensure there are no defects and products are safe when used in an ordinary manner;
2. Manufacturers have a duty to warn the consumer if they know or ought to know that there is a defect;
3. Manufacturers have a duty of care to avoid safety risks and make the product safe for its purpose;
4. Manufacturers have a duty of care to compensate for the cost of repairing a dangerous product.

The previous cases and information clearly illustrate the importance of a business, particularly those involved in manufacturing, to ensure that they take every precaution to keep the public safe. Strategic planning is the cure for the ill of product liability. Further, businesspeople must be aware that they must take every step to defend their company in a product liability lawsuit. Obtaining all of the information regarding the incident and all those involved—really, all documentation—are crucial steps. Naturally, the most important step is to contact the company's lawyer.

LO 4.3   4.3 Occupiers' Liability as a Tort

© R. Gino Santa Maria / Shutterfree, Llc | Dreamstime.com

As an **occupier**, the law dictates that you must take reasonable steps to make your property safe for anyone who comes onto it. This is generally an unintentional tort, and whether it is an intentional or unintentional tort depends on who exactly comes on your property. For example, a retail store (the occupier) where a customer slips and falls on a wet floor with no caution sign may be sued. Another example would be that a landowner who puts animal traps around his property may be sued if someone enters the property and is injured. So, the standard of care varies from situation to situation.

Occupier—a person, persons, or organization that may be the owner, landlord, tenant, or anyone who has responsibility, dictates the activities, and decides who enters the property.

For a claim against an occupier to be successful, three things must be proven by an individual:

1. The occupier made all reasonable attempts to keep the property safe.
2. The injury was as a result of the negligence of the occupier.
3. The individual suffered damages as a result of the injury.

As a businessperson, it is important that your policies and procedures and inspections and maintenance of the premises are in good order at all times. An occupiers' liability claim generally happens in restaurants, bars, and construction sites, but it can also happen in your home.

With an occupiers' liability claim, there is also the possibility that the court may decide the injured party too may have contributed to the injury and subsequent damages. If this is the case, some of the responsibility may be placed on the injured party. This is called **contributory negligence**.

Contributory Negligence—where the court apportions responsibility to the injured.

There are three classes of people who enter onto a property:

1. Tresspassers
2. Licensees
3. Invitees

It is important to realize that each province has an occupiers' liability act and that each of us should be aware of our responsibilities as occupiers, whether in a business or at home.

DID YOU KNOW?

You can find several provincial Occupiers' Liability Acts online:

Alberta: http://www.qp.alberta.ca/documents/acts/o04.pdf

Source: © Alberta Queen's Printer, 2000.

British Columbia: http://www.bclaws.ca/civix/document/id/complete/statreg/96337_01

Source: These materials contain information that has been derived from information originally made available by the Province of British Columbia at: http://www.bclaws.ca/ and this information is being used in accordance with the Queen's Printer License – British Columbia available at: http://www.bclaws.ca/standards/2014/QP-License_1.0.html. They have not, however, been produced in affiliation with, or with the endorsement of, the Province of British Columbia and THESE MATERIALS ARE NOT AN OFFICIAL VERSION.

Manitoba: https://web2.gov.mb.ca/laws/statutes/ccsm/o008e.php

Source: Manitoba Government.

Nova Scotia: http://nslegislature.ca/legc/statutes/occupier.htm

Source: 1996, c. 27.

Ontario: http://www.ontario.ca/laws/statute/90o02

Source: © Queen's Printer for Ontario, 1990. Current as of June 8, 2016. This is not an official version.

Prince Edward Island: http://www.gov.pe.ca/law/statutes/pdf/o-02.pdf

Source: Government of Prince Edward Island.

Let's take a look at each class of person who enters a property and the liability of the owner of the property.

For many, it is surprising to hear that an owner may still be held responsible for the injuries and damages incurred by a **trespasser**. Although another individual is breaking the law, this does not exempt you from also being held responsible for legal action under the *Occupiers' Liability Act*. For example, if a trespasser breaks into a business and severely fractures his or her back after slipping on a puddle caused by the business's ongoing water leak, he or she has the option to seek legal action for damages incurred if it can be proven based on the three items explained above.

Trespasser—a person, persons, or organization that enters the land of the occupier without legal right or permission.

LEGAL SCENARIO

I Didn't Know That I Would Get Injured!

Kenny and his friends were playing football near a resort. Their ball landed over the fence that separates the resort from a public area. The boys jumped over the fence and resumed playing football in the resort area. Kenny ran for a pass and crashed into a hottub that was empty for cleaning, resulting in a serious concussion. Kenny's parents sued the resort. Do they have a case?

Trespassers do not generally have the right to sue an occupier IF the occupier has not deliberately put up anything that would cause an injury in the event of a trespass. For example, again, in the use of an animal trap or another type of hazard on a property where someone who goes on the property could get injured, because the owner didn't use reasonable care in placing a hazardous item on their property they could be liable for the injury.

Another class of person, persons, or organizations that a person must be aware of and the liability of that person is that of the **licensee**.

Justin Kase z03z / Alamy

Licensee—a person, persons, or organization that enters the land of the occupier with permission.

An example of a licensee is when a person allows a friend to use their property for their own enjoyment. If that friend falls into a hole that was unmarked and was not informed there was a hole they should be aware of and was injured, the occupier may be liable. The standard of care, in this example, was that that occupier should have warned the friend that the hole existed.

In both classes of trespasser and licensee, businesspeople should know that any hazards that exist on a property need to be taken into consideration so that any liability can be avoided.

The area where the businessperson is especially vulnerable is where the person, persons, or organization is invited for their own benefit onto the premises.

This is where, in law, the metal hits the road for a businessperson. As a businessperson, by inviting a person, persons, or organization onto your premises/property, you wish to benefit from their attendance. For example a retailer, by virtue of being a commercial entity selling a product, invites the public to come onto their premises with the hope of selling the product. The occupier must ensure the safety of the public. This is where the standard of care is highest. The reasonable occupier will ensure that the safety of the invitee is paramount and will take all precautions to protect the **invitee**.

Invitee—a person, persons, or organization that enters the land of the occupier with an invitation so that the occupier benefits from the invitee's business.

One of the most referenced cases in the Supreme Court of Canada concerning occupiers' liability and an invitee is that of *Crocker v. Sundance*:

CASE STUDY

Crocker v. Sundance Northwest Resorts Ltd., [1988] 1 S.C.R. 1186

A competition was held at the Sundance Northwest Resorts Ltd. for two-person teams in an inner-tube to slide down a mogulled hill. Crocker entered the competition, signed the liability waiver without reading it, and paid the entry free. During the competition, there were two heats and during the first heat, Crocker suffered a cut above the eye because he was visibly intoxicated. Both the owner and the manager of Sundance asked Crocker if he was in any condition to participate in the second heat but did nothing to dissuade him from continuing. During the second heat, Crocker severely injured himself and as a result of his injuries became a quadriplegic.

The Supreme Court of Ontario found that Sundance was liable for 75 percent of the damages due to occupiers' liability and that Crocker was liable for 25 percent of damages through contributory negligence. The Ontario Court of Appeal overturned the trial judge's decision; the issue on appeal was whether or not the resort had a duty of care to prevent a visibly intoxicated person from participating in their event.

The Supreme Court of Canada allowed the appeal and found that the resort owed a duty of care to Crocker to remove him from the event. The resort did not take reasonable steps to prevent this foreseeable injury, the Court found. The trial judge's decision was upheld.

SCENARIO CHALLENGE!

Consider the situations below and find similar case law that would provide a solution:

- A trespasser on a private property gets injured when she slips on a newly painted deck.
- A person invited to an event who purchased a ticket becomes intoxicated and drives home.
- A cottage owner allows a family friend to use the cottage for the weekend and their child becomes injured in the hottub on the deck.
- A teenager gets caught in an animal trap hiking through the woods of a neighbour's property.
- An elderly woman slips on the steps of a public bus, breaking her hip.

FOR REVIEW

Questions

1. What types of professional associations would lawyers, architects, doctors, accountants, and engineers belong to? Do they have similar guidelines? If not, what are some differences? (LO 4.1)
2. What types of general occurrences would constitute a breach of fiduciary duty? (LO 4.1)
3. Describe the types of situations where a company could find itself in a product liability lawsuit. What type of strategies should the company have put in place? (LO 4.2)
4. What type of records management strategies should be in place in order to defend a lawsuit regarding product liability? (LO 4.2)
5. What steps can a business owner take to protect his or her business from a lawsuit from a trespasser, a licensee, and an invitee? (LO 4.3)

Activities

1. Contact a professional in your local area or research your provincial associations and societies and report what their guidelines are for that profession. You may look at the provincial bar society or the countrywide professional accountants' association. (LO 4.1)

2. Research and then discuss the construction trade and the types of professional liability that may exist. What types of professions belong to this area of business? What type of cases generally appear before the courts? (LO 4.1)

3. Research the top five product liability lawsuits that have made the news in the last 10 years. What do they have in common? Was the damage foreseeable? (LO 4.2)

4. Create a section that would exist in an operational manual for a retail store that outlines the strategies and tasks that should be in place to protect its customers. (LO 4.3)

CASES FOR DISCUSSION

Case #1

Hillary and Derrick are purchasing a house and property for the first time in a small town. They are excited about this big purchase. They do an online search for a lawyer who will handle the purchase. They find Simpson, a property law lawyer, and make an appointment with him. They provide Simpson with their documentation and he promises that he will have everything taken care of. There were several issues that became important during the process, such as which appliances were part of the sale and a boundary line that was not clear. The property closed nevertheless and it wasn't until after the sale when Hillary and Derrick had a boundary line dispute with the neighbours that they realized Simpson had also represented the sellers. What can Hillary and Derrick do? (LO 4.1)

Case #2

Meghan purchased a frozen pizza at the grocery store and baked it in her oven. When she bit into the pizza, sudden pain shot through her mouth and she lost a large piece of her dental bridge, which she swallowed along with the pizza. She went to her dentist and found out that she would need a replacement bridge, which would cost $5,000. What would you advise Meghan to do? (LO 4.2)

Case #3

Daniel's head hurt. He played on a AAA Midget hockey team and had just finished a playoff game. A puck had hit his helmet and there was a crack in the helmet. The impact was so severe that he may have a concussion. His helmet was advertised as passing all regulations for hockey helmets. Does Daniel have a case? Have there been cases of this nature in the Canadian courts? If so, what were the outcomes? (LO 4.2)

CHAPTER 5

ELEMENTS OF CONTRACTS, E-COMMERCE AND TECHNOLOGY

Learning Objectives

After reading this chapter the student will:

LO 5.1   Know what a contract is

LO 5.2   Know what separates a contract from an agreement

LO 5.3   Know why contracts are useful and needed

LO 5.4   Recognize the differences between an invitation to treat and an offer

LO 5.5   Understand the elements of a contract

LO 5.6   Know how valid consideration and intention affect a contract

LO 5.7   Recognize what option agreements are

LO 5.8   Understand the express and implied terms of a contract

LO 5.9   Understand the oral, written, and electronic forms for contracts

HELP!

As a businessperson, you may experience any of these scenarios:

- Help! You hired a contractor and she destroyed your office.

- Help! You sold an expensive product and you didn't get paid.

- Help! You bought a computer and it doesn't work.

- Help! Your local art gallery promised to sell you a painting but they sold it to someone else instead.

- Help! You exchanged information about your company's services through e-mail with a potential client and they are now insisting that you have entered a contract with them.

- Help! You clicked the "I agree" button on the terms and conditions of a website without actually reading what you were agreeing to.

LO 5.1   5.1 What Is a Contract?

Of all the legal relationships you may enter into over the course of your life, the ones based on **contracts** will be the most common and wide ranging. Everyone can describe a contract: a very formal, written agreement covering important business transactions. This common view is only partially correct. While contracts can be in writing, only a few have to be in writing because of the law. While having a contract in writing makes it easier to determine all of the terms of a contract, it does not necessarily determine a contract's validity. When you buy a cup of coffee from Tim Hortons you are entering into a contract that is just as valid as if you were buying a car, yet you have no formal written contract at the end. You have not negotiated with Tim Hortons about the product or the price. You have not determined potential consequences should they give you the wrong order. Or, we should say, you have not been *aware* of doing all of these things.

> **Contracts**—agreements that are enforceable through the law, agreed upon by two or more parties with benefits for all parties to the contract.

Contract law is the set of legal principles and rules that allow enforceable agreements to be created. It determines the rights and obligations a party has, whether they negotiated them directly or not. Contract law is primarily about a process that creates a framework within which a contract is created. With limited exceptions, parties have the ability to create any enforceable agreement that they desire. Our law provides what is known as "privity of contract." All **substantive aspects of contracts** are within the control of the parties, again with very few exceptions. The subject matter of the contract, its delivery, the terms for payment, and various other terms such as warranties, length of contract, and other matters are all left to the agreement of the parties.

> **Substantive Aspects of Contracts**—what a contract is actually going to do.

A contract is an agreement that the parties intend to be enforceable by the legal system. An agreement has often been called a "meeting of the minds." The minds of two, or occasionally more, people or businesses reach agreement on all the components of something yet to occur. Phrased another way, an agreement is an exchange of promises: two people agree to exchange something for something in the future.

When these minds meet, an agreement is formed. If the parties intend for this agreement to be enforced by the courts, and other details discussed in this chapter are met, then they should have a contract.

© Cacaroot | Dreamstime.com

LO 5.2   5.2 Contract vs. Simple Agreement

We enter into agreements all the time. The difference between a simple agreement between friends and a contract is that a party can use the courts to enforce a contract. You can't do so with a simple agreement. If you and a friend agree to meet for dinner and she doesn't show up, you cannot sue her for that. However, arranging for a dinner meeting with a client, and having them not show up, could allow you to sue them to recover the cost to you of their failure to attend.

Every contract is made up of terms. *Express terms* are those terms negotiated specifically by the parties. *Implied terms* are those terms imported into the contract from other sources. These could be from other laws or legislation that applies to the contract, from past behaviour by the parties in previous contracts, or from industrywide practices in that area of contracts.

DID YOU KNOW?

Simple Contract

Even the simplest contract will often involve multiple pages. This is because the best time to prevent problems, which may occur under a contract, is when you are agreeing to it.

The following link takes you to a simple, six-page contract for coaching a national sports team in Canada. It is a template shared by the Coaching Association of Canada (CAC), which was established in 1970. Since its inception, the CAC has developed into a world leader in coach training and certification. Each year, more than 60,000 coaches take a National Coaching Certification Program (NCCP) workshop, and since it began, more than 1M coaches have participated in the program.

http://www.coach.ca/files/CAC_Sample_Coaching_Contract_EN.pdf

Source: Coaching Association of Canada—www.coach.ca.

LO 5.3   ## 5.3   Why Are Contracts Needed?

Business Certainty

Contract law is the basis of commercial liability. It provides the basic protection of a person's rights in a commercial deal. Although many special rules have been created by government to deal with more specific areas of contracts—for example, employment law and sales of goods—when those rules fail or do not apply, contract law may still offer a resolution. Contract law is very black and white. The rules that are to be applied are simple and straightforward—it is applying the rules to the various fact situations that is hard. Courts do not want to interfere with contracts except in cases where there are clearly problems that the parties cannot resolve. The courts will not save a person from a contract that is bad for them, as long as it does not violate the rules of formation or performance. Knowing contract law makes a person a smarter consumer and less likely to be taken advantage of.

Statistics Canada reports that in 2009 Canadians placed internet orders for goods and services totalling $15.1 billion. The agency also reports that the more a person shops online, the less concerned they are with security. As online commercial activity grows, both consumers and businesses need to be aware of how the old rules of contracts apply to this new form of business.

Like consumers, governments and business both national and international have recognized the rise of e-commerce. The *Uniform Electronic Commerce Act* (UECA), adopted by the Uniform Law Conference of Canada, was designed to provide a template for federal, provincial, and territorial governments to enact a consistent set of laws to deal with e-commerce. The UECA and subsequent federal, provincial, and territorial acts did not seek to rewrite contract law. Its purposes were first to recognize that electronic contracts were as valid as any other form of contract to which the basic rules of contracts apply, and second to clarify how those rules apply in the unique situations caused by electronic contract formation.

LO 5.4   ## 5.4   Before the Contract: Invitation to Treat

You enter the drive-through at your local Tim Hortons and order a large coffee, double-double. Without knowing it, you have engaged in the first stage of contract formation, getting the agreement. Agreement is one of the simplest concepts in contracts; every contract goes through this process before it is formed. There has to be a valid offer from one party, and valid acceptance from the other. During a negotiation, the parties can switch roles and the **offeror** becomes the **offeree**. There are, however, clear rules as to what makes an offer and acceptance valid. The process actually starts off with an effort that in law we call an *invitation to treat*.

Offeror—the person making an offer.

Offeree—the person to whom the offer is made.

An **invitation to treat** is simply an announcement of a willingness to form a contract, communicated by one of the parties. In a retail environment, it is signalled simply by the store opening its doors for business. Most advertisements are also invitations to treat, as are postings on internet sites such as Kijiji, or classified ads in the local newspaper. These are inviting potential customers to negotiate a contract. In our example, the Tim Hortons menu at the drive-through is an invitation to treat. It is inviting you to buy a coffee. You have to be careful, though, because the enticements used to get you into the negotiation stage may or may not be enforceable as part of the final contract!

Invitation to Treat—anything that shows a willingness to conduct a business transaction.

LO 5.5   5.5 Introduction to Contract Requirements: Offer, Acceptance, Consideration, Intention

When one party decides that they want a coffee, and the other party has coffee to sell, a business transaction using a contract may be possible. To form a contract, one needs to satisfy the following four requirements:

- Offer
- Acceptance
- Consideration
- Intention

Sometimes offer and acceptance together are referred to as reaching an agreement; however, that approach complicates understanding by combining separate concepts. We will now look at each of the four steps.

Offer

You know something is an **offer** and not an invitation to treat if it specifies the *parties*, the *product*, and the *price*. This means that each side knows who is involved in the potential contract, what they are getting (or how it will be determined), and what they will be paying (or how it will be determined). If any of the three are missing or invalid, then an offer has not been made. If there are additional terms that a party wishes to have as major terms of the contract they also must be in this offer. If any of the three P's is missing, then an offer has not been made.

Offer—a promise to enter into a contract, under complete and specific terms, once there is a communicated acceptance.

Acceptance

For the contract to be formed, one of the parties must accept the offer made by the other party (see Figure 5.1). It takes very little to accept an offer. Acceptance has to be total; any alteration of the offer is a counter offer and simply continues the bargaining process. Acceptance will be valid when it is received by the offeror, and it usually requires the accepting party to perform a positive act signalling acceptance. This can be simply communicating the acceptance directly. Not doing anything or silence will be acceptance only if the parties have previously agreed that this is a reasonable method for acceptance. Other ways to accept can be by a method set out in the offer, as long as it is a reasonable method. If not set out in the offer, acceptance can be signalled by some other reasonable method.

Figure 5.1: **Forming the Contract**

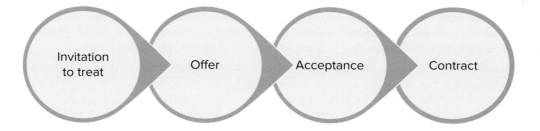

Consideration

In a contract, each party must give and receive something of value. This is called "mutual consideration." Most often one party provides goods or services to the other, who provides money to the first party. Mutual consideration can also take the form of an exchange of goods or services.

DID YOU KNOW?

Mutual Consideration

Mutual consideration occurs when a store sells a pair of shoes (a thing of value) to a customer for money (also a thing of value). Mutual consideration can also take the form of barter, such as when an electrician repairs his plumber friend's light switch in exchange for his plumber friend fixing his toilet.

Intention

The last key requirement to forming a contract is for both parties to have the intention that the agreement will be enforceable through the court system if necessary. Typically, in a commercial or business situation, if the parties go to the trouble to negotiate and reach an agreement the law assumes that the necessary intention was present.

LO 5.6   5.6 Beyond the Basics: Completeness, Revocation, Communication, Promises, Special Situations

The basic law of contracts is fairly straightforward. Unfortunately, there is always more law—more details that need to be understood. Offer, acceptance, consideration, and intention each become relatively complex topics once they are looked at in greater detail.

Offer

Depending on the situation, an offer—if made in written form—could be anything from a couple of sentences to many words filling dozens or occasionally hundreds of pages. A very basic deal might start with an offer that contained the identification of the item being purchased, the price, the date and method of delivery, any standards that the product has to meet, and perhaps a few more basic terms.

Once the offer is made it does not last forever. Offers can end in various ways that might result in ending negotiations, continuing negotiations, or a contract being formed. Here are some ways that an offer can end:

- There is a set time limit to the offer, set out in the offer. When this time limit passes, the offer is finished and cannot be accepted.
- There is a natural time limit to the offer. How long is it reasonable to expect an offeror to wait for an answer from the other party? In law, *reasonable* means that it is determined on a case by case basis depending on the circumstances. If I offer to sell you a vacation that starts next Sunday, I have to give you enough time to determine whether you can go. You, however, have to give me enough time to make the offer to someone else if you refuse.
- The offeror revokes the offer. Just as the other party is free to accept or turn down an offer, the person making the offer has some control of the process before a contract is actually formed. Remember, the law always likes to balance the rights of the parties. As long as it is done before a valid acceptance is made, and it is communicated clearly to the other party, a person can withdraw their offer. In some cases, if direct communication has not happened but the other party can be said to have reliable knowledge that the offer has been withdrawn, then the courts will deem a revocation to have taken place.
- The person making the offer dies, goes bankrupt, or suffers a severe mental breakdown. Any of these situations changes the legal capacity of the offeror to carry through on the contract formation. Note, however, that if you have proof a contract has been formed and can still be carried out it is a valid contract. Contracts that can't be carried out would be something like a personal contract of service. If you hired a clown to perform magic at a party and the clown died in a horrific card trick accident, that contract would not be enforceable.
- The other party can simply say no to the offer. This ends the offer completely; if the rejecting party comes back later trying to accept it, they are in fact making a new offer.
- The other party makes a **counter offer**, which is really a **rejection** and a new offer—with the original offeror now in the position to reject, accept, or counter offer.
- Acceptance both ends the offer and creates the contract. As it is the final step in the process it has its own criteria to be valid. An acceptance must be made and communicated while the offer is open. The acceptance must be complete and accept all the terms of the offer. If it does, an agreement is formed. If changes are made, conditions added, or the acceptance is not in any way a complete "yes," then there is no agreement. There is simply a continuing negotiation—a counter offer, as discussed above. An acceptance can be made by words, or occasionally by conduct.

Counter Offer—a new offer that also rejects the previous or original offer.

Rejection—a negative statement that terminates the current offer.

LEGAL SCENARIO

Offer and Counter Offer

Consider this offer: "I would like to buy this pair of shoes from you." We now see that this offer is not complete. It is not specific enough on one or more of the three P's (parties, products, or price). It needs to be something like, "I would like to buy this pair of size 10 red Nike shoes for $124.99. I will take them with me now. I want a guarantee that they will last at least 6 months." We now have a more complete and specific offer.

The ball is now in the store's court. Not willing to provide such a guarantee, their reply is "Yes, but we will not agree to provide any guarantee. This is not an acceptance."

"Yes, but" is a counter offer. A counter offer is in fact another form of offer. It ends the current offer but continues the negotiations should the original offeror—who is now the offeree—wish to. The negotiations could go on until an offer from either party gets the response "yes" (an acceptance) or "no" (a rejection of the offer).

Acceptance

Not only must the offeree accept the offer, but that acceptance must be communicated to the offeror. Negotiation does not always take place face to face and so acceptance could be communicated via e-mail, fax, phone, other electronic means or even using the surface mail system.

Sometime the offer specifies the method of communication to be used for acceptance. In that case the specific means must be used if the terms of the offer are to be agreed to. Otherwise, any reasonable methods will suffice.

Modern communication is usually instantaneous or nearly so and therefore there is little concern over when the acceptance is communicated, although it is clear that the acceptance must actually be received.

Early case law has established an exception to the rule that communication must be received and that at that point in time an agreement is formed. The exception is called the **post box rule**. If acceptance is made via the postal system, agreement is deemed to occur when the acceptance is posted. This is so even if the acceptance is never received. This exception seems to also apply to acceptance using courier companies.

> **Post Box Rule**—an offer is accepted when the acceptance is given to the postal service, not when it is received by the offeror.

Figure 5.2 illustrates the possibilities in responding to a contract offer.

Figure 5.2: **Responding to a Contract Offer**

DID YOU KNOW?

How an Offer Is Terminated

Offers (but not contracts) can be terminated by the following:

- Withdrawal or revocation of the offer by the person who made it
- Lapse of the offer after a specified or reasonable period of time
- The decline of the offer by the person to whom the offer was directed
- A counter offer from the person to whom the offer was directed
- Acceptance of the offer

DID YOU KNOW?

E-Commerce

From *Electronic Commerce Act, 2000* of Ontario

Formation and operation of electronic contracts

19. An offer, the acceptance of an offer or any other matter that is material to the formation or operation of a contract may be expressed,
    (a) by means of electronic information or an electronic document; or
    (b) by an act that is intended to result in electronic communication, such as,
        i. touching or clicking on an appropriate icon or other place on a computer screen, or
        ii. speaking.

Source: © Queen's Printer for Ontario, 2000. Current as of June 2, 2016. This is not an official version.

DID YOU KNOW?

Browse-Wrap vs. Clickwrap Agreements

Generally website owners use two types of agreements to contract with customers regarding purchases and terms of use for software. These agreements are known as browse-wrap and clickwrap agreements. Courts are of two minds when it comes to the enforceability of these agreements. While clickwrap agreements are generally found to be enforceable, browse-wrap ones are more problematic and will usually not be enforced unless a user takes an action that clearly consents to the terms of the agreement.

Browse-wrap agreements

Browse-wrap agreements are almost universally used on websites. They are the small hyperlinks at the bottom of a page that direct users to a "Terms of Service" page. The customer does not necessarily have to follow the hyperlink to be bound by the terms, although doing so and then continuing to use the website would be a clear consent to the terms to a court's satisfaction.

Clickwrap agreements

By contrast, a clickwrap agreement requires the user to review the terms of an agreement, which they must accept by clicking on a button signalling their agreement with the terms before proceeding. These terms are usually set out in a series of pop-up windows. Because the website has put these terms right in front of a user, and required positive action from them to continue, it is easy to see why they are regarded by the courts as more enforceable than browse-wrap agreements.

The following is the link to the Canada.com browse-wrap agreement: http://www.canada.com/aboutus/termsofservice.html.

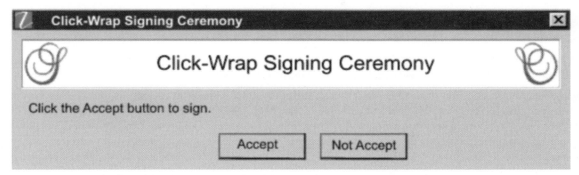

Reprint Courtesy of International Business Machines Corporation, © International Business Machines Corporation.

An accepted offer is an agreement. To form a contract, we also need consideration and intention to contract.

Consideration

A friend tells you that he has just purchased a new car. You have two primary questions you wish to ask: What kind of car, and how much did he pay? These two questions sum up the basis of consideration.

Consideration is simply the obligation that each side in a contract agrees to perform. As with most concepts in contracts, the rules of consideration are relatively straightforward, although the application of them may be difficult. In order to have an enforceable contract something of value must go from the offeror to the offeree, and in addition something of value must go from the offeree to the offeror.

> **Consideration**—the obligations each party owes to the other under the contract.

In some contracts this exchange takes place almost simultaneously with the formation of the contract. In a retail transaction, consideration is the product received and the price paid.

In other cases, one or both of the parties may not be expected to perform their side of the bargain until a future date. Consider the case where a painter is hired to paint a house and the owner is to pay for the work after it is completed. In this case, at the time the contract is formed the consideration takes the form of an exchange of promises. The painter promises to paint and the owner promises to pay the painter after the work is complete.

Of all the essential elements of a contract, consideration may arguably be the most important.

- Consideration does not have to be equal in value, as long as each party receives some sort of benefit. The law will not rescue you from a bad deal. This is where the concept of "buyer (or seller) beware" comes in. The law expects you to be fully knowledgeable as to the value of the goods or services bought.
- The benefit must be tangible—or, if not tangible, then recognizable as a benefit. For example, a psychic reading your future is not providing you with any tangible benefit. You cannot sue the psychic for getting the prediction wrong. However, the psychic is providing you with entertainment. Entertainment is recognized by society as a benefit that can be purchased. If the psychic performs poorly, you could sue them.
- Something done with no expectation of payment is a **gratuitous promise** or a favour and is not consideration. Even a promise of payment, made after you had committed to perform the favour, is not enforceable as it is similarly regarded as a promise.
- Consideration does not have to occur simultaneously. A promise for future performance of an obligation is valid consideration.
- When one party's obligation is a service, rather than a product with a tangible value, the law will set the consideration at the market value for similar services, referred to as **quantum meruit**.
- Final consideration does not have to be determined during contract formation, as long as the method for determining the consideration has been established. For example, a lawyer may bill you by the hour. You know what his hourly rate is but not the total hours needed to complete the work. This, however, is valid consideration as both parties know how the final bill will be determined.

Gratuitous Promise—doing, or agreeing to do, something for another person with no expectation of getting anything in return.

Quantum Meruit—a Latin phrase meaning "what one has earned"; it is how contract law determines that a reasonable price has been paid for a service.

 ## CASE STUDY

Intangible Consideration

Anyone who plays online video games is familiar with an end-user licence agreement (EULA). These are the terms that you agree to when you click the "I accept" button that allows a game to be installed onto your computer. Most of the time, people don't read these terms before accepting them.

In 2010, as an April Fools' Day prank, British retailer GameStation included a clause in its EULA stating that if you placed an online order on April 1, 2010, you granted the company a claim on your soul.

By the time the day was finished, 7,500 people had unwittingly sold their souls to GameStation (don't worry, the company rescinded this clause later!).

This scenario highlights two problems, one with contracts generally and one with online contracts specifically:

- From a consideration point of view, a soul is an intangible benefit and therefore cannot be exchanged.
- It could prove to be very dangerous to simply agree to a contract online without bothering to read what you are agreeing to.

Clearly this is an area where businesspeople and consumers must take care.

Intention

Generally, agreements negotiated for a business purpose are initially presumed to be intended to be contracts—agreements enforceable by the courts. However, agreements between family members are presumed not to be enforceable by the courts. An agreement that a parent will lend money to a college student is considered a matter for "family justice," not a matter that would involve the courts. However, it is possible to set up a contract that is enforceable by creating an agreement that contains terms similar to those found in a bank loan—interest, repayment schedule, default provisions, etc.

Intention is a relatively simple element of contracts. It does, however, determine whether or not the parties meant for the agreement to be enforceable by the law as a contract. Intention is determined by the relationship of the parties to each other.

If the relationship is commercial, then the agreement is presumed to be a contract and is therefore enforceable by the courts under contract law. If the relationship is social or domestic, then the agreement is presumed to not be a contract and is not enforceable by the courts under contract law.

The issue becomes more complicated in circumstances where elements of both relationships exist. If you ask an accountant an income tax question at a party, would you expect to be billed for her time? If she told you to make an appointment to see her you would expect to be billed. It is under circumstances such as these that determining the intention of the parties becomes difficult.

When you have a situation where there is a potential issue as to the intention of the parties, the best thing to do is to clearly state the intention at the outset.

CASE STUDY

Balfour v. Balfour, [1919] 2 KB 571

This is a case from England almost 100 years ago. Mr. and Mrs. Balfour were vacationing in England when Mrs. Balfour became ill and needed medical attention. They agreed that Mrs. Balfour would remain behind in England while Mr. Balfour returned to Ceylon (Sri Lanka). Mr. Balfour would pay Mrs. Balfour £30 a month until he returned. Eventually the relationship between the two soured and Mr. Balfour stopped making the payments.

The issue before the court was whether Mr. Balfour's offer to support his wife was intended to be legally binding.

The court decided that the law of contracts was not made for personal family relationships. As there was no intent to be legally bound when the agreement was agreed upon, there can be no legally binding contract. The relationship here was not commercial but was domestic, so there was no presumption that there was an intention for this agreement to be legally binding under contract law.

LO 5.7   **5.7** Option Agreements

Option agreements are enforceable contracts that prevent an offeree from withdrawing an offer prior to the date specified. Recall that an offer can be revoked at any time prior to acceptance. A promise to keep the offer open where no consideration is given by the potential purchaser is a promise, not a contract. However, it is possible to have a specific contract, an option agreement, where consideration does go in both directions. The potential purchaser needs to provide consideration, typically a fee, to the offeree.

> **Option Agreements**—contracts between a potential buyer and the seller of some item whereby in exchange for a fee the seller gives the potential buyer the first chance to buy the item, up to a certain date.

CASE STUDY

Dickinson v. Dodds, {1876} 2 Ch D 463 (CA)

This is a case from England over 140 years ago. On June 10, Dodds delivered a written offer to Dickenson, offering to sell his property to Dickenson. The offer stated that it was open for acceptance until 9 a.m. on June 12. Prior to 9 a.m. on June 12, Dickenson "heard" that Dobbs was revoking his offer because he would be selling the property to someone else. At 7 a.m. Dickenson delivered his acceptance, but Dobbs refused the acceptance because the property was already sold to another.

The court confirmed that an offer is not a binding document, it is not a contract, and so the offer could be revoked at any time, even though a promise to keep it open had been made.

If a party wanted to follow this process today and revoke an offer before the promised time that party would be well advised to clearly revoke the offer and communicate the revocation to the other party. There has been much criticism of this case on the basis that the revocation was not clear enough—simply delivering a revocation through the grapevine may not be sufficient in today's business world.

LEGAL SCENARIO

Your business wishes to buy widgets at the lowest price. Company A offers you 100 widgets for $300. You know that widgets are in short supply, but you think there is a small chance you can buy them elsewhere at a lower price. You enter into an option agreement with Company A for $25 wherein it promises to hold the order open to you for 10 days. This option agreement allows you to search for other widgets without risk that, if you don't find cheaper ones, Company A may sell all they have to other customers.

LO 5.8   **5.8** Terms of Contracts

Express and Implied Terms

There are two basic types of provisions, called "terms" by lawyers, in a contract: *express terms* and *implied terms*. **Express terms** state the provision explicitly. In a written contract, they are the terms that actually appear in the document. But even terms written down may be subject to interpretation because they are unclear, or because the parties disagree on the meaning of the words. Generally the usual dictionary definition of words is used, although many contracts actually define exact meaning to certain words at the beginning of the contract. It is important, when writing a contract, to make sure that the wording is clear and unambiguous.

Express Terms—in a written contract, the terms that actually appear in the document.

Implied terms are items occasionally added to the contract by judges in situations where the contract reaches the courts. Clearly implied terms are not actually in the contract. They are added, rarely, by judges to give meaning to the words or to more clearly reflect what the judge believes was the intention of the parties at the time the contract was entered into. The ability of judges to add implied terms is very much limited by case law and the basic premise of contract law that the parties are free to negotiate their own contracts.

Implied Terms—items occasionally added to contracts by judges in situations where the contract reaches the courts.

LO 5.9

5.9 Oral, Written, or Electronic Contracts

Preference for Written over Oral Contracts

Whenever possible in business, written contracts are preferred for reasons of clarity and certainty. The reduction of an agreement to writing clearly focuses the mind on the exact nature of the deal. An oral contract, although legal in most cases, opens the door to disagreements. In addition, when brought before the courts oral contracts can be extremely difficult to prove.

LEGAL SCENARIO

You enter into a contract to buy widgets from Company B: 10,000 units at $2.75 each today, 7,500 units at $2.50 in 6 months, and 12,500 units at $2.65 in 12 months. The contract is oral, not written. Because the quantities and prices change with each order and a year goes by, the parties can now not agree on the price of the final shipments. This problem could have been avoided with a written agreement. Worse, if this goes to court you may not have sufficient evidence to win the case.

Requirements for Written Contracts

While most oral contracts are enforceable and valid, a few are not. Four main exceptions exist. Contracts that need to be in writing include:

- Contracts relating to land, including sales and leases of land
- Contracts where the promises made are not required to be performed within a year of the execution of the contract
- Contracts of guarantee, where a party agrees to be responsible for the debt or obligations of another (in certain future circumstances)
- In some provinces, contracts for the sale of goods, above a small, stipulated monetary amount.

Any law that requires a document to be in writing can be satisfied electronically.

The Danger of Partially Written Contracts

It is important that written contracts be complete. Generally, parties can have a written contract or an oral contract, but not a contract that is partly in writing and partly oral. The parol evidence rule, a difficult and complex rule, states that oral evidence is not allowed in court to explain the written contract. You are basically limited to what you have written.

The Use of Electronic Contracts

With so many contracts being formed through electronic means these days, the rules in the UECA had to recognize electronic contracts as a valid form of contract. It does so through the use of "Functional Equivalency Rules." This impressive title simply means that contracts in electronic form are recognized as being equally valid as contracts that are in any of the other two accepted forms.

DID YOU KNOW?

E-Commerce

From *Electronic Commerce Act, 2000* of Ontario

FUNCTIONAL EQUIVALENCY RULES

Legal recognition of electronic information and documents

4. Information or a document to which this Act applies is not invalid or unenforceable by reason only of being in electronic form.

Legal requirement that information or document be in writing

5. A legal requirement that information or a document be in writing is satisfied by information or a document that is in electronic form if it is accessible so as to be usable for subsequent reference.

Legal requirement to provide information or document in writing

6. (1) A legal requirement that a person provide information or a document in writing to another person is satisfied by the provision of the information or document in an electronic form that is,
    (a) accessible by the other person so as to be usable for subsequentreference; and
    (b) capable of being retained by the other person.

    ...

Legal requirement to provide information or document in specified non-electronic form

7. (1) A legal requirement that a person provide information or a document in a specified non-electronic form to another person is satisfied by the provision of the information or document in an electronic form that is,
    (a) organized in the same or substantially the same way as the specifiednon-electronic form;
    (b) accessible by the other person so as to be usable for subsequent reference; and
    (c) capable of being retained by the other person.

    ...

Legal requirement re original documents

8. (1) A legal requirement that an original document be provided, retained or examined is satisfied by the provision, retention or examination of an electronic document if,

(a) there exists a reliable assurance as to the integrity of the information contained in the electronic document from the time the document to be provided, retained or examined was first created in its final form, whether as a written document or as an electronic document; and

(b) in a case where the original document is to be provided to a person, the electronic document that is provided is accessible by the person so as to be usable for subsequent reference and capable of being retained by the person.

Source: © Queen's Printer for Ontario, 2000. Current as of June 2, 2016. This is not an official version.

Standard Form Contracts

Standard form contracts are contracts drafted by one party without any negotiation with the other party. One example is rental car contracts. If you want to rent a car from a major car rental company you must do it on their terms or not at all. Not surprisingly, standard form contracts are written in a way that greatly benefits the car rental company.

There is little in the law that protects the customer in such a situation. The main protection is that unusual or particularly onerous provisions must be brought to the attention of the customer. This is often done by having the customer initial such sections.

FOR REVIEW

Questions

1. Explain the difference between an offer and an invitation to treat. (LO 5.4, 5.5)
2. Explain the term "counter offer." (LO 5.6)
3. Name the four ways an offer can be terminated. (LO 5.1, 5.2)
4. Explain the four basic requirements needed to create a contract. (LO 5.5)
5. Explain the concept of consideration. (LO 5.6)
6. What is a "gratuitous promise"? (LO 5.6)
7. What is the difference between a "clickwrap" and a "browse-wrap" agreement? (LO 5.6)
8. How does intention determine the enforceability of an agreement? (LO 5.5, 5.6)
9. What is a "functional equivalency clause" in e-contracts? (LO 5.9)
10. Explain the difference between express and implied terms in a contract. (LO 5.8)

Activities

1. Browse newspapers, magazines, or websites and other periodicals for a recent contract law case. Explain the background of the case, the issues of the case, and provide the outcome. (LO 5.1, 5.3)
2. Count up the number of contracts you have entered into over the past five days. What was common among them? What was different? (LO 5.1)
3. Discuss how contracts can be used to reduce risk. (LO 5.3)
4. Why is intention an important element of contract law? (LO 5.5, 5.6)
5. Online, find an example of a clickwrap agreement and a browse-wrap agreement. Is there any common element among websites that use one type of agreement over the other? (LO 5.6)

6. Why is contract law not usually concerned with the consideration received by both sides being equal in value? (LO 5.5, 5.6)

7. How would a party determine that *quantum meruit* has been met in the price charged for a service? (LO 5.6)

8. Four types of transactions require a contract to be in writing. Why is that necessary for these types of transactions? (LO 5.9)

9. What is an example of a standard form contract that is commonly encountered? Why is it necessary for businesses to have standard form contracts? (LO 5.9)

CASES FOR DISCUSSION

Case #1

Arnold owned three building units (A, B, and C) in a commercial development. As a result of some financial difficulties, he e-mails to Bob as follows: "I will sell you one of my units for $150,000." Bob immediately e-mails back "I accept your offer." (LO 5.1, 5.4, 5.5)

a. Was Arnold's e-mail an offer? Why or why not?

b. Is an e-mail exchange such as this one valid in forming a contract?

Case #2

A friend buys you a cup of coffee at Tim Hortons during "Roll Up the Rim" time. You roll up the rim and win the grand prize. (LO 5.1, 5.2, 5.5, 5.6)

a. Is the prize yours to keep?

b. Do you and your friend have to share the prize?

c. Is the prize your friend's to keep?

Case #3

Monica invited Brody to the college New Year dinner and dance. Brody accepted the invitation and agreed to accompany Monica, who purchased the tickets and arranged a limo. Two days before the dance, Brody tells Monica that he is no longer interested in going to the dance with her. (LO 5.1, 5.2, 5.5, 5.6, 5.7)

a. What contract formation issue could determine whether a contract has been formed?

b. Would a court make a decision requiring Brody to go to the dance with Monica?

CHAPTER 6

CONTRACTS: PROBLEMS WITH FORMATION

HELP!

As a businessperson, you may experience any of these scenarios:

- Help! You and a competing business want to agree to restrict where you can each do business so as not to overwhelm the market.
- Help! You just entered into a two-year cell phone contract with a 17-year-old.
- Help! You mistakenly left out a zero in the price of a sales contract.
- Help! Your boss wants you to rent her your cottage, even though you don't normally rent it to non-family members.
- Help! You just purchased a business and found out the previous owner inflated the revenue figures for the last year.

LO 6.1   6.1 What Causes Problems in Contract Formation?

There are three requirements to a valid contract: each party must have the necessary capacity to enter into the contract, the contract must not be contrary to law, and the contract must be entered into voluntarily by each party, not as the result of a mistake or an unfair action by the other party.

A problem with any of these three elements may make the contract automatically invalid or a **void contract**, or allow one of the parties the option to end the contract, making it a **voidable contract**.

> **Void Contract**—a contract regarded by the courts as never having existed, with neither party able to enforce anything under it.

> **Voidable Contract**—a contract whose defect allows one of the parties to end the contract as if it had never existed.

LO 6.2   6.2 Introduction to Formation Problems in Contracts: Legality, Capacity, Voluntariness

When there has been an offer and acceptance, and consideration and intention have been determined, we have finished the initial stages of contract formation. There are three other elements that will determine whether a contract will be enforceable. These elements provide a safety valve to both society and the contractual parties, by looking at the purpose of the contract and the motivation for the parties to enter into it. These three elements are:

- Legality
- Capacity
- Voluntariness

Legality is the element that allows the contract's purpose to be evaluated by society. Capacity is the element to protect a vulnerable person from being taken advantage of. Voluntariness applies to everyone who enters into a contract and refers back to the privity of contract. So even though the law will not protect you from entering into a poor contract, it does recognize that a contract should be a voluntary undertaking by all parties and will review any factors—such as mistake, misrepresentation, undue influence, and duress—that impacted on the voluntariness of one party's agreement to the contract.

Legality

When dealing with the **legality** of the object of a contract, ask yourself the following question:

> Was the purpose of the contract legal, and even if legal, was the purpose one that should be enforced by a court of law?

If you and a friend have a bet on the hockey game that night, and you win, what happens if your friend refuses to pay? Most courts in Canada refuse to enforce gambling debts between private parties, even though they often resemble perfectly good contracts. The reason they are not enforced is usually cited as a **public policy** one: the courts do not want to promote activities such as gambling.

Legality—the purpose of the contract must be legal, and even if legal, must be one that a court of law believes should be enforced.

Public Policy—the purpose of the contract must not conflict with the interests of society.

Capacity

Capacity is used by the law to protect those people we consider vulnerable. Were the parties capable of understanding what they were getting into, and if not, should they be allowed out of the contract with few or no consequences?

Capacity can be denied based on a category of the party—age, mental infirmity—but sets conditions on the extent to which it can be used to render a contract unenforceable.

DID YOU KNOW?

Dealing with a Minor

According to Industry Canada's Consumer Trends Report, in 2002 minors ages 8–14 spent $1.7 billion of their own discretionary income. It is called discretionary income because the analysis shows that most of the necessary needs of minors are paid for by their household. As such, this discretionary spending does not fall into one of the categories of contracts to which a minor can be bound. Businesses have to be aware of this risk when dealing with minor consumers.

Voluntariness

Though the law expects each party entering into a contract to be knowledgeable, it also expects each party to play by the rules. When one party doesn't, it may open the door for the other party to get out of the contract because they entered into it with false expectations of the nature of the benefits to be received. The parties must enter into a contract with their eyes open, and not due to invalid actions by the other party.

LO 6.3   **6.3** Beyond the Basics: Legality

© Zerbor | Dreamstime.com

The purpose of a contract must be a legal one. Many students confuse legality with the actions taken in forming the contract. If I force you into a contract through the threat of violence, then that is an illegal act. However, it does not render the contract void because of the illegality. The contract itself, without regard to why I entered into it, may be a perfectly valid contract. As we will see, a party forced into a contract will be able to leave because of the voluntariness element of duress.

The legality of the contract has to do with the purpose of a contract. The parties have to ask themselves what the contract is for and whether its goals and obligations are legal. If I have a contract with you to steal a car for you, that is an illegal purpose and will not be enforced even though it has all the other essential elements of a contract. If you don't pay me, I cannot take you to court to sue you for payment. If on the other hand you do pay me but I don't do the job, you also cannot sue me for your money back.

The more subjective element of illegality concerns those contracts which, though not illegal because of a written law, a court decides are against public policy. These are matters for some object or purpose that the court feels society would not wish to promote. For example, you would not go to jail for gambling with your friends in a poker game at your house—it is not illegal. However, you would not be able to go to court to enforce a debt that arose from that poker game. Another example of this occurred in the 1980s when surrogate motherhood was not being regulated by the law. Courts decided that applying contract law rules to a family law issue was not desirable or in the public interest. Therefore, contracts for surrogate motherhood would not be enforced as commercial transactions, except for compensation for expenses. This issue has since been addressed by the *Assisted Human Reproduction Act*, which applies some regulation to the area.

As the above example shows, one of the great strengths and weaknesses of using public policy to determine the enforceability of a contract is that it can change over time as public attitudes change. If the public is strongly opposed to or in favour of a type of contract, the courts can vary their interpretation of public policy. A legislature could also take up the matter directly and pass a law either allowing or prohibiting such a contract.

A contract that has a purpose that is illegal or against public policy will be rendered void or unenforceable by a court. No compensation under contract law will be available to either party.

CASE STUDY

Kingshott v. Brunskill, [1953] OWN 133 (C.A.)

A farmer, Kingshott, sold a crop of ungraded apples to another farmer, Brunskill, whose business was grading and selling apples to the public. In Ontario at the time, it was illegal to sell ungraded apples. Brunskill refused to pay the full price for the ungraded apples and was sued by Kingshott for the full price. Even though Brunskill graded the apples before selling them to the public, the court ruled that as the original contract was for an illegal transaction, it would not be enforced.

Even in the face of illegality, a court will be hesitant to interfere in such an agreement, even if it means one party profits over the other. The parties should be aware of the consequences when entering into a contract that they should know is against the law.

LO 6.4

6.4 Beyond the Basics: Capacity and Voluntariness

It is important to understand the effect the lack of capacity will have on a contract. Unlike the other essential elements of contracts, **capacity** is determined by placing the parties to a contract into a category. If that category has been deemed to be vulnerable, then that person may have lacked the capacity to enter into a contract with full understanding of the obligations and consequences that come with it.

> Capacity—the parties must be capable of understanding what they are getting into.

A capacity issue may make a contract voidable. This means it can be terminated by the party lacking capacity without any negative consequences. However, the contract will continue until that party, or someone on their behalf, acts. Note that this doesn't mean a person gets the benefit of the contract for free. Before ending the contract, both sides must meet their obligations. Also note that it is only the party without capacity who can end the contract. This option is not available to the other party.

People without Capacity

Minors (or Infants)

Minors, or infants at law, have always been recognized as being vulnerable in contract situations. Because of this it is a general rule that contracts made by minors will not be enforced against them but will be enforced for them. A minor has the option of not performing or ending a contract with no liability.

There are two exemptions to this general rule. The first is an exception for beneficial contracts of service and for the provision of necessaries. The second concerns the consequences when a minor repudiates a contract where the other party has already fulfilled all or part of their obligations.

A beneficial contract of service is, at its most basic level, a job or apprenticeship. As long as the minor is not being exploited and is deriving a benefit from the contract it will be enforceable against both parties under contract and employment law.

A contract for necessaries covers such things as food, clothing, lodging, medical and legal attention, and transportation to and from work. However, as with beneficial contracts of service, there can be no evidence of exploitation of the minor. Exploitation means that the cost to the minor must be a reasonable one under the circumstances.

CASE STUDY

Mosher v. Benson (2008), 269 N.S.R.(2d) 376 (Small); 860 A.P.R. 376

A minor purchased a vehicle from the defendant. The minor's parents brought a claim seeking, in effect, to reverse the transaction. The Nova Scotia Small Claims Court allowed the claim. The motor vehicle in this case was not a "necessary of life" and therefore the contract was voidable if the minor or the minor's guardians so wished. The minor would return the vehicle, and get his money back.

Capacity does not allow a minor to profit from a contract wrongfully; it only allows them the option to get out of a contract that would otherwise be binding.

Diminished Contractual Capacity

Where the law relating to minors only requires objective proof that the person was a minor when they entered into the contract, the law relating to diminished contractual capacity requires the party wishing to overturn to prove the following three things if they want to be released from their obligations:

1. That the person at the time the contract was formed suffered from some recognized condition that affected their ability to appreciate the nature of the contract to which they were agreeing. This could arise from mental impairment due to intoxication—both voluntary and involuntary—or mental, physical, or emotional conditions. Note that a physical condition such as advanced age or injury does not automatically lead to the conclusion that the person suffers from diminished contractual capacity.

2. That the other party to the contract knew, or should have known, of the condition at the time the contract was formed. This may be almost impossible to show, especially when the contract is negotiated through the mail, or by the internet or telephone.

3. That the person claiming incapacity, or someone with authority to act on their behalf, took immediate steps to terminate the contract as soon as it was practical to do so upon becoming aware of it or regaining capacity.

Other Entities with Limited or No Capacity

Corporations, labour unions, and people who are bankrupt have their ability to enter into contracts limited by statute law. This usually restricts the type and extent of contracts that they can enter into. In Ontario, community colleges can only enter into contracts that are within their mandate and further their organizational purpose.

DID YOU KNOW?

Entities with Limited or No Capacity

- Corporations: The capacity of public bodies, such as colleges, may be limited by legislation
- Labour unions: Status varies by province as to the type and nature of contracts a union has the capacity to enter
- Enemy aliens: Contracts are void or suspended with citizens of countries with whom we are at war
- Aboriginal peoples: Status Indians have a restricted capacity to contract while living on a reserve
- Bankrupt debtors: Undischarged bankrupts must notify potential contracting parties of their status and limited capacity

Voluntariness

The final element that a court will examine in contract formation is why a party entered into that contract. If a party's entry into a contract was without the necessary voluntariness, it can be used to end the contract. This is more likely to be effective if they can show that the other party either deliberately, or in some cases accidentally, actively denied them this voluntariness. As such, a mistake will probably not let you out of a contract, but a deliberate misrepresentation by the other party will.

LO 6.5   ## 6.5 Mistake

If a party enters into a contract under a basic misunderstanding, a court may give them some relief from the contract. However, the old legal maxim that "mistake of law is no defence" applies because the court presumes all parties to know the law. A party who does not know the law may have only themselves to blame should the contract not be what they were expecting. The court also will not repair a mistake of judgment in entering into a contract because both parties are presumed to have done their due diligence in assessing the obligations and benefits of a potential contract before entering into it.

There are two types of **mistakes** recognized by courts that may allow for some remedies to be applied. A distinction is made between these two types:

1. Mistakes about the terms of the contract, and
2. Mistaken assumptions about the subject matter of the contract.

Mistakes about the terms of a contract may occur because one party inadvertently used the wrong words in stating the terms. The court will grant relief if a reasonable person would have recognized that a mistake was made.

> **Mistakes**—wrongful beliefs about the terms of a contract that cause a person to enter into it.

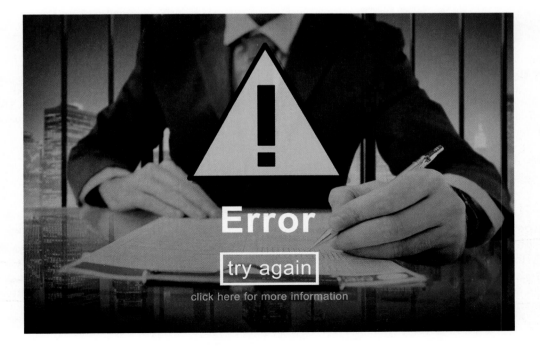

Rawpixel.com / Shutterstock.com

Sometimes a mistake can be made in recording the agreement in writing. This could be something as simple as a typo. The court will solve the problem if:

- The parties were in complete agreement
- There were no further negotiations to change the contract
- The change in the written document is most easily explained as a mistake of recording

The usual remedy for situations like this is called rectification. That simply means that the court will correct the mistake in the contract.

Sometimes misunderstandings about the meaning of words will arise if the parties have different interpretations of an ambiguous or unclear term. In these cases, the court will give the term the meaning that is the most reasonable under the circumstances. Where one or both of the parties change their position or pass on an opportunity because of a mistake in a contract, the court will grant relief if the results will be reasonably fair to both parties. Solutions may require ingenuity or imagination in the exercise of discretion. If no remedy appears available, the loss will often be left to lie where it fell.

A party may make a mistake about the existence of the subject matter of the contract. If the subject matter of the contract was destroyed prior to contract formation, the contract is void.

A special type of mistake is known as *non est factum.* This is where a mistake has been made about the nature of a signed document. This arises where one of the parties had to rely upon another person—not the other party—to tell them what a contract was about. If there is a misunderstanding in what obligations the person has agreed to because of this reliance, the party can get out of the contract. Blind and illiterate people and those who are unable to read the language of the document are usually protected since these people must ultimately rely on the integrity of people to explain to them accurately the terms of a contract.

A contract made under *non est factum* is voidable if:

- The signer could not read it
- The signer was not careless
- The subject matter is completely different than the signer believed

 CASE STUDY

The Mistake of *Non est factum*

According to the Supreme Court of Canada decision in *Marvco Color Research Ltd. v. Harris*, [1982] 2 S.C.R. 774, a person signing a contract can avoid the consequences of a document he or she has signed only if

(a) the mistake is a serious one, and

(b) the signer has not been careless of his or her own interests.

In this case, Johnson, who was living with the daughter of the Harrises, asked them to guarantee a mortgage to a third party to help him in his business. They did so. At a later date, Johnson asked them to re-sign the documents to correct an error with the dates on the original. The Harrises did so without reading the document, trusting the assurances of Johnson that the only changes were to the dates. These assurances were the only reason they did not read the document, as both were educated people. When the third party was unable to pay back the loan, the Harrises found themselves responsible for the money owing. They unsuccessfully claimed the defence of *non est factum.*

What happens when one party to a contract mistakenly gives a benefit to the other party?

If you received the benefit knowing of the mistake, you must return the benefit. If you did not know of the mistake, the court will determine whether or not you have been *unjustly (unfairly) enriched* by the mistake. If so, reparations may have to be made to the other party.

E-Commerce

Ingram Publishing

Two particular concerns with mistakes made in e-commerce transactions have been identified and dealt with by the *Uniform Electronic Commerce Act* and its federal and provincial versions. The first concern recognizes that it is easy to hit the wrong key or click the mouse or screen at the wrong place, sending a command that has legal consequences. This is referred to as the "single keystroke error." Secondly, with the increase of transactions completed online the involvement of people in a face to face transaction has been reduced. To take the place of personal interaction, many websites rely upon electronic agents to complete their side of the contract formation. Unfortunately, an electronic agent cannot recognize or respond to a subsequent message that says "I didn't mean that!" The law deals with these concerns by setting out the criteria that would allow a natural person to get of a contract due to such a mistake.

These conditions apply to both the person claiming that they made a mistake and the website on which the mistake was made.

The person claiming the mistake must:

- Give notice of the error as soon as practically possible;
- Respond to instructions from the other party, and;
- Have received no benefit from the mistake.

In addition, the above conditions will apply only in situations where the online party did not provide a method for preventing or correcting an error.

DID YOU KNOW?

E-Commerce

From *Electronic Commerce Act, 2000* of Ontario

Errors, transactions with electronic agents

21. An electronic transaction between an individual and another person's electronic agent is not enforceable by the other person if,
    (a) the individual makes a material error in electronic information or an electronic document used in the transaction;
    (b) the electronic agent does not give the individual an opportunity to prevent or correct the error;
    (c) on becoming aware of the error, the individual promptly notifies the other person; and
    (d) in a case where consideration is received as a result of the error, the individual,
        i. returns or destroys the consideration in accordance with the other person's instructions or, if there are no instructions, deals with the consideration in a reasonable manner, and
        ii. does not benefit materially by receiving the consideration.

Source: © Queen's Printer for Ontario, 2000. Current as of June 2, 2016. This is not an official version.

LO 6.6 | 6.6 Misrepresentation, Undue Influence, and Duress

Unlike mistake, if misrepresentation, undue influence, or duress has occurred during contract formation the innocent party will have the option to void the contract.

Misrepresentation

There are two types of misrepresentation that contract law is concerned with: fraudulent and innocent misrepresentation. Both involve one party being misled by the other, but the knowledge of the misleading party determines whether or not the misrepresentation was fraudulent or innocent. This determination will have an effect on the remedies available to the innocent party.

Fraudulent misrepresentation, deliberately misleading the other party on an important term of the contract knowing that it was one of the reasons why the other party agreed to the contract, will allow the innocent victim two options. They can void or end the contract and sue for damages under the tort of deceit.

> **Fraudulent Misrepresentation**—a false statement made by one party about an important term in a contract that they know was a reason why the other party agreed to the contract.

CASE STUDY

Derry v. Peek (1889), 14 App. Cas. 33

This English case from 1889 established the test we still use for deciding whether or not a misrepresentation was fraudulent; that is, if the court decides that a statement was made:

(a) knowingly;

(b) without belief in its truth; or

(c) recklessly.

The defendant in this case was a builder of tramways. Originally these trams were pulled by horses, but these were gradually being replaced by trams that were driven by steam or other mechanical engines. The defendant issued a prospectus—information used by investors to decide whether to invest in a company—that they had been granted the absolute right by Parliament to mechanize their trams. The plaintiff, relying on this prospectus, invested heavily in the company. Unfortunately, the right was not absolute, and was denied on many sections of the tramways. Without the considerable cost savings that mechanical trams have over horse-drawn ones, the company went bankrupt. The plaintiff sued for recovery of his investment, alleging, among other things, that the prospectus was a fraudulent misrepresentation that caused him to invest. Unfortunately, in applying the test laid out above, the court found that the defendants had not committed fraudulent misrepresentation as they had made the statement in the honest belief that it was true.

Innocent misrepresentation involves a party being misled without the active intent of the other party. The law has to be careful to separate innocent misrepresentations from mistakes, as the innocent misrepresentation allows a party to void a contract if they so wish. This can only happen, however, if the innocent party does so promptly after learning of the misrepresentation and if no other innocent third party would be negatively affected. If the party who caused the innocent misrepresentation learns about it first, failing to advise the other innocent party turns the innocent misrepresentation into a fraudulent one, with the increase in remedies that go with it.

> **Innocent Misrepresentation**—a false statement, made by one party about an important term in a contract, which they in good faith believed to be true, that was a reason why the other party agreed to the contract.

Contracts of "Utmost Good Faith"

While most cases of misrepresentation involves a positive action by the party committing the misrepresentation (that is, they have do something to create the misrepresentation), some contracts allow for misrepresentation to occur by one party failing to say or do something that they are bound to do because of the relationship between the parties. These contracts give rise to a duty of **utmost good faith**.

> **Utmost Good Faith**—a duty of disclosure, arising out of a special relationship of trust between the parties.

Examples of such special relationships can arise because of the nature of the contract. Contracts for insurance are said to be ones of utmost good faith because the insured has a duty to disclose changes in circumstances—their health, for example—that might change their risk. This duty arose first out of common law, and later became a statutory duty under most provincial Insurance Acts.

DID YOU KNOW?

Duties of Utmost Good Faith

From the Insurance Act. R.S., c. 231, s. 1 of Nova Scotia

Duty to disclose

> 82 (1) An applicant for insurance on his own behalf and on behalf of each person to be insured, and each person to be insured, shall disclose to the insurer in any application, on a medical examination, if any, and in any written statements or answers furnished as evidence of insurability, every fact within his knowledge that is material to the insurance and is not so disclosed by the other.
>
> (2) Subject to Sections 83 and 86, a failure to disclose, or a misrepresentation of, such a fact renders a contract voidable by the insurer

Source: R.S., c. 231, s. 82 (1 and 2).

Contracts with Consumers

With the availability of online contracts for goods and services, courts have started to create special duties for suppliers when dealing with consumers. As most online contracts are formed by standard form contracts, the rules developed for such contracts are particularly relevant.

The duty is now on suppliers to point out terms that may be different from those that a consumer might reasonably expect.

CASE STUDY

Tilden Rent-A-Car Co v. Clendenning (1978), 83 DLR (3d) 400 (Ont Ca)

While renting a car from the plaintiff, the defendant Clendenning bought the extra insurance. It is obvious to the clerk that Clendenning did not read an exemption clause that limits what the extra insurance will cover. The clerk does not point this out. Clendenning gets into an accident and damages the vehicle. He pleads guilty to driving while intoxicated, although he later insists that he was not intoxicated. Tilden, claiming that the insurance does not cover this situation, sues Clendenning for the cost of the damage to the vehicle.

The court decided that the exemption clause was unreasonable and inconsistent with the claim to provide complete coverage for the added cost. It goes against the intention of the signer and Tilden could not rely on these clauses.

If a contract contains onerous and/or unusual provisions, it is the duty of the party seeking to rely on such terms to ensure that they are effectively called to the attention of the other party in order for the contract to be binding. The signer is bound by the terms of the document only if the other party believes, on reasonable grounds, that those terms express the signer's intentions.

Undue Influence

© Konradbak | Dreamstime.com

While **undue influence** can be determined by the circumstances of a relationship, it is more common for it to be presumed from the existence of a current relationship between the parties. For there to be a finding of undue influence, there must be a mental domination of one party over the other to the extent that that person is robbed of free will. A contract reached through undue influence can be voided by the victim as long as they do so promptly.

> **Undue Influence**—influencing a party into entering a contract through the abuse of a position of dominance.

Such special relationships as teacher and student, spouses, and accountant and client give rise to a presumption of undue influence. This can be rebutted by the stronger party with evidence that at the time the contract was formed there was no undue influence. This means, however, that the best time to deal with this is at the point of contract formation—by taking steps such as getting independent legal advice or setting a fair market price for the contract.

CASE STUDY

Bank of Montreal v. Duguid, 2000 CanLII 5710 (ON CA)

This leading Canadian case on undue influence established the current view of that issue.

In 1989, Duguid and another party applied to the Bank of Montreal for an investment loan in a tax-driven condominium investment. While the Bank was not prepared to make the loan based on the assets of Duguid and his colleague, they agreed to make the loan provided that Mrs. Duguid was also on the covenant of the promissory note. Contrary to its written policies, the Bank did not suggest to Mrs. Duguid that she obtain independent legal or financial advice. The Bank also did not disclose its concerns about the financial viability of the condominium project. The loan was not repaid and, Duguid having become bankrupt, the Bank sued Mrs. Duguid for repayment of US$87,243.84 plus interest.

The court conceded that a party may set aside a transaction where they were induced to enter into it by another's undue influence. There are two types of undue influence, actual and presumed. Undue influence is presumed for certain relationships of trust and confidence or it may be presumed for any de facto relationship of reposed trust and confidence. Where a complainant relies upon a presumption of undue influence, the court must look to the nature of the relationship and determine whether the potential for domination exists as a matter of fact or whether it may be presumed. The relationship between a husband and wife is not one that categorically gives rise to a presumption of undue influence; rather, it is a relationship that may give rise to the presumption because a spouse may be able to demonstrate that his or her relationship was one for which it is reasonable to presume undue influence in the procuring of a transaction.

The Bank in this case knew of the possibility of undue influence, yet failed to take reasonable steps to make sure she was entering into the obligation freely. Mrs. Duguid established presumed undue influence arising out of the circumstances of the marital relationship when she signed the note. This meant that the Bank seeking to uphold the transaction must rebut the presumption of undue influence by proving that Mrs. Duguid co-signed the loan freely—for example, by showing that she received independent legal advice. As the Bank could not do so, they therefore cannot enforce the promissory note against Mrs. Duguid.

DID YOU KNOW?

Presumption of Undue Influence and Independent Legal Advice

Undue influence is presumed in:

- Family relationships with inequality
- Relationships where one party possesses special skill or knowledge
- Relationships where one person is in dire straits

Presumption may be rebutted by independent legal advice. Independent legal advice is simply where a person facing a decision seeks advice from an outside lawyer who advises them of the rights, obligations, and risks they face. The lawyer then provides that person with a letter that states they have been advised of those rights, obligations, and risks and have an understanding of them.

Duress

Duress is a form of threat that forces a person into entering a contract against their will. The law recognizes three types of threat that can allow a contract to be voided by the victim for duress. These three types are threats that cause harm to the person, reputation (for example blackmail), or finances (threatening to fire someone if they don't agree to the contract. For a court to allow a person to void a contract under duress, they must act promptly once the threat is removed and prove that they had a reasonable apprehension of the threat being realistically achievable.

> **Duress**—coercing a party into entering a contract through the threat or use of harm to their person, their reputation, or their finances.

CASE STUDY

Barton v. Armstrong [1976] AC 104 Privy Council

Although not a Canadian case, *Barton v. Armstrong* outlines duress quite well.

Armstrong was the chairman and largest shareholder in Landmark Corporation Ltd. Barton, Bovil, and Cottrel were the other three directors of the company. After internal disagreements over how Armstrong was running the company and abusing his privileges as chairman, the other three directors asked him to resign. Armstrong refused to do so. The others then managed to take control of Landmark's subsidiary companies and remove all credit facilities from Landmark Corp. When Armstrong discovered this, he made a number of death threats to Barton. This pressured Barton into purchasing Armstrong's shares in the company for substantially more than they were worth. Barton agreed to this partly due to the threats but also due to the fact that it would mean Armstrong would no longer have controlling interest. Although Barton believed he would be able to turn the company around without Armstrong's dealings, the company became insolvent soon thereafter. Barton sought to have the contract set aside.

The Court decided that the contract could be set aside. Where there is duress to the person there was no obligation to show that he would not have entered the agreement but for the threat, it simply being sufficient that the death threats were a cause.

Once all of the essential elements of contract formation have been met, then a valid contract is formed. Most problems with contracts can be anticipated during the formation process, which is why it is such a vital part of contract law. It is better to deal with anticipated problems at this stage than to wait and have them develop through the life of the contract.

FOR REVIEW

Questions

1. What is a void contract? (LO 6.1)
2. What is a voidable contract? (LO 6.1, 6.4)
3. What does it mean if a contract is "illegal by statute"? (LO 6.3, 6.4)
4. What does it mean if a contract is "against public policy"? (LO 6.3)
5. In what types of contracts will a minor be bound? Why are these exceptions necessary? (LO 6.2, 6.4)
6. What three things must a person prove if they wish to get out of a contract due to intoxication? (LO 6.4)
7. What three conditions must be met for a person to get out of a contract they agreed to online by mistake? (LO 6.1, 6.5)
8. What is the difference between fraudulent and innocent misrepresentation? (LO 6.6)
9. What is the difference between duress and undue influence? (LO 6.6)
10. What is independent legal advice? (LO 6.6)

Activities

1. What kind of things should a court look at when deciding whether a contract should be unenforceable due to public policy concerns? (LO 6.2)
2. Why has the emergence of online shopping made capacity to contract more difficult to identify in contracts? (LO 6.4)
3. Why does contract law presume undue influence exists in certain relationships? (LO 6.6)
4. A person who blackmails another person into entering into a contract renders the contract voidable under duress. Why is it not a matter of illegality? (LO 6.6)
5. In dealing with electronic agents, why does the law include a provision to limit the claiming of an error in contract formation if the online merchant has a mechanism to prevent or correct an error? (LO 6.5)
6. Why are courts hesitant to overturn contracts on the basis of a mistake? (LO 6.5)

CASES FOR DISCUSSION

Case #1

John, who is in the electronics business, sold a car stereo system on credit to Miles, a 17-year-old. The equipment cost $1,500 and Miles made an initial payment of $500 and agreed to pay the balance in 10 monthly instalments of $100 each. (LO 6.1, 6.2, 6.4)

a. Which of these parties must honour the contract?
b. Why can the other party get out of the contract?
c. What is the effect if the party who can end the contract chooses to do so?

Case #2

Peter offered to sell his restaurant business to Denise. Before accepting, Denise requested the financial statements for the business. Peter delivered them but he inflated the revenue figures on the income statement to make it look like the company made more money than it actually did. After reviewing the statements, Denise agreed to purchase the business. She has now discovered that the business is not very profitable. (LO 6.1, 6.2, 6.6)

a. Can Denise get out of this contract? If so, on what basis?

b. Can Denise choose to remain in the contract? If so, is she entitled to be compensated in any manner?

c. What are Denise's options if she doesn't wish to remain in the contract at all?

Case #3

Today, Jim entered into an agreement to sell his cottage to April for $150,000. Unknown to both Jim and April, the cottage was totally destroyed last weekend when a large pine tree fell on it during a severe windstorm. (LO 6.1, 6.2, 6.5)

a. What happens to this contract?

b. What determines the outcome in this case?

CHAPTER 7

CONTRACTS: ENDING CONTRACTS

Learning Objectives

After reading this chapter the student will:

LO 7.1	Understand the obligations owed by each party during the life and performance of a contract
LO 7.2	Know what problems can arise in performing a contract
LO 7.3	Examine the effect a problem in performance will have on a contract
LO 7.4	Describe the ways that a party can exit a contract, with or without consequences
LO 7.5	Recognize the differences between a breach of warranty and a breach of condition in a contract
LO 7.6	Understand the remedies that can be applied to a breach of contract

HELP!

As a businessperson, you may experience any of these scenarios:

- Help! The company that renovated your office left it in such a mess that you had to hire a professional cleaner.

- Help! The company that was supposed to pave your driveway has called and cancelled the day before they were to start the job.

- Help! The company that redecorated your offices is demanding full payment for the job even though there are still a couple of things to be completed.

- Help! It's Christmas time and your online ordering server has been down for a week while you wait for it to be repaired.

- Help! You have hired a famous singer to appear at the grand opening of your business and they are now saying that they won't be coming.

- Help! You arranged a vacation through an online travel agent in Tennessee and the tour company went bankrupt the day before you were to leave.

LO 7.1   ## 7.1 Performance of Contracts

Once a contract has been formed, the parties are entitled to **performance** of the contract according to the terms of the contract. Each party must also know when the contract has ended. This is important because the ending of the contract releases each party from further obligations. Formally, this is known as the discharge of contracts. Obligations end when each party to the contract has performed or completed their obligations to the satisfaction of the other party. If the performance is not completed or is not to the reasonable satisfaction of one of the parties then a **breach** may have occurred. If the breach is important enough it may also end the contract. No matter what type of breach occurs, the innocent party has legal rights for a remedy to repair the breach.

> **Performance**—the completion of a party's obligations under a contract to the reasonable satisfaction of the other party.

> **Breach**—the failure of a party to perform their obligations to the other party's reasonable satisfaction.

DID YOU KNOW?

Ways to End a Contract

- A contract may be ended by:
  - Performance
  - Agreement
  - Frustration
  - Operation of law
  - Breach

Both businesses and consumers have to be aware of when their obligations and rights under the contract have come to an end.

LO 7.2   7.2 Introduction to Discharge of Contracts

Once the formation of a contract has been completed, it may seem that all the hard work has been done. This actually couldn't be further from the truth. The formation of a contract simply sets up the relationship between the parties. They now have to manage that relationship to an endpoint. How they manage that relationship will determine how satisfied each party is in the benefits received under the contract. The five ways that a contract can come to an end are:

- Performance
- Agreement
- Frustration
- Operation of law
- Breach of contract

Performance means that all—or most—of the obligations under the contract have been met to the reasonable satisfaction of each party. *Agreement* means that the parties have agreed either in the contract itself or in a mutual agreement that the contract has finished. *Frustration* means that, through no fault of the parties, the contract has become impossible or unnecessary to perform. *Operation of law* means that a statute has imposed a **condition** on the contract that requires it to end. *Breach* means that there has been a failure by one party to perform an important enough term of the contract to make it necessary for the other party to terminate the contract and move on.

> **Condition**—an essential term of a contract.

Performance

© Yurolaitsalbert | Dreamstime.com

When determining whether a contract has been completely performed, ask yourself the following question:

> Have all of my reasonable expectations under the contract been met by the performance of the other party?

If they have been met, then the contract has been completely performed and now comes to an end. If they have been almost entirely met, so that a neutral party would say that they have been "substantially" performed, then the contract can be said to be ended. If a minor part of the contract has not been performed satisfactorily, than a breach has occurred but the contract has not ended, and the innocent party may take steps to remedy the breach. And if a major part of the contract has not been performed, then a major breach has occurred and the innocent party can treat the contract as having ended and take steps to obtain a remedy.

DID YOU KNOW?

"Reasonable" Expectations under a Contract

Lord Steyn (a South African judge who sat as a Law Lord in the British House of Lords from 1995 to 2005) suggests that "The function of the law of contract is to provide an effective and fair framework for contractual dealings. This function requires an adjudication based on the reasonable expectations of parties."*

A party has the right that a contract will be performed to the level that is "reasonable" under the contract. This means, in light of all the terms of a contract, what a "reasonable person" would expect for performance.

For example, if you pay $800 to have your car painted, you are allowed to expect that you will receive a service that warrants the $800 price tag. You do not have to accept performance that is more in line with a $300 cost, nor can you demand performance that is closer to what you would receive under a $3,000 custom paint job.

Both businesses and consumers have to be aware of this limitation of their expectations. Should one want a different level of performance, then that needs to be specified in the contract itself.

* "Contract Law: Fulfilling the Reasonable Expectations of Honest Men" (1997) 113 *LQR* 433 at 434.

Agreement

A contract can end when the parties agree not to perform the contract. These types of agreements can take place as follows:

- Waiver of an agreement means the parties have chosen not to proceed with the performance of a contract that already exists. A waiver can be gratuitous, which means that one party releases the other party from their obligations with no benefit for doing so. However, if a party has partially performed their obligations under the contract, a waiver will be binding only if the province that covers the contract has a statute that allows part performance in satisfaction of a debt binding.
- A new agreement may be substituted for the original one. This has the effect of discharging the original contract.
- A contract may contain clauses that discharge the contract when a condition precedent or subsequent occurs, or it may have an **option to terminate** that gives one or both of the parties a right to discharge the agreement without liability as long as they follow the process outlined in the contract.

Option to Terminate—a condition, for example giving notice, that allows a party to end the contract.

Frustration

A contract can also end by something called frustration. In these cases, discharge results when it becomes impossible to perform the contract. Sometimes, frustration occurs when the purpose of the contract no longer exists.

Frustration must be related to an event that occurs after the contract is made. If the possibility of the frustrating event was known at the time of contract formation, than the parties should have taken steps to prevent it.

The frustrating event must also make performance impossible. It cannot just make the contract harder or more expensive to perform. Frustration must also not be caused by one of the parties, either deliberately or through negligence.

Operation of Law

A contract can also be ended by certain circumstances described by statute. For example, if you declare bankruptcy in Canada, then your credit card contracts are terminated by the *Bankruptcy and Insolvency Act*.

Breach of Contract

Under certain circumstances, a breach of a contract will end the contract. For this to happen, the entire contract must be breached or an essential term of the contract must be breached. Additionally, the innocent party that suffers the breach must choose to treat the contract as being ended.

Remember, however, that no matter what type of breach occurred, and no matter whether the innocent party chose to end the contract, that party is entitled to some type of remedy for the breach.

LO 7.3   7.3 Beyond the Basics: Performance

Performance

Most contracts end by the performance of their obligations. This is the expectation of most parties when they enter into a contract. Usually, the parties can expect that all obligations under the contract have been performed to the reasonable satisfaction of the other party. The exception to this is something called **substantial performance**. When one party has performed almost all of their obligations under the contract, they can require the other party to perform their obligations under the contract. This is to prevent a party from using a minor failure of performance to claim breach of contract and refuse to perform their part of the contract. A court may, however, reduce the obligations owed to allow for the incomplete performance of the other party.

> **Substantial Performance**—occurs when all except for a trivial part of the contract obligations have been performed.

Sometimes a party may wish to preserve their legal rights to enforce a contract or receive compensation for a breach by another party refusing to fulfill their obligations. If you know that the other party is not going to fulfill their obligations, say for example because they found a cheaper supplier than you, it is best to perform a **tender of performance**. This simply means that you show you are willing to perform your obligation in full. Doing so is accepted by the court as performance, allowing you to sue the other party for compensation for failing to perform the contract at all.

Tender of Performance—an attempt by one party to a contract to perform its obligations under the contract. Indicates a willingness, readiness, and ability to complete the contract.

Recent case law in Canada has now implied a duty of "good faith" as an organizing principle in contract performance. Simply put, this means that in certain types of contracts the court imposes a duty on the parties to perform their obligations under the contract without misleading the other party as to that performance. Essentially, what the court has done is brought in a safeguard against fraudulent performance, which is similar to the protection against fraudulent misrepresentation in contract formation.

 CASE STUDY

Bhasin v. Hrynew, 2014 SCC 71, [2014] 3 S.C.R. 494

In this case, the party known as C markets education savings plans to investors through retail dealers, known as enrollment directors, such as Bhasin (B). They had a three-year contract that would automatically renew at the end of three years unless one of the parties gave six months' notice in writing that they did not want it to renew. Hrynew (H), another enrollment director and a competitor of B, wanted to capture B's lucrative niche market and had previously proposed a merger of their agencies. He also actively encouraged C to force the merger. B had refused to participate in such a merger. Despite B's concerns, C appointed H to audit the records of all of the enrollment officers. C also discussed with the government Commission his plan to merge B's agency with H's agency. At all times, C lied to B about the potential merger.

When B continued to refuse to allow H to audit his records, C threatened to terminate the 1998 agreement and in May 2001 gave notice of non-renewal under the agreement. At the expiry of the contract term, B lost the value in his business in his assembled workforce. The majority of his sales agents were successfully solicited by H's agency.

The Court identified that a duty of good faith in performance existed in the following contracts:

- Contracts expressly requiring cooperation of the parties to achieve their objects;
- Contracts involving the exercise of contractual discretion;
- Situations where a contractual power is used to evade a contractual duty;
- Contracts in the employment context in the narrow sense that the manner of termination must be done in good faith;
- Contracts in the insurance context; and
- Contracts in the tendering/procurement context.

In such contracts, the court said that the duty of honest performance is as follows:

1. It "means simply that parties must not lie or otherwise knowingly mislead each other about matters directly linked to the performance of the contract";
2. It does "not impose a duty of loyalty or of disclosure" or "require a party to forego advantages flowing from the contract"; and
3. It is a "simple requirement not to lie or mislead the other party about one's contractual performance."

Quite simply, this means that in some types of contracts there are duties between the parties that are more than just performing their specified obligations. They must do so in an honest and open manner.

LO 7.4   7.4 Beyond the Basics: Agreement, Frustration, and Operation of Law

Agreement

Remember that contract law does its best to allow the parties to manage their relationship. Just as the law says you freely enter into a contract, it also allows for the parties to freely leave a contract under certain conditions. A contract can end when the parties agree not to perform the contract. These agreements can take the following forms:

- A waiver is an agreement not to proceed with the performance of a contract already in existence. If one party has already performed their part of the agreement and gives up their benefit, it is called a **gratuitous waiver**. This will be effective only if the waiver is given under **seal**, which essentially makes the waiver a binding promise. If there has been part performance of the contract, however, the waiver is binding only in provinces that allow a release of obligations for part performance.

- Sometimes a new agreement can be substituted for the original agreement. This new agreement ends the original contract. This may occur by material alteration of the terms of the original agreement, by accord and satisfaction or by novation.

- A contract may contain a clause that discharges the contract upon the occurrence of a condition precedent or subsequent, or it may contain an option to terminate which gives one or both of the parties a right to discharge the agreement without liability.

Gratuitous Waiver—the release by one party of the other party from performing their obligations under the contract. It is gratuitous because the releasing party does not receive the benefit to which they are entitled.

Seal—a mark on a contract that signifies the intention of the parties to be bound by the terms even in the absence of any consideration.

DID YOU KNOW?

Substituted Agreement, Accord and Satisfaction, and Novation

- Substituted agreement
  - A substantial change in the terms of the contract
  - Requires that a new or further benefit be received by all parties
  - Requires mutual consent of all parties
- Accord and satisfaction
  - An out of court settlement to end the contract on different terms than those contained in the contract
  - Substitutes new contract and ends all obligations under the old contract
- Novation
  - Replacement of party to the contract with a new party, or
  - A change to the subject matter of the contract
  - Requires mutual consent by all parties

A contract may include terms for its discharge within its own terms. A lease agreement, for example, may allow for one of the parties to end the lease upon giving a certain number of days' notification. There may be a clause that ends a contract when a certain condition necessary for the contract to be performed is not met (a **condition precedent**) or when a certain occurrence happens while the contract is being performed that will end the contract. For example, there may be a rising cost clause in a contract that states the contract will be ended if the price of a necessary item for the contract rises above a certain level. This is called a **condition subsequent**. These conditions, however, must be specified as such in the contract terms.

Condition Precedent—a clause that ends a contract when a certain condition necessary for the contract to be performed is not met.

Condition Subsequent—an uncertain event which, if it occurs, ends the contract.

Gustavo Frazao / Shutterstock.com

Frustration

Sometimes, through the fault of none of the parties, the performance of a contract becomes impossible or at least purposeless to proceed. This is referred to as the doctrine of **frustration**. There are several key elements to frustration. First, the frustration must relate to an event that occurs after the making of the contract. Second, the frustrating event must make performance impossible and not just create an unforeseen hardship. Note that "impossible" may not mean it is physically impossible to perform, but rather that the nature of performance has been altered radically. Finally, the frustration must not be self-induced.

Frustration—an unforeseen outside event that makes a contract impossible to perform, or changes it completely from what the parties intended.

CASE STUDY

Krell v. Henry [1903] 2 KB 740

The defendant, Henry, rented a flat in London from the plaintiff, Krell, to watch the coronation procession of King Edward VII. Although the contract did not mention the purpose of Henry's use, the housekeeper had assured him he would have an excellent view of the procession. He was to pay 75 pounds for the two-day rental. Unfortunately, the King fell ill and the procession was postponed. Henry refused to honour the agreement.

Krell sued for the money owing under the contract as he claimed that the contract—namely, the rental of his flat for two days—could still be performed. Henry claimed that as the purpose for the contract no longer existed for a reason outside the control of either party, the contract was now impossible to perform. He countersued for the return of his deposit.

The court agreed with Henry. When the basis of a contract was known, or should be known, to the parties at the time they agreed to the contract, performance will be excused when that basis is frustrated by an unforeseeable intervening. A contract's purpose or basis does not have to be explicitly stated but may be inferred from surrounding circumstances.

DID YOU KNOW?

Frustrating Event

- Impossible performance
  - Some event, such as the destruction of a rented premises, makes it impossible to perform the obligations under the contract
  - Any natural event that makes performance impossible is said to be an *Act of God*
    - "Natural" is defined as anything that is beyond human control where no one is responsible
- Operation of law
  - A change in the law now makes the performance of the obligations under the contract illegal
- Change in the reason for the contract
  - The frustrating event prevents the purpose of the contract from being performed
  - The purpose, although it can be inferred from the events surrounding the formation of the contract, must be obvious to the parties

The effect of frustration is very straightforward. A frustrating event discharges the parties from further performance. At common law this meant that each party had to bear their own losses caused by the frustrating event. As is often the case, however, statute law has softened the common law's hard line. Most provinces have a Frustrated Contracts Act that allows recovery of expenses from deposit or from the person who received a benefit before the frustrating event. This means that you have to pay for any partial benefit received before a contract was frustrated. It also means that if one party incurred expenses, for example supplies, you can deduct those expenses from any deposit received from the other party.

DID YOU KNOW?

Frustration

From Frustrated Contracts Act, R.S.O. 1990, c. F.34 of Ontario

Adjustment of rights and liabilities

<u>3. (1)</u> the sums paid or payable to a party in pursuance of a contract before the parties were discharged,

(a) in the case of sums paid, are recoverable from the party as money received for the use of the party by whom the sums were paid; and

(b) In the case of sums payable, cease to be payable. R.S.O. 1990, c. F.34, s. 3 (1).

Expenses

<u>(2)</u> If, before the parties were discharged, the party to whom the sums were paid or payable incurred expenses in connection with the performance of the contract, the court, if it considers it just to do so having regard to all the circumstances, may allow the party to retain or to recover, as the case may be, the whole or any part of the sums paid or payable not exceeding the amount of the expenses, and, without restricting the generality of the foregoing, the court, in estimating the amount of the expenses, may include such sum as appears to be reasonable in respect of overhead expenses and in respect of any work or services performed personally by the party incurring the expenses. R.S.O. 1990, c. F.34, s. 3 (2).

Benefits

<u>(3)</u> If, before the parties were discharged, any of them has, by reason of anything done by any other party in connection with the performance of the contract, obtained a valuable benefit other than a payment of money, the court, if it considers it just to do so having regard to all the circumstances, may allow the other party to recover from the party benefitted the whole or any part of the value of the benefit. R.S.O. 1990, c. F.34, s. 3 (3).

Source: © Queen's Printer for Ontario, 1990. Current as of June 2, 2016. This is not an official version.

Operation of Law

Sometimes a law passed by the government may step in to end a contract. For example, when a person files for bankruptcy they are released from many contractual obligations. This fits in with the purpose of bankruptcy law, which is to allow a person to get out from under contractual obligations that they are not capable of fulfilling.

DID YOU KNOW?

The Special Case of Bankruptcy and Student Loans

Bankruptcy law in Canada does not wipe out all debts. Certain kinds of debts will survive a bankruptcy and remain owing even though all other debts are forgiven and discharged. Examples of these surviving debts include:

- Fines imposed by a court;
- Alimony, maintenance, and support payments;
- Damages awards arising from civil proceedings for bodily harm, sexual assault, or wrongful death;
- Debts and liabilities arising out of fraud; and
- Student loan debts.

Student loan debt was excluded from bankruptcy protection because of increasing numbers of student loan defaults; increasing loan losses; and the perception that students were abusing the bankruptcy process to rid themselves of their loan obligations.

Student loan debt will not be discharged by a bankruptcy if the bankruptcy occurs within seven years of the person ceasing to be a student. To try to retain some fairness in the system, student loan recipients who declare bankruptcy within the seven-year period are able to make an application to have the loan discharged after five years if they are able to show hardship.

The *statute of limitations* is another law that can end the rights under a contract. In this case, it limits the time you have to enforce a contract through the use of the courts. Most contracts must be enforced within two years of a party suffering an injury to the non-performance or substandard performance of a contractual obligation.

DID YOU KNOW?

Operation of Law

From the Limitations Act, 2002, S.O. 2002, c. 24, Sched. B

Basic limitation period

4. Unless this Act provides otherwise, a proceeding shall not be commenced in respect of a claim after the second anniversary of the day on which the claim was discovered. 2002, c. 24, Sched. B, s. 4.

Discovery

5. 1. A claim is discovered on the earlier of,
       (a) the day on which the person with the claim first knew,
            i.   that the injury, loss or damage had occurred,
            ii. that the injury, loss or damage was caused by or contributed to by an act or omission,
            iii. that the act or omission was that of the person against whom the claim is made, and
            iv. that, having regard to the nature of the injury, loss or damage, a proceeding would be an appropriate means to seek to remedy it; and
       (b) the day on which a reasonable person with the abilities and in the circumstances of the person with the claim first ought to have known of the matters referred to in clause (a). 2002, c. 24, Sched. B, s. 5 (1).

Source: © Queen's Printer for Ontario, 2002. Current as of June 2, 2016. This is not an official version.

LO 7.5   **7.5**   Beyond the Basics: Breach of Contract

Breach of Contract

Imagine this scenario. You have signed a contract to lease a new car. You show up at the car dealership excited to pick up your new vehicle, which you ordered in a nice red colour. When you get into the dealership, you see a car—the same model as yours—that is a rusty brown colour. The salesperson greets you and points to this car, proudly saying that it is your new vehicle. But, you protest, it is brown, not red! The salesperson explains that the rust brown colour is a type of red and that's what the contract stated. Needless to say, you are not happy. You think they have breached the contract and want to walk away from it. Here is the dilemma you face. Whether or not a breach of contract will allow the innocent party to treat the contract as being ended or discharged depends on whether the breach was of a major term or a minor term of the contract. A condition is a term of the contract that is determined to be major. In other words, if a party would not have agreed to this contract if this term were different, then it is probably a condition. On the other hand, if the term were such that it was not one of the main reasons why a party agreed to the contract, then it is referred to as a **warranty**. You have to ask yourself, would you have agreed to lease this car if you could not get it in red? If the answer is yes, then it is a warranty. If the answer is no, then it is a condition. However, for it to be a condition it must have been clearly stated at the time the contract was formed that the colour of the car was of such importance to you that you would not accept any other colour. As long as the other party agreed to that, then it is a condition. If they didn't agree to it, or were unaware of it, then the court will determine whether the colour of a car is of sufficient importance to be considered a condition.

> **Warranty**—a minor term of a contract. Any term less important than a condition is assumed to be a warranty.

© N.l | Dreamstime.com

A breach of contract occurs when one or other of the parties fails to live up to its obligations under the contract. Failure to do so will open the party up to a claim for **damages** by the other party. These damages may include the ending of the contract and monetary compensation to fix the unperformed obligations. There are also some special remedies that may be used, such as an injunction or specific performance.

> **Damages**—a remedy that is in the form of money.

© Jovani Carlo Gorospe | Dreamstime.com

LEGAL SCENARIO

Terms That Are Warranties in a Contract

The leading Canadian case of *Fraser-Reid v. Droumtsekas, [1980] 1 SCR 720, 1979 CanLII 55 (SCC)* has an important statement on what is a warranty under a contract. As stated by Justice Dickson, at p. 731:

> A *warranty* is a term in a contract which does not go to the root of the agreement between the parties but simply expresses some lesser obligation, the failure to perform which can give rise to an action for damages, but never to the rights to rescind or repudiate the contract.

There are three ways that a breach may occur:

1. Express repudiation;
2. An action by a party that makes performance impossible;
3. Failure to perform a term of the contract.

The first two would be treated as a breach of condition, while the third could be either a breach of condition or a breach of warranty.

Express Repudiation

If a party to a contract advises the other party before the date for performance that they will not perform any of their contractual obligations, then they have committed a repudiation of the contract. This can happen either verbally, in writing, or through conduct. If it happens before the contract is to be performed then it is referred to as an "anticipatory" breach. The innocent party can treat the contract as being at an end and can seek a replacement contract. They can also sue the breaching party for damages.

Sometimes the anticipatory breach is implied rather than **express repudiation**. Whether this has occurred has to be determined from what the party does or fails to do. Not showing up at a scheduled time to start a contract may be an **implied repudiation**. If the innocent party does not accept this repudiation—for example, they keep emailing the other party to reschedule—then it is not repudiation and the contract cannot be treated as being at an end by the innocent party. Figure 7.1 illustrates the process of express repudiation.

Figure 7.1: **Process of Express Repudiation**

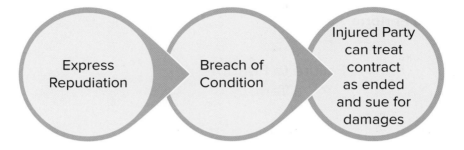

Express Repudiation—a stated intention by a party not to perform any of their obligations under a contract.

Implied Repudiation—an intention by a party not to perform any of their obligations under a contract that can be presumed by their actions or lack thereof.

Rendering Performance Impossible

If a party does something deliberately or though negligence that makes performance of the contract obligations impossible, then they have breached the contract. If, for example, we have a contract for me to buy your lawnmower and you sell it to someone else before I can come and get it, then you have made it impossible to perform the contract. I can treat the contract as being at an end and sue you for a remedy. Figure 7.2 shows the process of rendering performance impossible.

Figure 7.2: **Rendering Performance Impossible**

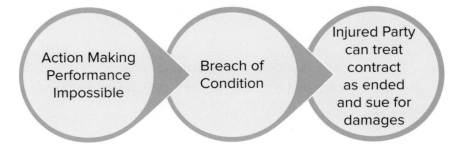

Failure to Perform

As already discussed, if a party to a contract fails to perform a term of the contract that is vital and essential (a condition), the innocent party can treat the contract as being at an end. If the party fails to perform a minor term of the contract or there is a minor defect in the performance of an important term then they have committed a breach of warranty. In this case, the innocent party must still perform their contractual obligations. They do, however, have the right to sue for a remedy. Failure to perform is illustrated in Figure 7.3.

Figure 7.3: Failure to Perform

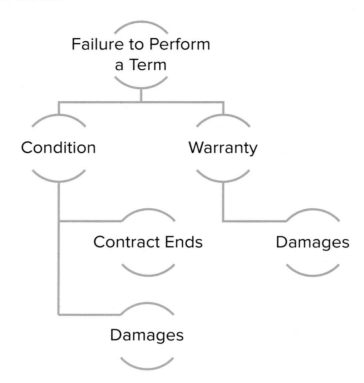

DID YOU KNOW?

Breach of Condition and Breach of Warranty

- Consider the following when dealing with a breach of condition and breach of warranty:
    - The circumstances of each contract will determine whether the breach is of a condition or a warranty
    - Minor or insignificant terms that would normally be considered warranties can be considered to be conditions if the parties stated that intention in the contract
    - Important or essential terms that would normally be considered conditions can be treated as warranties by the parties if it was specified in the contract

LO 7.6   7.6 Remedies for Breach of Contract

When one party breaches a contract, the other party is entitled to a remedy. As noted in Chapter 3, a remedy is what the court can provide to the party who has been harmed by the breach of the contract. The most common remedy provided by courts is money.

Limiting Liability in the Event of Breach

As the cost to a breaching party may be extremely large, a number of strategies have been developed to try to limit the cost of a remedy. Parties can attempt to limit their exposure to large damages by using one of three contract clauses:

1. **Limitation of liability clause**
2. **Liquidated damages clause**
3. **Exclusion clause**

> **Limitation of Liability Clause**—a term in a contract that places a limit on the amount of damages that would follow a breach of the contract.

> **Liquidated Damages Clause**—a genuine negotiated estimate of the amount of damages that would follow a breach of the contract.

> **Exclusion Clause**—a term that removes liability and damages after certain specified breaches.

LEGAL SCENARIO

The company you work for sells motor controls. You sell a starter to a customer, Company A, for $300. The starter is used to start and stop a production machine that is worth more than $1 million. Your starter fails and this failure results in severe damage estimated at $300,000 to your customer's production machine. Your customer sues you for the damage in the amount of $300,000 plus legal costs. Without a clause in the contract of purchase and sale for the starter that limits your responsibility, your company may have to pay for the damage.

Continuing the Legal Scenario example, because your company's starter motor damaged your customer's machinery it was not able to produce or deliver its product, which was in high demand. Your customer, Customer A, was supposed to deliver $450,000 of its product to its customer, Company Z. As a result Company Z sued Customer A for damages resulting from non-delivery. Company Z was successful and was awarded $450,000 in damages.

The contract between your companies *did* include an **indemnification** clause. This clause stated that your company would have to reimburse Customer A for any damages resulting from failure of your starter motor. As a consequence, your company is also responsible to reimburse Customer A for the damages of $450,000 awarded to Company Z.

> **Indemnification**—a promise by one party to bear the monetary costs for losses or damages incurred by another party.

Remedies in the Event of Breach of Contract

Whenever a breach occurs, the innocent party has the right to sue for a legal remedy. A legal remedy is an order that a court is entitled to issue in a civil lawsuit to enforce a right or to redress harm. The legal remedies available in a breach of contract lawsuit are:

1. an award of damages;
2. an order of specific performance; and
3. an injunction.

Of these three types of remedies, an award of damages is the most common. It makes sense because contracts are, at their essence, commercial transactions with an established monetary value. An award of damages simply uses that value to compensate the innocent party in an amount necessary to fix the injury done by the breach of the contract.

Specific performance and an injunction are regarded by the courts as extraordinary, equitable remedies. They are used only when it has been demonstrated that the circumstances of the contract breach cannot be adequately addressed by a financial award.

Award of Damages

© Photozoo | Dreamstime.com

The purpose of an award of damages is to put the victim in the same economic position they would have been in if the contract had been completed. Sometimes compensation is set at an amount to punish the party who breached the contract. These types of damages, called *punitive damages*, are not common in Canada. Our courts regard an award of damages as compensation, not punishment.

LEGAL SCENARIO

You buy a new carpet from a company. The price also includes installation of the product. After three months' use, you notice that the carpet is beginning to wear in certain places. It is determined that the company installed the wrong grade of carpet for such an area. The carpet has to be replaced. However, the only way that the problem will not reoccur is if it is replaced by a substantially better grade of carpet. This type of carpet is much more expensive than the original one. It could be said that you are getting an upgrade over what you had originally purchased. However, as the more expensive carpet is necessary to repair the injury that was caused by the original company's breach (selling and installing a carpet that they knew or should have known was not suitable for your purpose), the award of damages will be calculated at that higher amount.

The calculation of an award of damages is complicated. The damages must be said to "flow naturally from the breach." The damages cannot be too remote. This means that losses that could not have been foreseen as a consequence to a breach will not be compensated. Neither will the court allow the innocent party to get more from the award of damages than they were due under the original contract. An upgrade of a product is not going to be paid for under an award of damages unless it is shown to be necessary to fix the problem caused by the breach. These are called *consequential damages*.

 ## CASE STUDY

Hadley v. Baxendale (1894), E.R. 145

This English case helped establish the principles used in calculating damages owed under a breach of contract.

Hadley, a mill owner, contracted with Baxendale for a new mill shaft. They gave the broken mill shaft to Baxendale to use as a pattern for the new one. The replacement was supposed to take only a day to make and deliver. Instead, it took a week. During this time the mill could not operate and Hadley was not making any profits. Hadley sued for the profits lost due to the delay.

The court found that the lost profits were not damages that should be compensated. They were too remote from the breach.

When a contract is breached damages should be what the two parties have reasonably contemplated them to be. If there are special circumstances, both parties must be aware of the circumstance for a breach to amount to damages that would ordinarily flow from a breach of these special circumstances. This awareness depends on what was communicated or obvious to each party.

This discussion of the principles of damage calculation informs such calculations even today.

The **test for remoteness of damages** is as follows:

1. Did the damages arise naturally from the breach?
2. Was it in reasonable contemplation of the parties as the probable result of the breach? Were they foreseeable and probable consequences of a breach?
3. Were any special circumstances communicated or obvious to the parties at the time the contract was formed?

> **Test for Remoteness of Damages**—the cost and effect of a party's breach of contract must have been something that could have been predicted at the time the contract was formed.

If a person expected to make a profit from a contract, then they can be compensated for the loss of profit caused by a breach. These are called **expectation damages** and are calculated based on the profit that a person anticipated earning from the contract. Because the contract was not performed, the party has suffered a loss of profit, and the damages awarded will put them into the position they would have been in if the contract had been performed properly.

> **Expectation Damages**—compensation for the loss of profit caused by a breach, calculated based on the profit a person anticipated earning from the contract.

These expenses were incurred because one party relied upon the other party to perform their part of the contract. These are referred to as **reliance damages**. The effect of these types of damages is to put the injured party in the position they would have been in if they had not entered into the contract; that is, putting the injured party back in its precontract position.

> **Reliance Damages**—compensation for expenses incurred because one party relied upon the other party to perform their part of the contract, intended to put the injured party back in its precontract position.

With all types of damages, however, there is a duty placed on the injured party as well as the breaching party. The duty to mitigate requires that the injured party take reasonable steps to minimize or reduce the cost of the breach of contract to them. A failure to satisfy the court that these steps have been taken, even if they were ultimately unsuccessful, could result in the court reducing the amount of damages owed to the injured party.

Normally contract law does not compensate an injured party for any type of loss that is not purely financial. Because they are commercial relationships, there is usually no consideration of the emotional consequences of a breach of contract. Sometimes, however, the nature of a contract may have an emotional element in it. If this is the case then there may be some compensation awarded for mental anguish.

CASE STUDY

Jarvis v. Swan Tours [1972] 3 WLR 954 Court of Appeal

Mr. Jarvis was a solicitor who got only two weeks' vacation per year. One year he decided to take a ski holiday in Switzerland through a travel company called Swan Tours. In the company's brochure, Jarvis was promised that his holiday would take place at a "wonderful little resort" with beautiful ski runs, gourmet dining, hospitable owners who spoke English, and nightly professional entertainment.

Unfortunately, the resort failed to live up to any of these promises. The ski runs were in terrible condition. The owners spoke no English. The meals provided were barely edible. And the nightly professional entertainment was a local citizen who, after spending the day working at his regular job, would came and yodel until he passed out from the free beer which was his payment.

Mr. Jarvis sued for damages for mental suffering resulting from the breach of the contract.

Lord Denning, the judge in the case, held that the statements in the brochure were representations or warranties. This meant that a failure to live up to them gave rise to breaches of the contract and gave Mr. Jarvis a right to damages.

It was in calculating the damage, that Lord Denning did something radical. He said:

> In a proper case, damages for mental distress can be recovered in contract breach... One such case is a contract for a holiday, or any other contract to provide entertainment and enjoyment. If the contracting party breaks his contract, damages can be given for the disappointment, the distress, the upset and the frustration caused by the breach.
>
> Damages should include loss of entertainment and enjoyment, which he was promised, not just cost of the vacation.*

* http://www.bailii.org/ew/cases/EWCA/Civ/1972/8.html.

Equitable Remedies for Breach of Contract

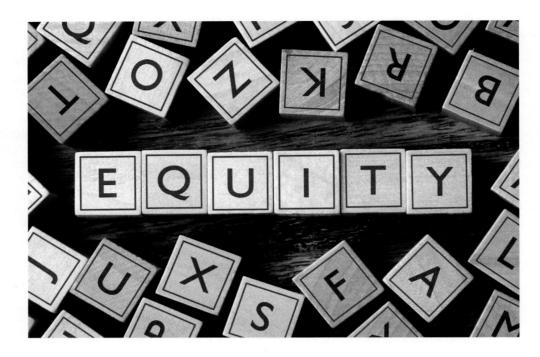

schatzie / Shutterstock.com

Sometimes the loss caused by a breach of contract cannot have a monetary value placed upon it. In cases like this, the common law has created a set of more practical remedies. These are known as:

1. Rescission;
2. Injunction;
3. Specific performance; and
4. *Quantum meruit.*

Because the courts regard these as extraordinary remedies, they will be denied under a number of circumstances. If the injured party does not have "clean hands"; that is, if their own actions contributed to the breach, or if they delayed unreasonably in bringing the action, then they lose the right to an equitable remedy. It will similarly be denied if there was only nominal consideration or the consideration was only a promise under seal. Finally, if the equitable remedy would affect an innocent third party, it will not be awarded. If these remedies are not available, then the injured party must make do with damages.

The first type of equitable remedy, *rescission*, simply means that the parties are restored to their original positions. In a retail environment, this remedy is very common. If you purchase a product that doesn't work, you return it to the store and get your money back. This is a form of rescission.

The second type of equitable remedy is an injunction. An *injunction* is a court order stopping a person from doing something that they are not supposed to do under a contract or that is inconsistent with the contract. The most common example of an injunction is the enforcement of a non-competition clause in an employment contract. If your contract with your employer says that if you resign you cannot work for another company in the same industry for a year and you proceed to so do, then your former employer can get an injunction ordering you to stop working for that other company.

Specific performance is the third equitable remedy. Where monetary compensation will not be adequate to repair the damage caused by a breach of contract, a court may order a party to fulfill the contractual obligation. This type of remedy is common for contracts for the sale of land and for contracts involving unique goods whose value is beyond money. Specific performance will not be ordered if it requires the supervisor of the court to ensure that the party will complete their obligations. It will also not be ordered in contracts for personal service, for example a contract featuring a particular entertainer.

Finally, there is the equitable remedy of *Quantum meruit*. This term is Latin for "As much as is deserved." It means that if a party completed part of the contract before repudiating it, they are entitled to be paid for the work they had done. However, they will also have to pay damages to the other party for the costs of breaching the contract.

Enforcing E-Contracts

For the most part, the principles and remedies governing the performance and breach of contracts apply whether they are in traditional or electronic form. The issue that arises with electronic contracts, however, is choosing which law should apply to the contract and where the court proceeding should be held. This is an issue with electronic contracts because they can often involve parties that are not present together except via the Internet.

So whose law should govern in cyberspace? This question actually involves two issues: jurisdiction and governing law. Often the contract will state the forum (that is, where the case will be heard and which law should be applied). This will normally be accepted by the court unless there is a "balance of convenience" argument that strongly favours another forum.

A balance of convenience argument means that if parties have not chosen a governing law, the courts will use the system that has the closest and most real connection with the transaction and the parties.

Such things as the locations of the content provider's website and host server will be taken into account. As will the actual location of the parties and any intermediaries used in the negotiation of the contract. The court will also look at any representations made by the product or service provider as to where they are located.

Because of the meteoric rise of online retail transactions, many Canadian provincial governments have stepped in to provide some clarity and protection for consumers. Note that these rules apply only to business to consumer transactions, not business to business transactions. In Ontario, for example, choice of law rules are subject to the *Consumer Protection Act, 2002 (Ontario)*. If the Act applies, the parties cannot waive or override it.

DID YOU KNOW?

Consumer Protection Act, 2002 (Ontario)

- "Internet agreements" are consumer agreements formed by text-based Internet communications.
- Disclosure and cancellation provisions of the Act apply if "total potential payment obligation" under the consumer agreement is greater than $50.
- Suppliers must provide consumers with an express opportunity to accept or decline the agreement and to correct errors prior to entering into it.

When all is said and done, most contracts proceed smoothly from formation through performance. Even when there are issues in the performance, these can often be solved on a practical basis by the parties. When the problems can't be solved, it is best to have made sure that expectations of performance, and the consequences of poor or non-performance, are stated clearly at the time the contract was made.

FOR REVIEW

Questions

1. What are the five ways a contract may be discharged? (LO 7.1, 7.4)
2. What is novation? (LO 7.4)
3. What are the differences among tender of performance, performance, and substantial performance? (LO 7.1, 7.3, 7.4)
4. What is a breach of contract? (LO 7.5)
5. What is repudiation? (LO 7.5)
6. How are the two types of repudiation different from each other? (LO 7.5)
7. What is the difference between a breach of condition and a breach of warranty? (LO 7.5)
8. What does "frustration" mean in the context of contracts? (LO 7.2, 7.4)
9. What is a liquidated damages clause? (LO 7.6)
10. What is an equitable remedy? (LO 7.6)
11. What is "balance of convenience"? (LO 7.6)

Activities

1. Browse newspapers, magazines, or websites and other periodicals for a recent contract law case that ended with an award or equitable remedy. Can you explain the outcome? (LO 7.3, 7.6)
2. Why do courts allow for substantial performance to satisfy a contract's obligations? (LO 7.2, 7.3)
3. Why does the innocent party to a breach often have the choice to accept the breach and continue with the contract? (LO 7.1, 7.2, 7.5, 7.6)
4. Why does contract law prefer an award of damages as the remedy for a breach of contract? (LO 7.1, 7.3, 7.6)
5. How is a liquidated damages clause different from punitive damages? (LO 7.6)
6. What kind of circumstances might give rise to a court ordering an injunction? (LO 7.5, 7.6)
7. Why are courts reluctant to order specific performance as a remedy for the breach of a contract of personal service? (LO 7.5, 7.6)
8. In dealing with electronic contracts between parties in different countries, how will a court determine whose law should apply and where the dispute should be heard? (LO 7.6)

CASES FOR DISCUSSION

Case #1

Lisa hired Mark to renovate her kitchen. The work was completed on time and mostly to her satisfaction; however, there were a few issues with some of the work. The cupboard handles were not the ones Lisa had selected. The lighting fixtures were in slightly different spots than she had chosen and the drawers, even though they were installed with the hardware Lisa had chosen, did not close as smoothly as she would like. Mark is now demanding that he be paid in full. (LO 7.1, 7.2, 7.3, 7.6)

a. Has Mark completed his part of the contract?
b. Does Lisa have to pay Mark the agreed upon price?
c. Is Lisa entitled to any compensation for the work not done to her satisfaction?

Case #2

Kane, a landlord, rents an office to Lawrence on a five-year lease. After a year and a half, Lawrence tells Kane he has bought another business and will be moving his operation there. He offers to pay Kane rent to the end of the year, but to leave the premises immediately so that Kane can rent them to someone else. Kane refuses and says that if Lawrence leaves he will sue him for the rent owing until the end of the five-year lease. Lawrence leaves, and when the five years is over Kane sues him. (LO 7.1, 7.2, 7.3, 7.6)

a. What type of breach has Lawrence committed?

b. What type of remedy is Kane entitled to? How will the damages be calculated?

c. Is there anything that could have been done when the contract was made that would have helped prevent this situation?

Case #3

Denise is excited. She has booked a trip to Hawaii for her family. She found a great deal online through a travel agent in another province. Unfortunately, the week before she was to leave, the tour company went bankrupt and the trip was cancelled. Denise had already paid for the trip with the travel agent. She now wants to get her money back. She also bought a brand-new wardrobe suitable for Hawaii's warm weather. (LO 7.1, 7.6)

a. Whom should Denise sue in this case?

b. How will Denise decide where to begin her lawsuit and which province's law will apply?

c. How will her damages be calculated? Can she get compensation for her disappointment over the trip being cancelled? What about the new clothes she bought?

CHAPTER 8

EMPLOYMENT LAW

Learning Objectives

After reading this chapter the student will:

LO 8.1   Understand the definition of employment law

LO 8.2   Describe the relationship between employer and employee

LO 8.3   Understand labour laws, regulations, and employer(s) rights in Canada

LO 8.4   Understand an employment contract

LO 8.5   Explain the concepts of unjust (wrongful) dismissal and the grounds for dismissal

LO 8.6   Understand collective bargaining and labour disputes

HELP!

As a businessperson, you may experience any of these scenarios:

- HELP! I have just been tasked with hiring a new employee. What should I know about this process?

- HELP! I have a difficult employee. What am I legally able to do?

- HELP! The business where I work doesn't have proper bathrooms for staff. Is this workplace following the law?

- HELP! What labour laws do I need to know as an employee and as a manager?

- HELP! My employer wants me to sign an employment agreement. What is it?

- HELP! We are a unionized environment shop. What does that mean?

LO 8.1   8.1 What Is Employment Law?

In all organizations, individuals are either part of management or an employee. As a result, there are laws and regulations that govern the management/employee relationship. Businesses need to be aware of their own rights as well as the rights of those they employ. There are very specific laws and regulations that pertain to the employment relationship and businesses need to ensure that they obey them. Failure to do so can mean a significant drain on time and financial resources, along with serious legal implications for the business.

> ## DID YOU KNOW?
>
> ### Human Resource Management and Employment Law
>
> Human resource (HR) management is a specific area that is growing in today's modern businesses. Specialists in this area are trained and knowledgeable in the laws, regulations, and responsibilities of employers and employees. This specialty allows businesses to know they are "doing the right thing" for their employees and, as a result, avoiding risk of legal suits for such issues as wrongful dismissal.

Rawpixel.com / Shutterstock.com

Some businesses also have the additional responsibility of being governed by a union contract. In a union environment, the relationship between employer and employee is outlined in a union contract. We will be examining this relationship later in this chapter.

The fair treatment of employees by their employer means that a business will benefit from loyal and productive employees. Businesses can gain a competitive advantage by either hiring and keeping valuable employees or knowing when to end an employment relationship for those not fitting their business. Further, an employer's solid knowledge of the contract in a unionized environment encourages a stable relationship where work stoppages are rare. The reputation of business as a "great place to work" is often gained or lost based on the employer/employee relationship.

DID YOU KNOW?

Risks and Benefits in Understanding Employment Law

Benefits:

- Makes for a comfortable and safe work environment for employees and management

- Leads to fair treatment for everyone

- Creates understanding of concepts like fair hiring/firing practices, discrimination, overtime, pay, child labour, and other areas

Risks:

- NONE! Knowledge is important for businesses. When unsure, contact an HR specialist or your lawyer.

 ## CASE STUDY

Pate Estate v. Galway-Cavendish and Harvey (Township), 2013 ONCA 669 (CanLii)

The case of *Pate Estate v. Galway-Cavendish and Harvey (Township)* is a case of wrongful dismissal, malicious prosecution, and reputational injuries as well as other issues. It is also a famous case where the damages awarded were in the unprecedented amount of $550,000.

In this case, John Pate, a 10-year employee of the Corporation of the Township of Galway-Cavendish and Harvey in Ontario, was fired in 1999. Pate, the building inspector for the Township, was dismissed on the alleged basis that the Township had uncovered discrepancies with his building permit fees. Pate was not provided with the details of these discrepancies. The employer told Pate that if he resigned, they would not contact the police. Pate refused to resign.

Pate was dismissed and the employer, after an investigation, turned over information to the Ontario Provincial Police (OPP). The Township then exerted some influence on senior OPP officials to lay charges, which they did. Pate went to trial against the OPP-based charges but was acquitted after only a four-day trial. Although the trial only lasted a few days, Pate was in the public spotlight from when he was wrongfully dismissed in 1999 until the end of the trial. He was unable to obtain employment in his field and passed away in January 2011.

After his acquittal in 2003, Pate sued the Township for wrongful dismissal, malicious prosecution, and reputational injuries, as well as special damages for costs of the criminal trial defence costs, punitive damages, and aggravated damages.

In the first trial between Pate and the Township in 2009, Pate was awarded a total award of $279,094 and $25,000 in punitive damages for his claim but the court denied the malicious prosecution claim.

Pate successfully appealed the Supreme Court of Ontario's decision to the Ontario Court of Appeal on the grounds that the Court erred in not awarding him with malicious prosecution and for awarding him only $25,000 in punitive damages. The appeal was allowed and two re-trials were allowed on the separate issues of malicious prosecution and the low punitive amount.

In one re-trial for malicious prosecution, Pate was awarded one dollar ($1.00), which the parties had agreed to; in the other re-trial for punitive damages, the court found for Pate in the amount of $550,000 (which would be added to the initial punitive damage award of $279,094).

The Township appealed the decision of $550,000 in punitive damages to the Ontario Court of Appeal, where the decision of the court was to disallow the appeal and award Pate's estate (he had died and his estate represented his interest).

As you can see in the above case, a business or organization can lose a significant amount of money and go to great expense when defending their actions against an employee.

LO 8.2   8.2 The Employer and Employee Relationship

It is important to understand the various relationships that businesses have with those they pay for services. An **employee** is someone who works for a person or an organization and is provided money and possibly benefits for the work they do. Managers manage employees and make decisions concerning their employees. The **employer** is the person who tells the employee what to do (and other terms of their employment, such as hours to be worked) in exchange for money.

Employee—a person who is given direction and supervision along with the resources to do the job in exchange for money for work they do below a management level.

Employer—a business or organization that gives direction and supervision to a person and provides the resources to do the job in exchange for money.

There are other types of relationships where employers pay for work performed but they are not covered under the employer–employee relationship. In those instances the employee acts as an **independent contractor**. The service they render is dictated by a quote or contract and they provide their own tools; contractors are not directly involved in the operations of the business. The employer is not responsible for the contractor's employees and is not responsible for deductions, vacation pay, and so on.

Independent Contractor—performs a service for an employer and renders an invoice or bill.

LEGAL SCENARIO

Employee or Contractor?

Indicate the status of the person in each situation:

- A transcriptionist who works from her home office transcribing medical reports for medical specialists
- A wedding decorator and caterer
- A travel agent who works in the head office of a large corporation
- A private investigator who works for only one law firm
- An insurance adjuster
- A Microsoft trainer/instructor

Explain whether or not you can indicate the described individual's status as an employee or contractor. What other information do you need to have? Is this information readily available online?

LO 8.3

8.3 Labour Laws, Regulations, and Employer/Employees' Rights in Canada

In Canada, labour laws, regulations, and employer/employees' rights are found on both a provincial/territorial and a federal level. First, we look briefly at the federal acts a business should know when dealing with its employees.

Employers can visit http://www.servicecanada.gc.ca/eng/about/publication/workers_rights.shtml to review Workers Rights in Canada. This page on the Government of Canada's website provides information such as:

- What are employment standards?
- What employment rights are protected by employment standards legislation?
- Do all workers have the same employment rights?
- Workplace Health and Safety
- **Human rights legislation**

> **Human Rights Legislation**—federal, provincial, and municipal legislation that is determined by the division of powers under the *Canadian Charter of Rights and Freedoms* to prohibit discrimination in all aspects of business.

The *Canada Labour Code* also outlines, in detail with accompanying Acts, labour relations, occupational health and safety, standard hours, wages, and vacations and holidays. The Code also regulates about 12,000 enterprises and 820,000 employees in such industries as banks, marine shipping, air transportation, railways, pipelines, telephone, telegraph, cable, Crown corporations (owned by the government but self-controlled, for example Canada Post), and many First Nations activities.

The Standards and Equity page of the Government of Canada's website, http://www.esdc.gc.ca/en/jobs/workplace/employment_standards/index.page, provides the following information for employers and employees:

- Federal labour standards:
  - Hours of work
  - Vacation and general holidays
  - Leave (sick leave, maternity leave, etc.)
  - Termination, layoff, or dismissal
  - Wages, pay, and deductions
  - Sexual harassment
  - Employer compliance

- Federal construction contracts
- Wage Earner Protection Program (WEPP)
- Minimum wage database for every province and territory
- Equality and inclusion

Another important website with information for employers on human rights and employers' obligations is the Canadian Human Rights Commission, http://www.chrc-ccdp.ca/eng/content/organizations-and-businesses, which deals with the obligations of employers, what happens when a business is named in a discrimination complaint, and ways that a business can improve its workplace. The Canadian Human Rights Commission website also deals with questions that the general public might ask.

For those businesses not outlined in the Canada Labour Code mentioned above, employees are governed by the province or territory.

Alberta	http://work.alberta.ca/employment-standards.html
British Columbia	http://www.labour.gov.bc.ca/esb/
Manitoba	http://www.gov.mb.ca/labour/standards/index.html
New Brunswick	http://www2.gnb.ca/content/gnb/en/departments/post-secondary_education_training_and_labour/People/content/EmploymentStandards.html
Newfoundland and Labrador	http://www.gov.nl.ca/lra/index.html
Nova Scotia	http://novascotia.ca/lae/employmentrights/
Northwest Territories	http://www.ece.gov.nt.ca/advanced-education/employment-standards
Nunavut	http://www.gov.nu.ca/labour-standards-act
Ontario	http://www.labour.gov.on.ca/english/
Prince Edward Island	http://www.gov.pe.ca/labour/
Quebec	http://www.cnt.gouv.qc.ca/en/home/index.html
Saskatchewan	http://www.saskatchewan.ca/work
Yukon	http://www.community.gov.yk.ca/es.html

So, you may ask, which level of government has the most authority in **employment law**—is it the federal government or the provincial/territorial governments? In essence, those industries that fall under the *Canada Labour Code* as mentioned above (telecommunications and marine shipping, for example) are governed by the federal government, and all other industries/enterprises are governed under the provincial government's regulations in the province where they reside.

Employment Law—an area of law that governs the relationship between the business and its employees.

The one common element that businesses encounter regardless whether they are a federally or provincially regulated business is that they have the Rand Formula. The **Rand Formula**, named for an arbitration that ended a strike in Windsor, Ontario, in 1946, recognizes that the union speaks for all employees who benefit from a union's activity in the workplace. The idea was to foster labour peace and fair treatment for workers in the same employment situation and not allow workers to get the benefit of union representation without participating, through the payment of dues, in the union.

Rand Formula—states that regardless of an employee's union status, they must pay their labour union dues.

LO 8.4   8.4 Employment Contracts

It is important for businesses to understand when an **employment contract** exists and what the responsibilities are for the employee and employer. In Canada, a contract for a fixed period of one year or more must be in writing. However, in many situations, employment can exist on a simple verbal agreement when it is for an indefinite period of time and doesn't have specific requirements.

GoShiva / Shutterstock.com

Employment Contract—an agreement outlining the specifics of an employer and employee's responsibilities for a period of time; can be written or verbal.

In some occupations and in some industries, the running of a business may involve sensitive information. It could be something as simple as a recipe or as complex as a medical file, but regardless the employee must sign an employment contract with very specific requirements that the employee not take certain actions; these actions are set out in **restrictive covenants**. For example, where a trade secret exists the employee would have to sign an employee contract promising not to reveal the trade secret.

> **Restrictive Covenants**—items in an employment contract that outline conditions, promises, and restrictions of the employee with regard to the business.

Most businesses have a lawyer draw up the contract to ensure both parties are protected. However, some smaller businesses will purchase an online template. It is always wise to seek legal advice for any contract that is complex in nature or that limits either party significantly and would not hold up in a legal case.

LO 8.5   8.5 Unjust Dismissal and the Grounds for Dismissal

The word "fired" is not a pleasant one to hear. In some cases there is a justified reason for the dismissal and in some cases there is not. An employee might be dismissed "for cause" if, for example, the individual's resume contained falsified information. Other situations could arise in which an employee has been dismissed without cause, which may constitute a wrongful dismissal. It is important for businesses to ensure that they have all the documentation required to justly dismiss an employee in the event of a legal action. Also, businesses must know the standard and duty of care in their position as an employer. It is critical that employers are up to date with their knowledge of the provincial labour laws as well as the federal regulations.

Minerva Studio / Shutterstock.com

When examining cases, keep in mind that the words "wrongful" and "unjust" are interchangeable when dealing with **dismissal**. The most commonly used term is **wrongful dismissal**.

Dismissal—occurs when an employer informs an employee that they are no longer employed at their business.

Wrongful Dismissal—occurs when an employer does not have the basis to dismiss an employee; there is no cause for dismissal under their contract or under a statute of law; also called *unjust dismissal*.

An employee who does not have a collective agreement (unionized) and has been employed for 12 consecutive months with the same employer is protected from unjust dismissal. There is a process that the employee must go through in order to file a complaint for unjust dismissal. The federal government outlines the process for an employee to make a formal complaint at http://www.esdc.gc.ca/en/reports/labour_standards/unjust_dismissal.page. This website offers a wealth of information including case studies of real situations that may help you and your business stay out of hot water.

Situations may arise in which the terms of an employee's employment are so significantly changed, or the employee's position within the organization is made so difficult, that the employee believes the employer has essentially dismissed them from their original position; this is called **constructive dismissal**. As a result, the employer effectively forces the employee to quit.

Constructive Dismissal—occurs when the employee has not been fired but believes the employer has not complied with the terms of the employment contract.

DID YOU KNOW?

What can employees do if they feel they were unjustly dismissed?

The *Canada Labour Code* states that employees who feel they were unjustly dismissed can:

1. Request, in writing, a written statement from their employer giving the reasons for dismissal. The employer must reply within 15 days after the request is made.
2. File a complaint alleging unjust dismissal at any Labour Program office no later than 90 days from the date of the dismissal.

The complaint may be made by the dismissed person or by a representative, such as a lawyer. The complaint must identify the employee, state that the employee was dismissed, include the date of dismissal, and claim that the dismissal was unjust.

Initially an inspector will try to settle the dispute through negotiation for a settlement. If that does not work, then an adjudicator will be appointed—which requires the Minister of Labour to decide whether or not the dispute should be heard by an adjudicator. If the matter can be heard by an adjudicator, a hearing is held and the adjudicator has the power to render a decision.

The adjudicator can make the business reinstate the employee, with or without compensation for lost wages; not reinstate the employee nor provide compensation for lost wages; or another remedy that the adjudicator deems suitable.

Further, an employee can also sue the employer for wrongful or unjust dismissal—and this can even happen during the investigation by the inspector.

Source: Title: Unjust Dismissal. URL: http://www.esdc.gc.ca/en/reports/labour_standards/unjust_dismissal.page#h2.11 Employment and Social Development Canada, 2016. Reproduced with the permission of the Minister of Employment and Social Development Canada, 2016.

If the employee is unionized, there is another process which we will look at later in this chapter.

DID YOU KNOW?

There are three general grounds for disciplinary action, according to Canadian Labour Standards:

1. Incompetence—where the employee does not have the skills or ability to do the work
2. Negligence—where the employee may ignore their duties or is careless in carrying out their duties
3. Misconduct—where the employee breaks the rules

There may be a fine line between where an employee has been incompetent or negligent and where they have broken a rule and been justifiably dismissed. In some cases, it may be a small rule that was broken or an action that was not meant to hurt anyone so the actions of the employee could be corrected. Sometimes, it is not. The important thing is that employers set up a system so that infractions or actions can be identified and corrected and that dismissal is the last resort.

Source: Title: Unjust Dismissal. URL: http://www.esdc.gc.ca/en/reports/labour_standards/unjust_dismissal.page#h2.11 Employment and Social Development Canada, 2016. Reproduced with the permission of the Minister of Employment and Social Development Canada, 2016.

Now that we have an understanding of the basics, let's look at a case of wrongful/unjust dismissal.

 CASE STUDY:

Higginson v. Babine Forest Products Ltd., 2010 BCSC 614 (CanLII)

Larry Higginson, the plaintiff, was employed for 34 years at Babine Forest Products Ltd. in British Columbia, and over the years had risen to a manager's position. Mr. Higginson was dismissed in October 2009 without notice and without a severance package.

Mr. Higginson sued Babine Forest Products for wrongful dismissal, alleging that his dismissal was because of the acquisition of Babine by another forestry company (Hampton Lumber Mills). Mr. Higginson alleged that in order to avoid paying severance packages to its long-term employees, Babine created a hostile and dismal work environment hoping that employees would eventually leave on their own. When Higginson didn't leave, he alleged, the company made up false reasons for his dismissal.

The Supreme Court of British Columbia gave Mr. Higginson the amount of $809,000, which included $573,000 in punitive damages in a jury trial. The jury found that Babine's conduct was improper and awarded, at the time, the largest punitive damages in an employment law case.

Higginson v. Babin illustrates the importance of treating employees well and maintaining a positive work environment, as well as having documentation that proves the dismissal of an employee was conducted properly. For example, some red flags that should stand out in this case are the poor work environment where it was hostile and the push was to make employees leave; poor documentation so there wasn't any evidence of wrongdoing on the plaintiff's part; and other areas that directly show the fault of the defendant.

So what constitutes wrongful dismissal? If an employer has "just cause," meaning a good reason to fire an employee, they can dismiss the employee. And what constitutes just cause? Here are a few examples of actions that may be grounds for dismissal:

- Using drugs or alcohol at work
- Being unable to do the work because of lack of skills or knowledge
- Being dishonest
- Disobeying a supervisor
- Disobeying the rules of the organization
- Having a conflict of interest
- Being involved in an activity contrary to the employer's interests

An employer can fire an employee for some of the above causes without notice or with pay instead of notice. An employer can simply say "you are fired!" and does not have to give a reason. Employers do, however, have to give notice, in writing, to an employee they are firing. If the employer does not give notice, the employee is entitled to receive pay for the time they would have been paid had they not been fired and had been given notice.

As stated previously, businesses need to keep in mind that each province and the federal government has legislative rules about how an employee is to be dismissed, so check the province's legislation where the business resides to ensure you are being fair when dismissing an employee. There are guidelines for how much notice an employee should be given, depending on a variety of elements such as years with the company. Also, it is important to recognize that **termination pay** is not the same as **severance pay**.

Termination Pay—payment by the employer to the employee when an employee is fired for the time they would have been paid had they not been fired and been given notice. This happens when an employer does not give dismissal notice.

Severance Pay—where the employee is provided termination or separation pay based on the specific duration of their employment and they lose their job. It's most common when massive layoffs occur. It is most commonly calculated by the employee's salary multiplied by the number of weeks/years worked up to a specified number of weeks/years. These calculations do vary, however, and are determined by the employer.

LEGAL SCENARIO

I Have to Work on Fridays?!

Sarah rolled her eyes and her mouth thinned with determination as she approached Colin. Colin, a security and system administration employee, was sitting at his messy desk with headphones on listening to music and typing on a social media site. Colin had been employed for the past four months at Simpson & Sons, a property rental company. Colin's first month was comprised of training on their security and administrative systems and later he was to work independently on his own group of rental properties. It had recently come to Sarah's attention that Colin rarely, if ever, came to work on Fridays. She, as Colin's direct manager, had been informed by a few of her staff because they wondered when they would get a Friday off, if some employees had flex days or different schedules.

Sarah had been monitoring Colin from time to time and found his performance to be average. He got the job done but not much else. There was very little initiative. It was clear that there were other people who would do this job far better. The absent Friday issue was definitely a deal breaker.

Sarah sent Colin an e-mail invitation to meet with her earlier that day but he did not show up. Now she approached his office determined to have a first disciplinary meeting with him. She asked for him to come to her office immediately so they could chat. When he sat down in her office, she asked him why he didn't come in to work on Fridays. He said he didn't think he had to because he got his work done in four days. Further, when he was in school, he only went to school Monday to Thursday.

What advice would you give to Sarah?

LO 8.6   ## 8.6 Unions: Collective Bargaining and Labour Disputes

One of the greatest challenges a business faces is the complexity of a unionized environment. Union contracts and labour disputes are very serious matters and can often leave a business and its employees splintered. However, a unionized environment provides a stable workplace with very few surprises in terms of the guidelines the organization and its employees are governed by.

Canada is a country with the freedom for employees to gather together and form a **union** so that their rights are protected. In areas such as fair wages and safe working conditions as well as many other segments, unions are a necessary and helpful component to many successful businesses. Even the Labour Day holiday celebrates our country's access to labour unions and the battle that was fought for the rights of employees that goes back centuries.

> **Union**—a collection of employees in a trade or employment organization formed to protect and further their rights and interests through the negotiation with management and establishment of a signed contract that outlines every aspect of the employment relationship for a specific duration.

© Rwmoulton | Dreamstime.com

Does every business have a labour union? No, a union is not always formed in a business. The main consideration in a union environment is the requirement for a contract. There are other considerations, but much of the focus is on the negotiation of the terms of the employment relationship in the form of a **union contract**. For a business or a manager in a business, the answers and solutions for most employment issues are prescribed within a union contract.

> **Union Contract**—a legal document between employees and management that outlines the rights, terms, conditions, and benefits that all employees of that union can expect for a specific period of time; also called a *collective agreement*.

Who can join a union? Anyone has the right to join a union in Canada. In some cases, unions are specific to a trade that exists all over Canada, for example steelworkers or federal employees. In some cases, it is specific to a group that works for an organization or business, like teachers or nurses in a specific province.

The jurisdiction of unions is found under labour law in the provinces, though some are under the federal government (i.e., telecommunications, marine). In Canada's territories of Nunavut, Northwest Territories, and Yukon, the federal government has jurisdiction regarding labour. The forming of a union follows a very specific process.

DID YOU KNOW:

How Are Unions Formed?

- Employees express an interest to form a union
- Membership cards (cards that state the person on the card is or will be represented by the union) are collected

- Significant support of the membership is shown by a legally required percentage of employees that have signed their membership cards (varies in each province and territory)
- Cards are submitted to the provincial or federal labour relations board with an application for union certification (membership and voting for a union is confidential—employers will not know who supported the union)
- Labour Relations Board may either legally recognize or require a secret ballot among employees—depending on the province or territory
- Once the union is legally certified, the first union contract (collective agreement) can be negotiated

Source: Adapted from International Union of Operating Engineers, "Your Rights/Forming a Union," http://www.iuoe.org/join-iuoe/your-rights-forming-a-union.

Each province and territory has a calculation for the percentage of employees within an organization that are required to agree to form a union. For example, if more than 50 percent of employees within an organization have signed their membership cards, they can be certified as a union in Quebec. However, in Newfoundland and Labrador more than 65 percent is required in order to advance to certification.

If you or your business is involved in union certification, contact a labour relations lawyer to assist you and your organization with this process. Further, you will require a highly skilled labour relations lawyer to negotiate the first and all later union contracts.

Collective Bargaining

Jim West / Alamy

Once the provincial (or territorial) labour relations board has approved union certification, the union is in a position to bargain with management for the collective union agreement.

Collective bargaining is an important factor in the labour relationship. Why is it important? It's all about negotiation and agreement. When you have two distinct groups—the union and the company/management—they must "come to the table" with what they want and be able to negotiate and agree on conditions and rules of the employer–employee (or management–union) relationship.

You can visit the following websites for resources and statistics regarding **collective bargaining** in Canada:

- http://www.labour.gc.ca/eng/resources/info/publications/collective_bargaining/collective_bargaining.shtml
- http://www.canadianlabourrelations.com/collective-bargaining.html

> **Collective Bargaining**—negotiation between a union and management to reach a union contract that outlines the rules that govern the relationship.

Labour Disputes

Despite the best interests of both, there sometimes comes a time when conflict arises between the union and management. This can occur when the collective agreement is active but generally it happens when both sides cannot agree on the entire or part of a proposed agreement. This may result in a slowdown of work or possibly a refusal to work by the union's members, generally referred to as a **strike**. Some of the terms you may encounter in this regard are:

- A **legal strike** occurs when there is no collective agreement to refer to;
- An **illegal strike** occurs when there is an active collective agreement and there is no basis for the employees to strike;
- A **wildcat strike** occurs when employees take sudden, unofficial action;
- A **lockout** occurs when the employer refuses employees access to the work premises.

> **Strike**—work stoppage in a unionized environment; can be a refusal to work, a slowdown of work, and various other options. A strike can be a legal or an illegal strike.

© The Canadian Press/Nathan Denette

Legal Strike—occurs when there is no collective agreement in effect.

Illegal Strike—occurs when there is a collective agreement and employees have no legal platform to strike.

Wildcat Strike—an unofficial action where employees walk out of their employment with no warning to the employer or to union officials.

Lockout—employers do not allow employees to enter the premises to work, usually during the bargaining process.

There are several terms that businesspeople should be aware of when dealing in a unionized environment but, again, in this complex area of law and industry it is critical to have legal advice throughout any union–management situation.

DID YOU KNOW?

Canada's record on labour dispute strikes is illustrated by some stories from the news...

Canada's record on wildcat strikes:
http://www.cbc.ca/news/canada/canada-s-record-on-wildcat-strikes-1.1189423

Chronicle Herald union says company refused call back to the bargaining table:
http://www.cbc.ca/news/canada/nova-scotia/chronicle-herald-strike-seven-weeks-1.3488557

Women fired while on maternity leave want better legal protection:
http://www.cbc.ca/radio/thecurrent/the-current-for-may-10-2016-1.3574840/
women-fired-while-on-maternity-leave-want-better-legal-protection-1.3574912

Saguenay mechanics set to return to work after 3-year lockout:
http://www.cbc.ca/news/canada/montreal/
saguenay-mechanics-set-to-return-to-work-after-3-year-lockout-1.3416960

Labour Dispute Resolutions

Finally, there comes a time when the labour dispute requires help in resolving the issues and the parties might turn to some form of mediation. Because there is a union contract, there may be some or many items that the two sides may not agree on. For example, where a company may want to change the number of working hours in the work week, or the union may want a change regarding working conditions, there may not be a meeting of the minds and both sides cannot agree. When this happens, the resolution may require a third party, such as an arbitrator, to help move it in a positive manner; in this case the parties might turn to the process we explored in Chapter 2 known as Alternative Dispute Resolution. This might involve an **arbitration** or **conciliation**, with an **arbitrator and/or conciliator** assisting the parties, or **mediation** with a mediator who will attempt to keep the discussion ongoing between the disputing parties. The process could result in **binding arbitration**, a decision by an arbitrator or an arbitration board that is final and cannot be appealed.

Arbitration—a final resolution where both parties agree to the decision of the arbitrator. Once decided, the decision cannot be appealed; the decision of the arbitrator is final and binding.

Conciliation—used when issues between the parties require resolution by a third party in a voluntary, flexible, and results-oriented manner.

Arbitrator and/or Conciliator—a third party who helps resolve labour disputes between a business and the union.

Mediation—occurs when a third party helps to resolve issues between the parties and assists in developing a solution. Not used in a union–management dispute.

Binding Arbitration—a decision by an arbitrator or an arbitration board that is final and cannot be appealed.

LEGAL SCENARIO

Which situations would you yourself deal with as a manager? Which situations would you instead refer to a lawyer?

- An employee goes wild and acts inappropriately at the annual year-end party.
- Your delivery person has the smell of marijuana on him regularly and you have had complaints from customers.
- The bouncer at your pub has been very aggressive with patrons who are intoxicated.
- A long-term employee has accumulated a large "on credit" bill at your clothing store.
- The receptionist at your office who was hired a month ago has complained of sexual harassment because a client calls daily and sends e-mails that have nothing to do with their work.
- After 10 years with your business, your top machinist is attempting to unionize your shop.

FOR REVIEW

Questions

1. In your own words, what is employment law and why is it important to an individual and to a business? (LO 8.1)

2. Describe the relationship between an employer and an employee and the relationship between the employer and a contractor. (LO 8.2)

3. Do employer/employee rights come within the jurisdiction of the federal government or the provincial/territorial governments? (LO 8.3)

4. What levels of government would you need to research if you were preparing a report for your manager on human rights legislation? (LO 8.3)

5. What website would you go to for information on what happens when a business is named in a human rights discrimination complaint? (LO 8.3)

6. Briefly explain what the Rand Formula deals with. (LO 8.3)

7. Briefly explain what a restrictive covenant is in an employment contract and provide an example. (LO 8.4)

8. What does the *Canada Labour Code* say employees can do if they believe they were unjustly dismissed? (LO 8.5)

9. What is constructive dismissal? Provide an example. (LO 8.5)

10. What is the difference between termination pay and severance pay? (LO 8.5)

11. What is collective bargaining? How does a union get involved in collective bargaining? (LO 8.6)

12. Why are labour unions important? (LO 8.6)

Activities

1. Visit your provincial government website and acquaint yourself with standards required under its labour code. What are the key points that a business should be acquainted with? Was there anything there you were surprised about? (LO 8.3)

2. Research various employment contracts you may find in a book or online. What are some common elements? What are some unusual elements? (LO 8.4)

3. Outline the process that follows the filing of an unjust dismissal claim by an employee under the *Canada Labour Code*, and discuss whether it is effective for resolving the issue between the employer and employee or whether the parties should take their issue to the court for resolution. (LO 8.5)

4. Research a local union contract online. What is contained in the contract? (LO 8.6)

5. Research the newspaper and online news for a labour dispute that has happened in the past year. What were the main items that were being disputed? (LO 8.6)

6. Research and discuss in a group the history of labour relations in your province. (LO 8.6)

CASES FOR DISCUSSION

Case #1

Siegi was angry. This was the second year in a row that she had missed her son's school play because her employer suddenly had a rush order and the employees were expected to drop all personal plans and work "whatever hours" required to get the order prepared to be shipped—and "whatever hours" often required 18 hours or more for two or three days straight. As well, there was no overtime paid, no vacation days in lieu of time worked, no bonus, and the employees were expected to cover their normal shifts as well. This happened several times during the year and the employer's explanation was always that it was not possible to predict when large orders might come in and if the employees don't want to work the time, they don't have to—"someone else would be happy to have the opportunity to take your place." These thinly veiled threats didn't sit well with Siegi either. She had seen the movie *Norma Rae*! She may not be Sally Field, but she knew what had to be done.

Siegi wants to create a union at her place of employment to deal with the awful working conditions and the blatant unfairness. (Did we mention her employer has two Porsche sports cars? One for summer and one for winter driving so the tires don't need to be changed.) She has come to you because her neighbour said you have taken a business course and know about employment matters. Advise Siegi on the requirements, processes, and timelines in your province for creating a union to represent the employees of a business.

Case #2

Adele, head of human resources at Techstellung, was becoming concerned about Estelle's work ethic. Estelle had been with the company for five years and had been a competent if not stellar employee. However, following a bicycle accident several months ago, Estelle's attitude toward her manager and her work had changed. For the past 4 months Estelle seemed to take short breaks often and no-one knew where she went. When she returned, there was a peculiar odour that came from her breath and on her clothes. Estelle's co-workers were complaining that she was not doing her share of the work anymore and they were having to cover for her. Estelle's supervisor recognized the mystery odour as marijuana and tried to speak with her about her behaviour. Estelle told him to "take a flying leap off a tall building" followed by some muttered words making rude suggestions.

As a result of the supervisor's report on Estelle's use of marijuana during work hours and his attempted conversation with Estelle, Adele decided it was time to cut Estelle loose and terminate her employment. Adele called Estelle into her office and gave her the news that she was terminated immediately because of her conduct, her use of drugs during work hours, and her display of lack of respect to her manager. Further, there would be no termination pay. Estelle became very upset and angry and claimed she was being unjustly treated due to her medical condition. Estelle said her doctor had prescribed the use of marijuana to deal with intestinal problems that arose following her bicycle accident and now she was being fired for following her doctor's orders.

a. Outline the issues raised by this fact situation for both Techstellung and for Estelle.

b. Advise Adele as to the proper process to be followed in this case.

c. Would your advice to Adele change if Estelle were not using marijuana under a doctor's prescription? If so, explain what changes you would make in your advice to Adele.

CHAPTER 9

PROPERTY LAW

Learning Objectives

After reading this chapter the student will:

LO 9.1 Understand the definition of property law

LO 9.2 Explain real, personal, and intellectual property

LO 9.3 Explain ownership rights of real property

LO 9.4 Understand the rights and obligations under a commercial lease

LO 9.5 Distinguish between types of bailment of personal property

LO 9.6 Explain the importance of copyright, trademarks, patents, industrial design, and trade secrets in carrying on a business

HELP!

As a businessperson, you may experience any of these scenarios:

- HELP! A customer left an antique ring to be sold on consignment through my store and a shoplifter stole it. The customer claims I have to pay him the value of the ring. Do I have to?
- HELP! The bank wants me to use my house to secure the line of credit for my business. What does that mean?
- HELP! The landlord wants a right of distress in the lease! What is that? I'm distressed already!
- HELP! My business is not doing well and I want to rent out the extra space I don't need. Do I have to tell the landlord?
- HELP! The bank is loaning me money to buy a delivery van but wants to register a general security agreement. What is that?
- HEY! (Just checking to see if you are still reading.) I designed a dynamite app for finding lost keys. How do I protect it from being stolen?

- HELP! I've invented a new app that my boss says belongs to her business because I used my office computer. But I developed it during my lunch hours! Does she have a right to it?
- HELP! I sold a sculpture of a flying loon to City Hall to hang in the lobby and they want to hang a wreath around its neck during December. That will ruin the effect of my sculpture. Can I stop them?

LO 9.1   9.1 What Is Property Law?

An interest in property determines whether an individual or organization owns an item, has the right to possession of the item, has the right to transfer an interest in the item, or has the right to stop someone else from using the item or occupying a space.

Property is either public property, owned by the government and available to the general public for use (sidewalks, a park bench), or it is private property, owned by an individual or business that is able to exclude others from using it without permission (a delivery van).

Operating a business always involves some form of property rights and duties. Examples of this include using a legal right of ownership over property to negotiate a royalty from someone who wants to use your company's trademark on a T-shirt, or ensuring the pointed tops on the fence around your storage yard can't injure someone if they climb over it.

Property law is a field of law that includes a broad range of legal rights and duties in the areas of real property and personal property.

> **Property Law**—a field of law that includes a broad range of legal rights and duties in the areas of real property and personal property.

LO 9.2   9.2 What Is Real, Personal, and Intellectual Property?

Real property is more commonly referred to as real estate and is the area of property law that deals with interests in land and anything permanently attached to land, such as houses, fences, and central air conditioning units.

> **Real Property**—land, including everything attached to it.

Personal property covers all other forms of property that are not real estate. There are two types of personal property: tangible personal property and intangible personal property. A car, your toothbrush, an oil painting, your transcript, and a cheque are all examples of personal property with a physical form that are referred to as **tangible personal property** (sometimes called *chattels*). The right to receive the money from a cheque when you cash it is referred to as **intangible personal property** (sometimes called a *chose in action*), because the right itself has no physical form although a physical item such as a cheque or a promissory note may represent it.

romakoma / Shutterstock.com

Personal Property—all property that is not real property.

Tangible Personal Property—things that can be touched that are movable, e.g., furniture, consumer goods, etc.; sometimes called *chattels*.

Intangible Personal Property—things that can't be physically touched, e.g., reputation, goodwill, etc.; sometimes called a *chose in action*.

Intellectual property is another type of personal property that arises from an individual's creative activities. An example of this is the right provided by ownership of a trademark to stop someone from using that trademark unless they have a licence from the owner allowing them to do so.

Intellectual Property—a type of personal property resulting from an individual's creative activities.

Zander was in the last semester of a two-year music program at her college. She had taken piano lessons for 14 years and guitar lessons for 10 years. Her passion, however, was the accordion! She had been learning to play it for the past three years and loved the sound and feel of the instrument. Zander wanted to share her enthusiasm for the accordion. Unfortunately, not many openings for professional accordion players existed in the city where she was studying. Not a single orchestra had answered her applications, and the offers from bands or music stores that responded to her requests for employment were nothing short of rude—very long hours for little or no pay. But Zander was not one to give up. She had taught some classmates how to play piano and guitar, and they had told her she was an excellent instructor. One of the classmates she had instructed won a scholarship to study guitar upon completing his music program. So, Zander thought, if she was going to put in the effort it might as well be for herself. She decided to put together a business plan, using some money from a small inheritance she had received from her uncle.

Over the course of this chapter we will follow Zander's progress and the issues she has to deal with in turning her decision into a reality.

LO 9.3   9.3 Real Property

The first thing Zander determined she needed was a place where she could provide music lessons to her students. After doing some research, she realized that she had a few options. One possibility would be to buy a house and renovate a couple of the rooms to use for teaching music. The other possibility would be to rent or lease a space in a building and fix it up as a music studio and classroom.

Zander knew that almost every business requires real property in some form to operate. Real property is usually referred to as real estate, and is generally defined as the land and buildings, including fixtures.

Fixtures are items considered permanently attached to the buildings or land, such as fences, in-ground pools, central air conditioning units, and so on.

> **Fixtures**—movable property/chattels that become permanently fixed to the land, such as a fence.

The ability to make laws for the purchase, sale, and use of real estate is within the powers of the provinces and territories. All land is owned by the government and is referred to as Crown land. The Crown grants the fee simple interest in real property to an individual or corporation. Title, or ownership, of the land is then shown as belonging to the individual, along with the rights that come from holding title. This **fee simple ownership** is the greatest interest in land possible and includes the right to buy, sell, and use land as security to borrow money, occupy, lease, or pass to another person through a will. Most people understand a fee simple interest as ownership, so for this chapter we will use the term *ownership*.

> **Fee Simple Ownership**—the most absolute form of land ownership, including the right to exclusive possession and the right to transfer the land for an indefinite period of time.

DID YOU KNOW?

Real estate law in Quebec is based on civil law

Provincial statutes that are similar in nature and content govern real property law in the provinces and territories. The law governing real estate in Quebec is based on civil law and found in the Civil Code of Quebec. You can read more about civil law in Chapter 2.

DID YOU KNOW?

Regulations govern the registration of a corporation intending to own real estate

In some provinces a corporation that intends to own real estate must be registered in that province or have a provincial licence for that purpose. It is best to seek advice from a lawyer in these circumstances.

The fee simple interest in real estate includes the right to use or occupy the land based on ownership, or to grant some right to the property, for example possession under a leasing agreement.

Andy Dean Photography / Shutterstock.com

LEGAL SCENARIO

Where Have All the Flowers Gone?

A potential purchaser of a piece of real estate to be used for the operation of a bed and breakfast inspected the property and was greatly impressed by the vendor's landscaping of the half hectare of land behind the house. The current owner was an avid gardener who had collected unique plants and shrubs and planted them in a spectacular display. The agreement of purchase and sale for the property was signed and the buyer looked forward to taking possession and opening a bed and breakfast operation in such a beautiful setting. On the day the buyer took possession of the property, she walked through the house, threw open the back doors onto the garden, and saw an empty half hectare of land with enormous holes where the plants and shrubs had been.

The buyer believed the plants were fixtures and as such were part of the real estate that she had purchased from the vendor. The seller had taken the plants with him believing they belonged to him since he had collected and planted them, and they were movable with a little effort and a shovel. If there is any doubt about an item qualifying as a chattel or fixture, it should be specifically addressed in the contract between the parties. It is easier and much less expensive to deal with the issue in a contract than to fight a court battle over it afterward.

Recording Ownership Interests in Real Property

The names of all owners of land in Canada are recorded under registration systems maintained by each province or territory. The two primary systems used in Canada are the registry system and the land titles system, and each province or territory uses some version of one or both systems. Registration of interests in land provides a public record of who owns the land as well as any encumbrances/debts that may affect title to the real property, such as a mortgage, and the date when it became effective.

A number of provinces have implemented or are moving toward a computer-based registration system that will allow for electronic registration of documents reflecting interests in land.

Registration Systems

The **registry system** merely records the documents that have been registered that affect the land under the provincial system. It does not validate or confirm ownership. The purchaser is required to check the validity of the seller's authority to sell the land by searching the government's files.

Registry System—a system of land registration operated by provincial governments to record interests in land; generally requires title to the property to be searched back 40 years for the current owner's interest to the land to be considered clear.

DID YOU KNOW?

Title is not guaranteed under the registry system

The provincial or territorial governments using the registry system do not guarantee the accuracy of the title that the vendor holds to land.

The **land titles system** operated by the government guarantees the accuracy of title to the land, subject to certain statutory limits. Documents registered under this system are checked to ensure they accurately reflect ownership. If an error is made that causes a party to experience a financial loss, that party may file a claim for compensation from a government-administered insurance fund.

Land Titles System—a system of land registration under which the provincial government guarantees the accuracy of the title to the land.

It is recommended that in the purchase of real property a lawyer be retained to perform the necessary searches to ensure that title to the property is accurate and clear of any encumbrances.

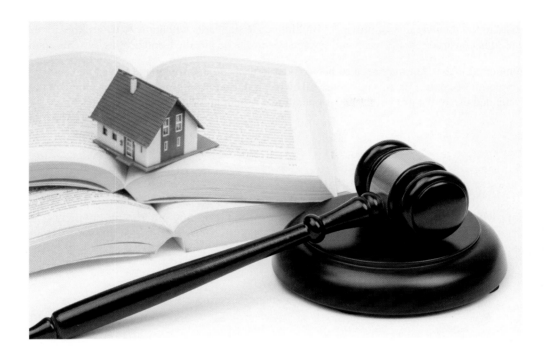

rallef / Shutterstock.com

DID YOU KNOW?

AKA "Torrens"

The land titles system of land registration is also referred to as the Torrens system.

Taxes

Land ownership gives rise to certain taxes at the provincial and municipal level of government. At the time of purchasing real property, a land transfer tax based on a percentage of the purchase price of the property is charged by the provincial and possibly municipal levels of government.

DID YOU KNOW?

GST and capital gains tax may apply to the sale of commercial real estate

The transfer of a commercial building will be subject to the Goods and Services Tax (GST)—or, in certain provinces, the Harmonized Sales Tax (HST)—along with any capital gains tax that may arise from the sale if the real estate is categorized as capital property.

Use of Real Property

Regulation of the use of real property is done primarily through zoning bylaws and building bylaws that control the type of activity the land can be used for and the nature of the buildings and structures that can be erected. These regulations are created at the provincial and municipal levels. Zoning regulations determine such matters as whether land can be used for operating a business or only for single-family residential housing, as well as the number of storeys a building may have.

Before starting construction on new buildings or renovations to alter an existing structure, building permits must be obtained and permit fees paid to the municipality or province. Building code standards will apply to determine, for example, the type of material to be used in construction, the water and sewage systems to be installed, and heating systems, among other things.

Provincial environmental legislation may need to be considered to avoid environmental issues that may restrict the use of the land, for example noise control or air emissions. Likewise, a licence from a provincial or municipal authority may be required for the intended use of the property, such as operating a restaurant or hotel.

DID YOU KNOW?

Environmental Cleanup Costs

The current owner of real property is responsible for cleaning up any environmental problems involving the land. Prior to purchase, it is strongly recommended the future owner request to have an environmental audit done.

BoBaa22 / Shutterstock.com

Mortgages and Real Property

Although Zander has a small inheritance to use for her business purposes, it is not enough to purchase the real property without finding more money to fund the transaction. In this case, Zander could discuss getting a mortgage, a loan secured by the property, with a financial institution or a private lender.

DID YOU KNOW?

A rose by any other name: Part I

The term "mortgage" is used under the older registry system for a loan secured by real property. Under the land titles system the term "charge" is used.

DID YOU KNOW?

A rose by any other name: Part II

"Hypothec" is the term used to describe a mortgage arrangement in the Province of Quebec.

A **mortgage** is a debt that is secured by the real property to ensure the repayment of the loan, whether for a set amount of money or a **line of credit**, to the **mortgagee** (the lender). The person borrowing the funds is referred to as the **mortgagor**. The mortgage is an agreement between the mortgagor and the mortgagee to borrow funds for a particular period of time, usually one to five years, known as the **mortgage term**. Several conditions usually are attached to the loan agreement, primarily the obligation to make the monthly payments on the loan, to pay annual property taxes to the municipality where the land is located, to maintain appropriate fire insurance on the property, to keep the property in good repair, and to repay the balance owing at the end of the term.

Mortgage—a debt using real property as security.

Line of Credit—a debt arrangement under which a lender agrees to make a maximum amount of money available to a borrower.

Mortgagee—the lender under a mortgage.

Mortgagor—the borrower/owner under a mortgage.

Mortgage Term—the length of time for which the mortgage loan is available to the borrower.

To alert any potential purchasers of the real property to the existence of the loan for which the land is being used as security, the mortgage is registered against the property under the appropriate land registration system. Registration also serves to protect the mortgagee's priority in the event a second mortgage is given against the land and registered on title. Under the land registration systems, the first party to register is the first party to be paid.

Generally repayment of the mortgage loan is made monthly or biweekly through blended payments of principal (the amount of the money borrowed) and interest on the loan. The amount of the blended payment is determined by the amortization period applied to the loan. The **amortization period** is the length of time required to pay off the entire debt, principal and interest, over a specified period of time. Usually a 25- or 20-year period is chosen in order to arrive at a monthly payment amount that can be maintained by the borrower/mortgagor.

> **Amortization Period**—the length of time it takes to repay a mortgage loan in full following the schedule of payments set out in the mortgage.

DID YOU KNOW?

Amortization Schedule

This amortization schedule shows blended payments of interest and principal for a three-year mortgage term on a mortgage loan of $200,000 at 3.25% interest calculated over a 25-year amortization period. The calculation results in monthly payments of $975. If a 15-year amortization period were applied, the monthly payments for this mortgage would be $1,405.

At the end of the three-year mortgage term, the balance of the principal must be repaid to the mortgagee/lender. For this purpose, either a new mortgage is arranged with another lender and the funds are used to pay off the balance of the previous mortgage, or the existing mortgage might be renewed for a further three-year term with the current mortgagee.

Date	Interest	Principal	Balance
Jan. 2016	$542	$433	$199,567
Feb. 2016	$540	$434	$199,133
Mar. 2016	$539	$435	$198,698
Apr. 2016	$538	$436	$198,261
May 2016	$537	$438	$197,823
Jun. 2016	$536	$439	$197,385
Jul. 2016	$535	$440	$196,945
Aug. 2016	$533	$441	$196,503
Sep. 2016	$532	$442	$196,061

Date	Interest	Principal	Balance
Oct. 2016	$531	$444	$195,617
Nov. 2016	$530	$445	$195,172
Dec. 2016	$529	$446	$194,726
2016	**$6,422**	**$5,274**	**$194,726**
Jan. 2017	$527	$447	$194,279
Feb. 2017	$526	$448	$193,831
Mar. 2017	$525	$450	$193,381
Apr. 2017	$524	$451	$192,930
May 2017	$523	$452	$192,478
Jun. 2017	$521	$453	$192,025
Jul. 2017	$520	$455	$191,570
Aug. 2017	$519	$456	$191,114
Sep. 2017	$518	$457	$190,657
Oct. 2017	$516	$458	$190,199
Nov. 2017	$515	$460	$189,739
Dec. 2017	$514	$461	$189,279
2017	**$6,248**	**$5,448**	**$189,279**
Jan. 2018	$513	$462	$188,817
Feb. 2018	$511	$463	$188,353
Mar. 2018	$510	$465	$187,889
Apr. 2018	$509	$466	$187,423
May 2018	$508	$467	$186,956
Jun. 2018	$506	$468	$186,488

Date	Interest	Principal	Balance
Jul. 2018	$505	$470	$186,018
Aug. 2018	$504	$471	$185,547
Sep. 2018	$503	$472	$185,075
Oct. 2018	$501	$473	$184,602
Nov. 2018	$500	$475	$184,127
Dec. 2018	$499	$476	$183,651
2018	**$6,068**	**$5,627**	**$183,651**
Jan. 2019	$497	$477	$183,174
Feb. 2019	$496	$479	$182,696
Mar. 2019	$495	$480	$182,216
Apr. 2019	$494	$481	$181,735
May 2019	$492	$482	$181,252
Jun. 2019	$491	$484	$180,768
Jul. 2019	$490	$485	$180,283
Aug. 2019	$488	$486	$179,797
Sep. 2019	$487	$488	$179,309
Oct. 2019	$486	$489	$178,820
Nov. 2019	$484	$490	$178,330
Dec. 2019	$483	$492	$177,838
2019	**$5,883**	**$5,813**	**$177,838**

Link to commercial mortgage professionals: www.greatlaw.ca

razihusin / Shutterstock.com

In the event of default in repayment of the mortgage loan, the terms of the mortgage agreement usually contain an **acceleration clause** that allows the mortgagee to demand full payment of the entire debt. Alternatively, the lender may look to other remedies that are either set out in the mortgage agreement or available through provincial legislation.

> **Acceleration Clause**—term in the mortgage agreement that permits the mortgagee to demand immediate payment of the full amount of the loan in the event of a default.

Generally, a lender will give "reasonable notice" before demanding payment following a default. In most cases, notices will be sent to the mortgagor confirming the default under the mortgage agreement and advising of the mortgagee's intention to enforce its security on the land if the default continues.

If default continues the mortgagee will have multiple remedies available. Most mortgage agreements contain a clause permitting the lender to sell the property in the event default continues for a set period of time after notice has been given. This **power of sale** remedy is relatively quick and easy to use provided the mortgagee follows the process exactly as set out in the agreement in terms of the type and timing of notice that is given to the mortgagor. If successful, in approximately 60 days from default the mortgagee is able to transfer ownership of the real property to a purchaser, free of any claim by the former owner/mortgagor. The mortgagee will apply the proceeds from the sale to pay the mortgage debt. The lender will reserve the right to sue the borrower for any deficiency if the sale proceeds are less than the amount owed. Likewise, if there is any money left over after paying off the mortgage loan, it will go to the mortgagor.

> **Power of Sale**—a remedy available to the lender under a mortgage allowing the sale of the real property in the case of default.

In some provinces, such as British Columbia, Ontario, and Nova Scotia, the lender will be able to sue the mortgagor for a court order of **foreclosure**. This court order passes title to the mortgagee in full satisfaction of the debt and eliminates any further obligation on the part of the borrower.

Foreclosure—a court action following which the lender obtains legal title to the real property after default by the borrower under a mortgage.

© Steveheap | Dreamstime.com

A third remedy available in most provinces is a **judicial sale** of the property by a sheriff at public auction or by tender under a court order. Funds from the sale are applied to the outstanding debt and the borrower remains personally liable for any shortfall between the sale price and the money owed.

Judicial Sale—a court-ordered and -administered sale of property after default under a mortgage.

DID YOU KNOW?

Determining priorities among mortgages

If acting as a lender under a mortgage, be sure to search title to the property before advancing the funds and follow up immediately by registering your mortgage on title. In a default under a mortgage, priority in payment is based on who registered first.

LO 9.4   ## 9.4 Commercial Leases

After giving it serious consideration, Zander decided that since this was a new business she might need to change locations in order to continue to grow and she did not want to tie up all her funds in the purchase of a property when she may need to do some renovations for a music studio as well as obtain equipment. After speaking with her real estate agent, Zander decided to consider the alternative of leasing commercial space in a building in an area of the city that would be easy for students to access, attractive to musicians for recording purposes, and convenient with lots of available parking.

The rules under which a commercial tenancy operates are very different from the rules governing a residential tenancy relationship. Each province has legislation that regulates many of the elements of the landlord–tenant relationship in a commercial setting. For example, in Ontario the *Commercial Tenancies Act* governs commercial tenancies. This Act contains many differences from the law that is applied to residential tenancies. There is also a significant amount of case law that has developed around the rights and remedies of landlords and tenants under a commercial lease.

> Link to a sample of a commercial tenancy lease:
> https://www.lawdepot.ca/contracts/commercial-lease-agreement

In a commercial leasing arrangement, the tenant has possession of the property while the landlord retains ownership. A **lease** is signed by both parties setting out the terms for the agreement, such as the length of the lease, the amount of rent and when it is to be paid, who is responsible for maintenance and repairs, and any restrictions on how the tenant may use the premises. Provided the tenant meets its obligations under the agreement, during the term of the lease the tenant is allowed exclusive possession and the landlord may enter the premises only under specific circumstances.

> **Lease**—a contract setting out the terms and conditions for the rental of a property.

There are different forms of leases depending on whether the property will be used for retail operations, warehousing, office space, or industrial manufacturing.

Leases are usually referred to as **fixed tenancy**, which are for a specified period of time such as one year or five years, or as **periodic tenancy**, which are for an indeterminate period of time. In a periodic tenancy arrangement, the lease continues until either the landlord or tenant provides notice terminating it. Provincial legislation, and usually the lease itself, sets out the period of time required for proper notice to be given. The timing and form of notice indicated should be carefully followed for effective termination of the lease agreement.

> **Fixed Tenancy**—a tenancy that has a fixed beginning and end date that can be for any period of time, from months to years.

> **Periodic Tenancy**—a tenancy that renews automatically at the end of the relevant rental period until terminated by the landlord or the tenant.

CarmenKarin / Shutterstock.com

There are generally four types of commercial leases:

1. A *net lease*, in which the tenant pays a fixed amount as rent as well as a percentage share (based on the size of the rented space) of the landlord's expenses relating to the operation, maintenance, and ownership of the property;
2. A *lease*, under which, in addition to the payments made under a net lease, the tenant pays for structural repairs to the premises as well;
3. A *gross lease*, in which the tenant pays a fixed amount as rent on a regular basis; and
4. A *semi-gross lease*, under which the landlord assumes responsibility for certain expenses under the base rent received from the tenant.

Along with rent, GST (and in some provinces, provincial sales tax) is payable by the tenant based on the rental rate under a commercial lease.

Lease Provisions

It is very important to make sure a lease is well drafted to meet the needs of the tenant and the landlord. Both parties should be aware of any provincial/territorial laws or municipal bylaws that may affect the use of the property. The tenant may have specific requirements concerning the use of the premises and the organization or setup of the business. The landlord may have certain obligations, such as noise restrictions imposed by a municipality or noncompetition clauses under leases with other tenants of the property. Generally, commercial tenants are not allowed to withhold rent as a way of self-help to force the landlord to meet its obligations under the lease. The lease should set out in clear language the rights and duties of both parties to the agreement in order to avoid any future misunderstandings or disputes.

Zander's plans for her new business include setting up a recording studio for musicians to rent, individual rooms for music lessons and practice, a space for displaying sheet music for sale and instruments for students to rent or buy, a waiting room, and an office for herself. This will require some construction and renovation work to be done on the property, which raises some issues. For example, as previously noted in this chapter, permits and fees for the structural changes to be made to the premises may be required by the municipality where the property is located. Who will be responsible for obtaining the permits? If Zander is responsible, will the landlord, as the owner of the building, be required to sign the applications? Will the landlord want the right to approve the plans before signing? And when the lease is completed, will Zander be required to put the premises back to the original condition? These are concerns that should be dealt with in the lease to make sure there is clear understanding and agreement by both parties.

Along with the term of the lease and any right to renew a fixed tenancy when the term is completed, the parties will want to consider who will be responsible for the repair and maintenance of the property while the tenant is in possession. Provincial law only requires landlords to maintain the basic safety of the property and to warn of any dangers. The tenant may want to have the landlord agree in advance to the intended use of the premises so that the tenant's right to **quiet enjoyment**, free from interference by the landlord, is established from the start in case other tenants complain. Will the fixtures—the shelves and built-in desks—that have been added to the premises stay when the lease ends and the tenant leaves, or will the tenant be allowed to remove them?

Quiet Enjoyment—the right of the lessee to occupy and use the leased premises without interference by the landlord. Also known as *quiet possession*.

If a business does not grow as the owner plans, it may become necessary to **sublet** all or part of the leased premises to other people to cut expenses. Generally, unless the lease does not allow it, tenants have a right to sublet. The tenant would remain responsible for the obligations under the lease and the subtenant would be responsible to her. Likewise, if the business does not work out at all, the tenant may want to transfer the balance of the term under the lease by an **assignment** to another party with the intention that that person becomes directly responsible to the landlord for the obligations under the lease. However, while there may be a right to assign, the **assignor** would remain responsible under the lease along with the new tenant (the **assignee**) unless the lease states the landlord will release the original tenant or the landlord agrees to this at the time of assignment.

Sublet—an arrangement under which the tenant leaves a leased space for a specified period of time and allows another person to occupy the leased space until the tenant returns to resume occupancy.

Assignment—an arrangement under which the tenant transfers the tenancy to another person for the balance of the term of the lease.

Assignor—a person who transfers rights to an assignee under an assignment.

Assignee—a person who receives rights from an assignor under an assignment.

A further reason for ensuring that obligations under the lease are clearly stated might arise in the event of a flood or fire on the property. In this event, the premises might not be useable for some time while repairs are done. However, the law indicates that the tenant's obligation to make payments for rent under the lease does not stop until the property can be used for business purposes again. If the tenant for whatever reason should decide to not pay rent, the commercial landlord has a couple of remedies to choose from. The landlord may choose to seize the tenant's goods located on the premises—computer systems, audio/video equipment, furnishings—and sell them to cover the outstanding rent. This is known as the **right of distress** and is not available to residential landlords. (This right of distress has nothing to do with an instructor's authority to mark assignments—just checking again to see if you are still reading.) Alternatively, the landlord may choose to take possession of the premises, usually by changing the lock. This is referred to as the **right of forfeiture** or re-entry. In this case, the tenant would need to apply to a court, pay the full amount of the outstanding rent, and ask for reinstatement of the lease. To avoid situations such as this arising due to a flood or some other disaster, it would be important to include a clause in the lease that allows the tenant to suspend payment of rent if the premises become unusable, and perhaps to terminate the lease if the repairs are significantly delayed to the point that it will affect the ability to continue the tenant's business operations in the future.

Right of Distress—the right of a commercial landlord to seize and dispose of the tenant's property following nonpayment of rent.

Right of Forfeiture—the landlord's remedy of evicting the tenant for breach of an obligation under the lease.

CASE STUDY

Emcan Bakery Equipment & Supply Ltd. v. DMI Property Management Inc., [2010] O.J. No. 2315

The case of *Emcan Bakery Equipment & Supply Ltd. v. DMI Property Management Inc.* illustrates two competing interests in a commercial lease situation.

Facts: A bakery bought a commercial dough mixer, oven, and related bakery equipment on an instalment plan for use on the commercial premises leased by the bakery. Under the credit arrangement, the equipment supplier retained ownership until the purchase price was paid in full. The bakery did not do well financially and stopped making payments on the equipment and also stopped paying rent on the leased premises. The landlord attempted to exercise the right of distress on the baking equipment, and the equipment supplier wanted to repossess its goods.

Decision: The court determined that the landlord could exercise its right of distress on the baking equipment only after it had paid the balance owing to the supplier.

After extensive research, Zander found an excellent location for her music studio and negotiated several key elements into her lease, including suspension of rent for whatever period of time the space might become unusable while the landlord made repairs following a flood or fire, and a two-week rent-free period during which she could access the premises to renovate and paint the space prior to opening for business (a "fixturing" period).

LO 9.5   9.5 Personal Property

While the rental premises were being set up, Zander began to look around for the various instruments and sound/recording equipment she would require for her music studio. She determined she could afford to buy items such as tambourines, triangles, and music stands. Other instruments and pieces of equipment, such as keyboards, bagpipes, microphones, and mixing boards for recording, she would need to borrow money to purchase. Some instruments that Zander wanted to have at the studio were so expensive she would need to pay for them in instalments over several years, such as a grand piano or (the love of her life) a deluxe, blazing red, state of the art electric accordion. To achieve her dream of acquiring these items for her studio—and to open her business on schedule—Zander needed to consider several options.

As discussed at the beginning of this chapter, everything that is not real property is personal property and is classified as a tangible item (chattels—cars, computers) or an intangible asset (choses in action—cheques, trademarks). Our focus in this part of the chapter is on the tangible items called chattels, usually referred to as "goods." Intangible assets, such as the copyright and trademark rights found with intellectual property, will be examined later in the chapter.

The ability of a business to exercise rights over the personal property (goods) used in its operations depends on whether the goods are owned by that organization or simply in its possession. Basic to the concept of ownership of property is the right to possess and use it. However, there are circumstances in which an owner of goods may grant the right of possession to another party while remaining as owner of the property.

When Zander rented steam-cleaning equipment to clean the floor carpeting in her music studio, she was given the right under the rental agreement to possess and use the equipment for a specific purpose over a set period of time. However, ownership of the steam cleaner remained with the company from which Zander rented the equipment.

A situation such as this, where the key elements of ownership and the possession of goods are split on a temporary basis for a specific purpose, is referred to as a **bailment** and is usually set up under a written contract. The owner of the goods is known as the **bailor** and the party in possession of the goods, such as Zander with the steam-cleaning equipment, is the **bailee**. The bailee is under a duty to take care of the goods while in possession of them. The standard of care that must be maintained under that duty depends on the nature of the bailment.

Bailment—the legal relationship that arises when the elements of ownership and possession of personal property are intentionally divided for a period of time.

Bailor—owner of the goods under a bailment.

Bailee—person in possession of the goods under a bailment.

For our purposes, we will look at two forms of bailment often found in a business setting:

1. Bailment for reward: including rental and consignment
2. Bailment for repair/services

Both parties will have certain rights and duties under the legal relationship established by the bailment. These are created through both the contractual terms and conditions agreed to by the parties and the common law. The common law rules for a bailment apply if there is no contract setting out the rights and duties, or if the contract does not address a particular issue. For example, the contract might contain a disclaimer clause aimed at limiting the bailor's liability should the goods being used under the bailment cause injury to the bailee, as might be the case if the steam cleaner backed up too quickly onto Zander's toe and broke it. It could also contain terms for the bailee to maintain the goods in a certain state of repair that might not be required under the common law. You can read more about the common law in Chapter 1.

Bailment for Reward: Rental

A bailment for reward is one in which consideration is exchanged between the parties. An example of this is a rental agreement. This is the most common form of bailment. It includes such arrangements as the rental of water coolers, cars, rug cleaning equipment, computers, and photocopiers, among other items. The common law standard of care is usually that by which a reasonably diligent person would take of the goods in the circumstances. Generally, this is the same standard as the reasonable person standard in tort law.

For example, if Zander (the bailee) rents guitars from Musical Instruments Inc. (the bailor) to use in teaching her students, there is an implied term that the goods will be useable for the purpose for which they are being provided. If the bridge on a guitar snapped because it had stress cracks and had not been checked by the bailor before being rented to the Zander, and a student's eye was injured by the guitar string when the bridge snapped, the bailor would generally be responsible for any losses suffered by Zander if the student sued for damages. Likewise, although the bailee generally is not liable for ordinary wear and tear on rented equipment under a bailment for reward, Zander has a duty to take care of the goods and could be sued by the bailor if the goods are damaged by an overenthusiastic student while in her possession.

CASE STUDY

Hadley v. Droitwich Construction Co. Ltd. et al., [1967] 3 All E.R. 911

The case of *Hadley v. Droitwich Construction Co. Ltd. et al.* illustrates some of the responsibilities in a bailment arrangement.

Facts: A construction company rented a crane and assigned its operation to Hadley, an employee with little experience in operating a crane. At the time the crane was rented its owners were aware that there was a need for some adjustments to be made to it, but the problem was not considered dangerous. On site the problem became worse and eventually caused an accident in which Hadley was injured.

Decision: The court held that under the bailment, the owners of the crane were liable as bailors because they had rented a crane that needed repair without warning the bailee of the condition. The court also found the bailee liable to Hadley because it had failed to properly service the crane before having its employee operate it.

Bailment for Reward: Consignment

To help pay her operating costs, Zander has agreed to display used musical instruments that her students wish to sell in her music studio alongside the sheet music. For each instrument sold, Zander will receive a commission. These instruments are placed in Zander's studio on a consignment basis.

Consignment is a bailment for reward. If the item is not eventually sold, it is returned to the owner. The owner of the instrument is the bailor and, in our running example, Zander's studio is the bailee under this arrangement. Unless the agreement between the parties states otherwise, the standard of care is the same as that outlined above and the bailee must exercise the care which an ordinary person would take of goods in the circumstances.

Consignment—the transfer of possession of goods from one person to another for the purpose of offering the goods for sale.

CoffeeFreak/Alamy

Bailment for Repair/Services

Another service being offered by Zander through her studio is the repair of stringed instruments such as guitars and violins. This is known as a bailment for repair or services, one in which the bailor, the owner of the instrument, pays the bailee, the repairperson, for providing a service. The bailee must make the repairs in a skilful manner (under a contract of repair), and while the instrument is in the possession of the bailee the common law of bailment states there is generally a duty to preserve the value of the goods at a standard as if the repairperson owned them.

LEGAL SCENARIO

The Case of the Vanishing Diamonds

Wanda had inherited an antique necklace set with three large, rare fancy canary yellow diamonds. The settings on one of the diamonds had become loose and Wanda decided to have it repaired before wearing it to her son's graduation ceremony. Wanda took the necklace to Ben Bijoux's Jewellery Emporium, located on a busy street in town, and arranged for Ben to repair the setting for the next day. Ben decided to work on the necklace immediately after Wanda left the store. He left the necklace on the counter while he went into the back room to get the necessary tools to make the repair. Ben was gone only a minute when he heard the store door open and close. Ben returned to the front counter immediately to find the counter empty. The diamond necklace had vanished.

Under a bailment for repair, the law places a duty on the bailee (repairperson) to take precautions to preserve the goods and their value at a standard as if the repairperson owned them. Wanda, the owner, swears she would never leave her diamond necklace on a counter next to a door on a busy street.

Personal Property as Security for a Debt

Although Zander can rent certain musical instruments for her studio, there are others for which it would be more cost effective for her business to either borrow money to buy them or pay for them over an extended period of time.

Rather than a bailment arrangement, goods can be used as security for the repayment of a debt. This might be created through a loan or the purchase of an item with payment to be made at some point in the future or over a period of time in instalments. In the event the debt is not repaid or a default occurs under the arrangement, the individual who is owed the money can seize the goods and sell them. If the sale price exceeds the debt, anything over the amount owed will be either paid to other lenders/ vendors according to their priority or, if there are no other lenders, to the owner of the goods who defaulted in payment.

Instalment Payments

For the most expensive items required for her music studio, such as a grand piano, Zander might consider leasing the instrument. This would be done through an equipment or financing lease. In an arrangement such as this, possession of the grand piano would be given to Zander at the time of signing the lease agreement, and ownership of the instrument would remain with the seller/lessor. Monthly payments would be made and Zander, the buyer/lessee, would have the option to purchase the instrument at the end of the lease for a small sum of money.

The vendor, who is in the business of selling goods and not lending money, will often sell its interest under the lease to a financing company that *is* in the business of lending money. The financing company holds title to the goods and receives the lease payments until the purchase option is exercised at the end of the lease. An equipment lease of this nature may be used in place of a chattel mortgage.

The common law provinces and territories have enacted *Personal Property Security Acts* (PPSA) governing security transactions involving personal property. A lien is filed under the PPSA by completing a financing statement that is registered under the province's or territory's electronic system. Registration "perfects" the lien and provides notice to the general public of the security interest created under a financing agreement over the personal property. For more on this topic, refer to Chapter 11.

Bakhtiar Zein / Shutterstock.com

DID YOU KNOW?

General Security Agreement

A lender may request a general security agreement when making a loan to a business. A general security agreement is a contract under which the debtor grants a security interest in the present and any future personal property of the business to a creditor to secure a commercial loan.

DID YOU KNOW?

Notice of a Security Interest

A lien under a PPSA is notice to the public that a security agreement exists against personal property to guarantee payment of a debt.

LO 9.6　　**9.6** Intellectual Property

Zander has completed the upgrades to the rental premises for her music studio; has bought the necessary music stands with cash; rented various musical instruments; purchased her sound recording equipment with monthly payments over the next year; and leased her flaming red, state of the art electric accordion and a grand piano. Zander's next step is to market her studio's services and prepare for its opening. For that purpose, she has designed a business card and retained the services of a friend to help her set up a website. In honour of the grand opening of her music studio and to bring the studio to the public's attention, Zander has composed a rousing marching song for electric accordion and flugelhorn that she has entered in a competition for contemporary Canadian music composers. The city has heard about Zander's composition and has approached her about possibly adopting it as the city's theme song. Zander is excited by this possibility, but wants to make sure she is credited as the composer and receives some monetary benefit if the city does adopt the song after the competition is over. Recognition is lovely but it doesn't pay the bills, she can be heard muttering to herself.

Zander's concerns regarding her original music composition are addressed by the area of law known as intellectual property, which can become an important asset for a business.

Intellectual property is a form of asset that falls within the definition of intangible personal property discussed at the outset of this chapter. The areas of intellectual property that we will examine in this chapter are **copyright**, **trademarks**, **patents**, **industrial design**, and **trade secrets**. Part of the value of intellectual property lies in the rights of ownership—which, if protected properly, allow the owner to commercialize the intellectual property rights through such things as licensing the use of a trademark or a piece of music, while retaining ownership and control.

Copyright—statutory protection of the intellectual property rights of the creators of musical, dramatic, literary and artistic works, and software.

Trademarks—identifiable features used to distinguish the goods or services of a business from those offered by another.

Patents—statutory grants of an exclusive right to make, sell, and use an invention within the jurisdiction in which it is granted.

Industrial Design—unique visual elements incorporated as part of a manufactured product's design.

Trade Secrets—confidential information regarding a product or production process that has commercial value to the owner.

Legislation concerning intellectual property rights is within the powers of the federal government and is applied the same way across Canada regardless of which province or territory the owner may live in. Information on various aspects of intellectual property, and the processes involved in protecting it, can be found at the website for the Canadian Intellectual Property Office (CIPO). This website is an excellent source of information and a good starting point for any questions you may have.

Link to CIPO website: www.cipo.ic.gc.ca.

Canada has signed a number of international conventions with other countries that are intended to extend the protection for intellectual property rights of inventors and authors into other countries. A legal adviser should be consulted if you are thinking of using intellectual property in Canada that originates from another country, or considering commercializing your intellectual property in another country.

Copyright

Zander has a legitimate concern in wanting to ensure that the music she is submitting to the competition cannot be taken by someone else and used without her permission as the composer—or, if it is used, that they pay her for its commercial value. The federal Copyright Act is intended to provide creative people like Zander with that protection.

Copyright in Canada covers any original literary, dramatic, musical, and artistic work, including computer programs, which are defined under the Act as literary works. Protection for copyright under the federal *Copyright Act* gives the owner of the copyright the exclusive right to publish, perform in public, or reproduce the original work, and the ability to prevent another person or business from copying or using such work for commercial purposes. Many other forms of protection also flow from copyright ownership.

Copyright protects the expression of an idea through an original work but not the idea itself. So, Zander's idea to combine the sounds of an accordion with a flugelhorn cannot be protected, but the actual composition, the musical expression she created using the two instruments, can be.

To be considered original, the work must have been created by the author and not copied from another source, and protection of the original work occurs automatically upon its creation. Registration of copyright is available, but optional at the decision of the owner and is not required in order to enforce rights in an original work. What it does provide is evidence of the existence of copyright and ownership as of registration.

Zander can register her copyright in her original musical work with the Copyright Office by submitting a registration form by mail or online for a small fee. She can expect a certificate of registration to issue within four weeks of submission of her application. However, Zander's copyright protection of her original composition will be in effect automatically from the date she composed it for the period of the rest of her life plus 50 years from the end of the calendar year of her death. If an original work has joint authors, the 50-year period is based on the death of the last surviving author. This term of protection applies to most copyrighted works in Canada with some exceptions that are set out in the Act.

While the author of a work is generally considered to be the first owner of the copyright, an exception to this occurs when the work has been created in the course of employment. In this situation the employee will still be the author but ownership of the copyright is held by the employer, subject to any contractual arrangement between the parties.

Under common law an author also holds the moral rights in a copyrighted original work. These rights allow the author to prevent his or her work from being modified or distorted, or used in a way that could harm the author's reputation. It is these moral rights that would allow Zander to prevent a literary group to which she had given permission to use her musical work at its meetings from using it as the rally song for a meeting in support of censorship and the encouragement of book burning.

Copyright in a work can be assigned in whole or in part by the owner. Generally, to be effective the assignment must be in writing and signed by the copyright owner. However, the moral rights of the author cannot be assigned and must be expressly waived by the author to be effective. An assignee that wants complete freedom to use a copyrighted work should require the waiver of the author's moral rights in writing as a term of the assignment agreement.

The reproduction or publication of a work or a substantial part of a work without the copyright owner's authorization would be considered infringement of the copyright. In Canada, there is an exception referred to as **fair dealing** under which, generally, it is not considered infringement to use a work for such purposes as research, review, education, satire, or private study. Copyright protection is also administered through copyright collectives such as SOCAN (Society of Composers, Authors and Music Publishers of Canada) and Access Copyright. A statutory system governing collectives is codified in the *Copyright Act*.

Fair Dealing—permitted use or copying of copyrighted material for specific limited purposes such as research and review.

© Arkadi Bojaršinov | Dreamstime.com

Link to SOCAN: www.socan.ca

Link to Access Copyright: www.accesscopyright.ca

Trademarks

Along with her music and website for marketing her studio, Zander has also designed a logo for her new business that involves music notes arranged to look like a stylized image of an accordion spelling out her name. She is very excited by its uniqueness and is certain it will help to distinguish her music studio and its services from any other in town. Zander considers it her trademark and wants to ensure that it is protected so that no other business can use it, or something that resembles it.

Zander's understanding of the purpose of her logo is correct. What she has described is a trademark—a word, symbol, or design that distinguishes the source of a particular product or service. In Canada, registration under the federal *Trade-marks Act* is not required for a trademark to be protected. However, without registration the protection available to the owner may be limited to the boundaries of the area where the trademark has developed a reputation. In Zander's case, it may be simply the city or the section of the city where her trademark is known as representing her music studio. With registration, the trademark rights are protected across Canada. So, as Zander's reputation grows, if she plans to use her trademark throughout Canada she should consider registering her trademark.

© Pressureua | Dreamstime.com

To qualify for registration, a trademark may not, among other things, be:

- Merely descriptive of the goods or services;
- Misdescriptive of the quality or nature of the goods or services;
- Confusing with an existing trademark; or
- In use by a prior user.

As well, the applicant must be able to show use of the distinctive trademark in Canada. If so, registration of wares, services, or both is possible for a term of 15 years, renewable for further periods of 15 years upon payment of a fee. The registration process involves procedural and legal elements that may best be undertaken with the assistance of a registered trademark agent.

If Zander's business grows and she is approached by another business to license the use of her trademark on T-shirts, she must maintain direct or indirect control over the quality of the wares or services for which the mark is licensed in order for the **licence** to remain valid. For several reasons, it is important that any licensing be done through a written agreement with the assistance of a legal adviser.

> **Licence**—a contractual right to use a trademark, copyright, patent, industrial design, or trade secret for a specified limited purpose and time.

Infringement of a trademark occurs when there is a sale or distribution of goods or services involving a similar or confusing trademark or trade name. In a situation such as this, the use of a confusing trademark by a competing business may give rise to a statutory infringement action, a common law action for passing off, or possibly a statutory action for unfair competition.

DID YOU KNOW?

Trademarks in Quebec

An exception for trademarks used in the Province of Quebec is available under the *Charter of the French Language* that allows a "recognized trademark" to be used in a language other than French unless a French version has been registered, in which case it must be used.

Patents

Zander has had a huge response to her offer to sell used musical instruments on consignment. As a matter of fact, her studio has become the go-to place for this purpose. The difficulty is the amount of floor space it takes up in her relatively small studio space. Late one night while eating pizza and pursuing her other passion, origami, Zander artfully folded a piece of paper in the shape of a flying bird (a blue heron) and absentmindedly used it to suspend a slice of pizza with a pencil stuck through it. Suddenly she saw the solution to managing her problem at the studio. Zander had created the shape for an item which, if made of strong, lightweight plastic, could be used to suspend musical instruments such as guitars and violins from the ceiling, freeing up much needed floor space. She knew this idea could make her a fortune. However, she is anxious to make sure she gets to benefit from her invention. Being creative is great, she muttered, but it doesn't pay the bills.

If Zander's creation comes within the definition of a new invention under the federal *Patent Act*, she may be able to claim the exclusive right to make, construct, use, and sell the invention and exclude anyone else from using it in Canada. Generally, the inventor, like Zander, is the owner of the patent unless the invention is created in the course of employment, in which case the employer is the owner unless the parties have an agreement that states otherwise. An employee should check his or her employment agreement for any terms dealing with ownership of intellectual property. If the employment agreement does not address this issue, it would be best to have any arrangement between the employer and employee in writing.

A patent may be obtained for any invention that is new, useful, and unobvious. This includes processes, machines, composition of material, and methods of manufacturing or any new and useful improvement thereof. However, a patent filed in Canada gives patent protection only in Canada. Patent protection in other countries should be discussed with a lawyer familiar with the patent systems available in foreign jurisdictions.

In Canada, a patent is issued to the first person to file an application for the new invention. Novelty is a requirement and there must be at least one or more new and inventive elements involved in the invention being submitted. Because of the requirement for novelty, it is recommended that an inventor not disclose information about the invention to other people until the patent application is filed. We discuss trade secrets, confidential information, and the use of nondisclosure agreements later in this section. If information about the invention is disclosed publicly before filing, the Act makes allowances for such situations provided the application in Canada is submitted within 12 months of the disclosure.

The process to obtain an issued patent is expensive and takes several years. A formal application is prepared setting out the necessary information relating to the invention. The way in which the claims for a patent on the process or material are drafted is critical to a successful application and should be done with the assistance of a legal adviser. The completed application is submitted to the Canadian patent office along with a fee and personal information about the inventor(s). The patent application proceeds through several stages of examination and, if considered allowable because it meets the necessary criteria, a patent issuance fee is paid and the patent is issued to the owner/inventor.

A patent owner has the exclusive right to use the patented invention in Canada for a period of 20 years from the date of the application. If another business infringes the patent, the owner can bring a court action to enforce the patent, stop the infringing actions, and, if appropriate, sue for damages or have the infringing party account for any profits they earned as a result of the infringing activity. Patents are only enforceable in the country for which they have been issued. If an item, like Zander's, has potential for international commercialization, patents should be applied for in the individual countries in which sales or competitors are anticipated.

faithie / Shutterstock.com

 CASE STUDY

Harvard College v. Canada (Commissioner of Patents) 2002 SCC 76

The case of *Harvard College v. Canada (Commissioner of Patents)* illustrates the Supreme Court of Canada's thoughts on patentable inventions.

Facts: Researchers at Harvard College developed a genetically altered type of mouse that was more likely to develop cancer following exposure to chemicals. This aspect of the mouse made it valuable for research purposes. The College applied to register a patent for the invention in Canada having already been issued a patent for the oncomouse in the United States and in a number of European countries.

Registration was refused by the Patent Appeal Board and by the Federal Court on the basis the process lacked the element of reproducibility that is required of a patent in Canada.

Decision: The Supreme Court of Canada held that the oncomouse could not be patented. Although some "lower" forms of life, such as genetically modified yeast, had been patented, the Court decided that patenting a higher life form would involve a radical departure from the traditional patent regime and can be done only under clear direction from Parliament.

If an inventor is unable to find the money to manufacture the invention she could sell the patent and assign ownership to another party who will be able to commercialize the invention. To be effective, the assignment must be in writing and signed by the current owner, in this case Zander. An alternative would be for the inventor to retain ownership of the patent and, as the **licensor**, license the patent rights to manufacture the invention to another party in exchange for a **royalty** on sales. If this licence is to be exclusive to the **licensee**, it must in writing and signed by the owner of the patent. If it is not an exclusive licence it is not required to be in writing, but for good commercial practices, it is strongly recommended that the parties set out the terms and conditions of the licence in writing.

> **Licensor**—the individual granting the right to use a copyright, trademark, patent, industrial design, or trade secret.

> **Royalty**—a payment made to the licensor in exchange for the use of a copyright, trademark, patent, industrial design, or trade secret; the amount usually is based on a percentage of sales or the number of units produced.

> **Licensee**—the individual receiving the right to use a copyright, trademark, patent, industrial design, or trade secret.

Industrial Design

Zander has been checking patentability issues on the Internet and is concerned that her creation will not meet the necessary elements to have a patent issue after spending the remaining money of her inheritance on it. However, she has read that if an item is ornamental and useful that it can be protected from being copied in Canada for several years. This might be an alternative that she can consider to make sure she gets the first opportunity to commercialize her new creation.

Zander could submit an application for registration of her "suspended bird instrument holder" under the federal *Industrial Design Act* and, if successful, she would have the exclusive rights to use the registered industrial design within Canada for a period of five years with the possibility of renewing it for a further five years. This is a total of ten years of protection for her creation, if the application is approved.

The Act defines industrial design as a functional item with "features of shape, configuration, pattern or ornament and any combination of those features that, in a finished article, appeal to and are judged solely by the eye" (*Industrial Design Act, R.S.C., 1985, C.I-9, s.2*). The item cannot be identical to an existing registered design or be so similar in appearance with some other design in the market that people would confuse them. The industrial design must be novel, primarily ornamental, but also useful.

Zander has already installed a flock of her suspended bird holders from the ceiling of her music studio and is concerned this means her creation would no longer be considered novel. In these situations, the Act allows an initial application to be submitted within one year of the item being made public in Canada or elsewhere. Once the industrial design has been registered, Zander will need to mark the item with the notice "Registered" or "Rd" with the year of registration in order to have full protection. Without the notice on the item, she would only be able to get an injunction to stop another person from commercial activity using her suspended bird holder. With notice, she has the ability to bring an action for infringement to get both an injunction and damages through an accounting for profits received by the infringer.

Trade Secrets

With costs mounting from renting the studio space, obtaining the necessary equipment, and marketing her new business, Zander is concerned that she won't have sufficient funds to get the protection needed for her intellectual property as well. She wants to be able to discuss her financial needs with possible investors interested in her business, but that would require showing them her drawings, business plans, financial plans, and other confidential information, which she is worried they might then use for their own purposes. Expressing interest is all fine and dandy, she was heard to mutter, but it won't pay for filing fees.

Zander's information has value for her business and it retains that value as long as it is not made available to her competitors and remains confidential. Her confidential information might include customer lists, how much she pays her suppliers, pricing policies, and future marketing plans for her business and inventions. It may also include a secret manufacturing process that is not patentable but is unique to her product that is kept as a trade secret.

© Antonio Mirabile | Dreamstime.com

 CASE STUDY

Apotex Fermentation Inc. v. Novopharm Ltd. (1998), 162 D.L.R. (4th) 111

The case of *Apotex Fermentation Inc. v. Novopharm Ltd.* illustrates the continuing obligations of confidentiality owed to an employer even when an employee leaves.

Facts: A former employee of the plaintiff, Apotex, accepted employment with Novopharm, a competitor of his former employer. The former employee of Apotex had confidential information about the manufacturing process for the drug Lovastatin, used for treatment of conditions involving cholesterol. Apotex sought an injunction restraining Novopharm from carrying out further research on the drug and for damages against Novopharm and the former employee.

Decision: The court found the employee and his new employer liable. The court stated that Novopharm knew or ought to have known the information was confidential and had been obtained from Apotex and consequently it was liable for the breach of trust of its new employee.

There is no statutory protection in Canada for trade secrets or **confidential information**. The only protection comes from common law principles such as those that prevent employees from revealing their employer's confidential business information. Once information is made public, the confidential element is lost and so is its commercial value. Contractual obligations requiring another person to keep information being provided to them confidential are one way a business can make information available while retaining the value of the information disclosed. Contracts of this nature are known as **nondisclosure agreements** or confidentiality agreements. These agreements are intended to protect the information exchanged by the parties who signed them, usually for a certain period of time, whether or not an actual business arrangement and contracts result from their discussions. They may also be used in an employer and employee relationship.

Confidential Information—information that retains its commercial value as long as the public or a competitor does not know it.

Nondisclosure Agreements—contracts between two or more parties to maintain information exchanged between them confidential.

If the terms of the confidentiality agreement are breached by one of the parties, enforcement is accomplished by going to court to obtain an injunction to stop the confidential information from being used or made public.

A trade secret is information that has value for a business as long as it is not known to the public. Provided the information is kept secret, it is protected. This might involve taking reasonable efforts to maintain the information's secrecy, such as keeping it in a locked cabinet and only showing it to individuals who are in a confidential relationship, for example an employee or someone who has signed a confidentiality agreement.

FOR REVIEW

Questions

1. Is the remedy of distress available under a residential tenancy? (LO 9.4)
2. State whether the following is a fixture or a chattel: (LO 9.3)
   a. A furnace
   b. A built-in dishwasher
   c. A dining room table
   d. A storage shed
   e. A circular saw stored in the storage shed
   f. An antique lampshade on a hall light
   g. A portable room dehumidifier
3. At what point is a lien on personal property considered to be "perfected"? (LO 9.5)
4. If a pre-existing environmental problem is uncovered following the sale of real property, is the vendor of the land responsible for the cost of cleaning up the problem? (LO 9.3)
5. What is the purpose for registering interests in land? (LO 9.3)

6. What are the two forms of personal property? (LO 9.5)

7. What is the purpose of a mortgage on real property? (LO 9.3)

8. Briefly explain what the term "blended payments" means under a mortgage. (LO 9.3)

9. Briefly explain the term "bailment" and give an example. (LO 9.5)

10. Briefly explain what is protected by an industrial design application. (LO 9.6)

Activities

1. With reasons, discuss whether a renewal clause would or would not be of benefit in a commercial lease. (LO 9.4)

2. What types of issues would you want to negotiate as part of your lease in the following circumstances: (LO 9.4)

    a. The premises are situated next to a river that tends to flood in the spring;

    b. The premises are under construction and already running behind for completion in time for your occupation and use;

    c. You have a large space and may want to rent part of the premises to another business if your business is slow to develop;

    d. You plan to spend $30,000 on shelving units and special directed lighting in setting up your business and want to take these with you at the end of the lease.

3. You have drawn up a strategic marketing plan for a new product that is unique and will be the first to be made available to consumers. What steps would you take to protect the plan and the information about the product as you discuss bringing the item to market with various suppliers and retailers? (LO 9.6)

4. Go to the Canadian Intellectual Property Office (CIPO) website and choose one of the tabs on the site (Trademarks, Patents, Copyright…). Provide a brief summary on the information available to you under that tab. (LO 9.6)

5. Discuss whether registration of a copyright with the government should be a requirement in order to have protection in that area of intellectual property law. (LO 9.6)

6. Discuss the benefits and drawbacks to the three remedies available to a mortgagee in the event a borrower defaults under a mortgage. (LO 9.3)

7. When is it more appropriate to sublet a rental property rather than assign your rights under a lease? (LO 9.4)

8. What is meant by the term "fair dealing" in reference to copyright law? Is it still relevant for contemporary business purposes? (LO 9.6)

CASES FOR DISCUSSION

Case #1

Hector was a well-known artist who specialized in sculptures of birds and animals. The town where he lived commissioned Hector to create a life-size sculpture of birds for the lobby at the town hall. The lobby was small, so Hector thought the best use of the space would be to suspend the sculptures from the ceiling. He proposed a small flock of Canada Geese because of their size and the V formation in which they fly.

The work of art was completed and installed to great acclaim by the town and the town's inhabitants. It became well known and as Hector's reputation grew, so did the crowds who came to admire his artwork. For a holiday season that was starting in December, the town council proposed that large red ribbons be tied around the necks of the Canada Geese in the lobby. It was discussed in council and approved that every year bows would be added to the sculpture to commemorate the festive season.

Unknown to Hector, bows were tied around the geese and the ribbon ceremony was completed. A few days later, a friend of Hector's mentioned that it was interesting to see how much the bows hide the necks on the geese, making them look deformed. Hector flew to the town hall to gaze dumbfounded upon his masterpiece looking like a decoration on the top of a gift parcel. "This doesn't fly with me," he muttered.

a. Discuss the issues raised by this fact situation. (LO 9.1, 9.2, 9.6)

b. What, if any, legal rights or remedies does Hector have to undo this action by the town council? (LO 9.6)

[See *Snow v. Eaton Centre Ltd.* (1982), 70 C.P.R. (2nd) 105.]

Case #2

Dan and Bre, recent graduates from a graphic design program, have decided to begin a graphic design business called "You Are Our Type." They are short of funds, so purchasing several pieces of expensive equipment as well as a rental location is prohibitive. Bre suggested that they use their own computers, printers, desks, couches, and items they individually have in their own apartments to create an office. As well, they would lease some office furniture and, rather than rent an office, would purchase a house close to downtown and set up their office there.

a. What advice would you give Dan and Bre? (LO 9.1, 9.2, 9.3, 9.4, 9.5)

b. Outline the areas of potential difficulties they may encounter if they go their separate ways in the business. (LO 9.3, 9.5)

Case #3

Vartoch had his eye on some land at the edge of town that he thought would be the perfect location for a restaurant with a takeout drive-through. It was close enough to the town that people could easily drive to it and it was large enough to accommodate a substantial parking lot and the driveway for takeout. Vartoch approached Wanda with his business plan and she loaned him $300,000, which was secured by a mortgage on the property when he purchased it. For over a year Vartoch struggled to get planning permission from the town for his project. The longer his application took, the harder it was becoming for him to be able to make the payments under the mortgage as funds were used up in making his application and arguing with the town council.

Unknown to Vartoch, the reason why the town's approval was delayed was because of planning discussions the town was having with the province about a new highway that would pass very close to the property Vartoch owned; the final decision and when construction would begin were still unknown. Wanda, as a member of the town council, was aware of the plans being discussed relating to the highway and that the value of Vartoch's property would go up considerably once the highway was approved. Needless to say, Wanda could not tell Vartoch anything about the highway plans because they were confidential. Eventually, Vartoch defaulted on his payments under his mortgage with Wanda.

Wanda, having heard that you took an excellent course in business law, has asked your advice on what her course of action should be. She confirms that the mortgage is two months in default and Vartoch is unable to make any payments.

a. Advise Wanda on the different remedies available to her as a result of Vartoch's default under the mortgage and the benefits and issues that each party may have. (LO 9.1, 9.2, 9.3)

b. Discuss whether Wanda's position on the town council should be considered an issue in these circumstances. (LO 1.4, 9.6)

CHAPTER 10

BUSINESS ORGANIZATION

Learning Objectives

After reading this chapter the student will:

LO 10.1	Understand the various forms of business organization for carrying on business
LO 10.2	Explain the nature of carrying on a business as a sole proprietor
LO 10.3	Explain the nature of a joint venture
LO 10.4	Explain the differences between a general partnership and a limited partnership
LO 10.5	Explain the nature of a corporation and the advantages or disadvantages of this form of business organization
LO 10.6	Describe the roles of shareholders, directors, and officers of a corporation
LO 10.7	Describe a franchise arrangement

HELP!

As a businessperson, you may experience any of these scenarios:

- HELP! I opened a candy store and used the name Tous Sweet for You. Now I'm told I have to file some form with the provincial government to carry on my business. Why is that necessary? I thought I just needed a place and a product.
- HELP! I hired a young man to help me sew buttons on the costumes for children that I make and sell. Someone said I would be responsible if a button wasn't sewn on correctly and a child choked on it. Seriously?!
- HELP! Without telling me, my partner bought an expensive lawn mower for our landscaping business that we can't afford. The dealership wants me to pay for it. I didn't agree to buy it. Why me?

- HELP! I've been asked to become a director of a company that transports and disposes of toxic waste as a business. There's no personal risk in being a director is there?

- HELP! Our company signed a contract to have a large and expensive conference room added to the building, and I just discovered one of our directors owns the construction company that was hired. That doesn't seem right, does it?

- HELP! My friend is a partner in a very successful business that operates white-water rafting adventures. She said they need more money to add skydiving to the business and is offering me a chance to get in on it. I have some extra cash to invest, but don't want to lose my other savings if someone is hurt and sues the business. Is there a way I can take part without taking the risk?

- HELP! I worked with a carpenter to make wooden chairs for a forest-themed restaurant. I provided the design, and he made the chairs. A patron sat down, and immediately stood up! A two-inch wood splinter was found to be the reason. The patron claims the carpenter is my partner, but I thought we were just working together on a project. Am I responsible for the patron being injured by the chair?

LO 10.1   10.1 Forms of Business Organization

An individual starting a grass cutting business on his or her own may be seen as a sole proprietor, totally responsible for the activities of their **sole proprietorship**. But if they link up with another person to offer grass cutting and garden care, the business may morph into a different legal entity—such as a **partnership**, in which each of them may be totally responsible for the activities of the operation, or perhaps a **joint venture**. If the operation grows large enough, they may choose to incorporate to limit their personal exposure to any lawsuits that may arise from the business's activities.

Sole Proprietorship—a business operated for a profit by one individual who is responsible for the debts and liabilities.

Partnership—a legal relationship between two or more persons carrying on a business for the purpose of earning a profit.

Joint Venture—a business activity, usually for a specific project or time period, carried on by two or more parties according to terms and conditions set out in a contract.

You can choose from among different forms for operating a business in Canada. The form chosen will depend on a number of factors, including such things as the number of people involved, the nature and size of the business, the risk involved with the products or services, financial requirements, and tax issues.

Business activities are highly regulated, and once the form for carrying on business is decided there may be a requirement to obtain municipal or provincial licences and to file paperwork with the government to indicate who is responsible for the products and services being offered to the public.

Garnet was in the last semester of a two-year entrepreneurship program at his college. Garnet's studies took up most of his time, and when he needed a break he would spend time on his hobby—raising tropical fish and birds. For most of his life, Garnet had kept tropical fish, breeding them to sell to pet shops and, one of his passions, developing new strains of angelfish.

At one point he'd had 12 fish tanks of different sizes in his room at home. Selling to the local pet shops helped him get the cash for his other passion, exotic birds. Garnet had a breeding pair of lovebirds, a few canaries, and, his pride and joy, a blue and gold macaw, a parrot that he had rescued from a local animal shelter when it was a young fledgling.

Garnet's hobby took up all the space in his room and he had not been able to add any more birdcages or aquariums for over a year. His parents had been on his case about how much space they took up and the constant chirping and birdcalls that could be heard throughout the house. His parents also kept asking what Garnet's plans were following the completion of his diploma at the end of the term, and how was he going to earn money to pay for his hobby.

One Saturday morning while Garnet drove his car across town to deliver a batch of young angelfish he had sold to a pet shop, he was thinking about his last term assignment for college, an analysis paper on starting up a new business. As Garnet entered the pet shop, with its gleaming rows of brightly lit fish tanks and the melodious chirps, cheeps, and songs coming from the wall of birdcages, it suddenly dawned on him—the answer to his space problems, his parents, and his last assignment. Garnet would open his own pet shop! Quickly pocketing the money from the sale of the angelfish, Garnet raced home and immediately booted up his laptop to start working on a business plan. He had a lot of the equipment and stock already at home and he knew a great deal about tropical fish and birds. It would be brilliant! It would be fun! He would make lots of money doing what he loved! He would get an A on his final assignment! On the spot, he decided he would name his pet shop "Water and Wings." (Note that marketing had not been Garnet's best class.)

Over the course of this chapter we will follow Garnet's progress and the issues he has to deal with in turning his decision into a reality.

LO 10.2   10.2 Sole Proprietorships

Garnet knew that the first thing he needed to determine was the form of business organization that would meet his needs. His plan was to keep his expenses low at the beginning by running the business on his own. Garnet would be responsible for all the decisions as to what stock to carry. All profit after paying for operating expenses would be used for him to draw a salary. Overhead would be minimal and he would keep the business as simple as possible, hiring an employee only after the business had become well established.

A sole proprietorship is a fairly simple form of business organization that is used when an individual owns a business and is solely responsible for its operations. This form of business structure is relatively easy to set up and is attractive for small businesses because the individual/owner makes all the decisions and receives all the benefits. Starting up can be as simple as choosing a name, registering it with the appropriate office of the provincial government, and obtaining the necessary licence to operate the business if one is required—for example, a liquor licence for a bar.

DID YOU KNOW?

Registration of a Business Name

If an individual uses a business name that includes their first and last name, they may not have to register the name with the provincial government. Some provinces, such as Saskatchewan, require the name to be registered even when operating under the individual's own name. The relevant statute should be checked for the province in which the sole proprietorship is operating.

DID YOU KNOW?

Your Form and Fee, Please

Registration of a business name is a straightforward process that can be handled by the business owner without a lawyer. It requires the completion of a form with such information as the name of the business, its address, and the name of the individual operating the business. Written instructions on completing the form are provided along with the form. A relatively small registration fee is paid and the form is filed with the relevant office of the provincial government. Generally, registrations must be renewed after a certain number of years that varies according to the jurisdiction. In Manitoba renewal is every three years, while in Ontario it is every five years. A penalty may be imposed on an individual operating a business that has failed to register when required.

One disadvantage of a sole proprietorship is that the individual is personally responsible for the debts and liabilities of the business, which means the owner's business assets (stock, equipment) and personal assets (car, house, bank account) are at risk if the business owes money or is sued. Unlimited personal liability for the business means that for sole proprietors insurance is an important element in managing the risk of running a business.

The ability to do tax planning is limited for a sole proprietor, because profits are taxed as personal income in the hands of the individual at their personal tax rate.

© Hofred | Dreamstime.com

LEGAL SCENARIO

The Absent-Minded Employee—Or, What Was I Thinking?

Helena operated a toy store as a sole proprietor. She had hired a student, Sam, from the local college on a part-time basis to help in the store. A delivery of small wooden rolling pins for a toy kitchen set arrived on Friday and Helena asked Sam to stack them on the shelves first thing the next morning.

To save time, Sam took the rolling pins out of the box and left them on the floor in front of the shelf so they would be ready for stacking before customers began to come in. On Saturday morning Sam arrived to hear the store phone ringing. He answered the call, responded to a customer's question, and then began to rearrange the display in the front window. Helena asked him where the toy rolling pins were. At the same moment they heard a customer cry out, followed by a heavy thump! "I've found them," Sam answered, rushing to help the customer who was lying on the floor surrounded by wooden rolling pins.

The customer suffered a concussion and severe back injuries and was off work for three weeks. Helena is being sued for $100,000 and is working with her insurance company to settle the matter. The injuries sustained by the customer were the result of the negligence of Helena's employee, Sam. On the basis of vicarious liability, Helena, as a sole proprietor, would be personally responsible for the damages caused by Sam's actions in the course of his employment.

Garnet realized that in selling fish to pet shops he had already started a sole proprietorship. This simple form of doing business appeared to meet his needs, so when he graduated from college Garnet found a small storefront location that was perfect for his business venture and registered his business name in compliance with the statute.

It did not take long for Garnet's business to establish an excellent reputation due to his knowledge and ability to develop a good relationship with his customers. Soon, Garnet was carrying new lines of equipment and unusual varieties of fish and birds that brought in customers from across town. Business was growing so well that the shop was becoming too small to handle it all. However, the growth allowed Garnet to hire an employee, which meant Garnet could spend time attending pet fairs to promote Water and Wings. It was at a pet fair that he met Aneka at the coffee bar. They began talking and she told him she had a Lhasa Apso. He asked if that was a type of latte and she explained patiently that it was a breed of dog.

Aneka was active in the dog show circuit with her Lhasa Apso show dogs, which she also bred and sold. She had a small dog grooming and dog supplies business, which had become so busy that she had outgrown her present location and was looking to move. Garnet and Aneka began talking and soon realized that if they combined their operations, they could afford to lease premises big enough for both their businesses and at a better rental rate. Further, each of them might do better from offering their customers more services.

Garnet and Aneka had several meetings to discuss how to structure this new, expanded pet shop. Both of them wanted to remain hands-on in running their areas of the store and making decisions, but they wanted to share costs to reduce their overhead. Neither of them wanted to set up anything too complicated. They discussed the possibility of making it a joint venture or perhaps going into a partnership. They decided to name the new business "Water, Paws, and Wings." (Hey—they chose it, not us!)

LO 10.3   10.3 Joint Ventures

A joint venture is a business activity, usually for a specific project or time period, that is carried on by two or more businesses.

DID YOU KNOW?

Joint Ventures and Contracts

Joint venture operations generally involve a contractual relationship of some form. There is no specific legislation in Canada governing joint ventures.

A joint venture may take the form of an *equity joint venture*, in which a separate legal entity is created such as a **corporation** or a partnership, with each party contributing capital or assets and participating in control through an ownership interest. A shareholder agreement or partnership agreement, depending on the type of separate legal entity created, is put in place to address such issues as dispute resolution or transfer of ownership interest.

Corporation—a legal entity created by government legislation that has a separate existence from its owners.

DID YOU KNOW?

Equity Joint Ventures

An equity joint venture is a separate legal entity to which the individual parties contribute capital or assets. Ownership interest in the legal entity entitles the parties to participate in control of the business and a share of the profits.

A second form of joint venture is the *contractual joint venture*. This form of business organization can be put together fairly quickly and is based on written contractual arrangements in which the parties address issues such as:

- Capital contributions and financing,
- The scope of the activities to be undertaken and what happens if the objectives are not achieved,
- Arrangements concerning management of operations,
- Allocations of profit and loss,
- Dispute resolution procedures,
- The ability of a party to transfer its ownership interest, and
- The relationship between the parties.

If the parties do not want the operation to be seen as a partnership, it is usually specifically stated in the contract.

DID YOU KNOW?

A Rose by Any other Name

A contractual joint venture is sometimes referred to as a strategic alliance, co-ownership, or teaming arrangement.

After doing some further research, Garnet and Aneka decided their plans did not reflect a joint venture arrangement. They began to explore the possibility of entering into a partnership.

© Diamondimages | Dreamstime.com

LO 10.4   **10.4** Partnerships

Each province or territory has passed specific legislation dealing with partnerships. Generally a **partnership** is defined as being "the relationship that subsists between persons carrying on a business in common with a view to profit" (*Partnerships Act* R.S.O. 1990, c. P.5 sec. 2). For our purposes, there are two main types of partnerships: a partnership (sometimes referred to as a general partnership) and a limited partnership. Each form has advantages and disadvantages for purposes of carrying on a business.

> **Partnership**—a legal relationship between two or more persons carrying on a business for the purpose of earning a profit.

DID YOU KNOW?

Formation of Partnerships in Quebec

In Quebec, a partnership is formed through a contract in which two or more individuals agree to carry on a business operation by providing property, knowledge, and/or activities, and to share the profits.

No partnership declaration in Quebec? In that case...

The province of Quebec recognizes the existence of an undeclared partnership where a partnership does not make the necessary declaration of partnership required under the provincial legislation.

General Partnerships

The advantage of a general partnership is the simplicity and informality involved in using it to organize a business. Generally, the only filing that is required is the registration of the firm's name if the partners are carrying on the business under a name other than their own. As well, a partnership may be required to register in each province or territory in which it is carrying on business.

No contract is required for the formation of a partnership as long as the statutory definition of partnership is met. A disadvantage is that a partnership may be established unintentionally by the parties, with all the responsibilities attached to being a partner, if the elements of the definition are found present in the business operations.

 CASE STUDY

Pinteric v. People's Bar and Eatery Ltd., [2001] O.J. No. 499

The case of *Pinteric v. People's Bar and Eatery Ltd.* illustrates that a partnership will be found to exist if the parties have acted as such, even in the absence of an express oral or written agreement.

Facts: The defendant claimed there was no express agreement of partnership between the restaurant and the individual who caused the plaintiff's injury. The plaintiff claimed an oral partnership agreement existed and the restaurant was responsible for the plaintiff's injuries caused by its partner.

Decision: The court held that because the individual had received "advances" rather than a salary, this indicated a partnership relationship between the restaurant and the individual.

The legislation sets out the rights and duties of the partners, such as the right to share equally in the profits of the business and an equal say in management decisions. However, the partners can modify this by a contract, called a **partnership agreement**, that clearly sets out the rights and obligations as the parties wish to arrange them among themselves. If a matter has not been covered by the partnership agreement, the legislation provides direction for resolving the issue. An example would be the dissolution of a partnership. The partners may arrange among themselves that the partnership will not dissolve upon the death or bankruptcy of a partner. However, in the absence of such a contractual arrangement, legislation generally states that a partnership will automatically dissolve upon the death or bankruptcy of a partner. It is usually recommended that the parties put their contractual arrangements in writing in the form of a partnership agreement, and that this be done when the partnership is formed.

Partnership Agreement—an agreement among all the partners in which such issues as management and procedures for carrying on the business, the division of profits and contributions, and dispute resolution are addressed.

A partnership is not a separate legal entity from the partners. For tax purposes, a partnership is very similar to a sole proprietorship as income is allocated to the individual partners according to their percentage interest and taxed at the partner's personal rate.

Stuart Miles / Shutterstock.com

A partner is considered an agent for the other partners and consequently a contract signed by one partner is binding on all the partners. Each partner is personally liable for the debts, actions, and obligations of the other partners in a partnership to an unlimited degree if the assets of the partnership are not sufficient. This liability is "joint and several." This means the partners would divide the liability according to their interest in the partnership, but also that each partner is individually responsible for the entire amount of any damages or penalty. For example, if a company had a judgment against the partnership for the price of a printer that had been sold to the partnership but not paid for, each partner would be responsible for contributing their share to the damages awarded under the judgment. If one or more partners are unable to pay, an individual partner may be responsible for paying the entire amount; that individual would then have to look to the other partners for their share of the amount that had been paid under the judgment. As a result, it becomes very important to have adequate and appropriate insurance to cover the risks involved in a business's activities.

As agents for each other, partners have a *fiduciary duty* that requires them to act in the best interests of the partnership. Among other things, a partner must disclose any conflict of interest he or she may have, must not compete with the partnership, and must not take personal advantage of information that becomes available through the partnership.

CASE STUDY

Blue Line Hockey Acquisition Co. v. Orca Bay Hockey Limited Partnership, 2008 BCSC 27 (CanLII)

The case of *Blue Line Hockey Acquisition Co. v. Orca Bay Hockey Limited Partnership* illustrates when a fiduciary duty comes to an end.

Facts: Three businessmen, Gaglardi, Beedie, and Aquilini, agreed to work together with the intention of purchasing an interest in the National Hockey League team the Vancouver Canucks.

After some months, the three men agreed that Aquilini would no longer be part of the group. When Aquilini tried to re-join the group, he was rejected. He then successfully negotiated on his own for an interest in the Vancouver Canucks. Gaglardi and Beedie brought a legal action against Aquilini claiming a partnership existed and they were the owners of the interest in the Canucks. They claimed the original decision among the three of them to work together had created a partnership. Consequently, Aquilini had a fiduciary duty to act in their interest as partners as well as a duty not to compete with them.

Decision: The court held that Aquilini was free to act on his own, as no partnership existed. All the parties had agreed to Aquilini leaving the group and he had not been allowed to re-join later when he asked. Any relationship with the other two parties ended when he left the group, and any fiduciary duties owed to them ended at that time.

Aneka and Garnet had a partnership agreement prepared that set out their rights and obligations in operating the expanded pet shop as well as the division of profits from the business. The firm's name was registered under the appropriate legislation and they began to look for new premises. Following a conversation on commercial leases with a friend of Garnet's named Zander, who had opened a music studio, they successfully negotiated a lease in an excellent location and were soon open for business.

Business continued to grow rapidly for the new partnership. Aneka's talents in dog grooming attracted more and more customers to the shop. Her reputation for breeding and selling show quality Lhasa Apso puppies was known across the province. They offered new lines of dog toys and leashes. Garnet was known for the variety of freshwater tropical fish he had for sale, and the selection of exotic birds he had available. People were driving an hour or two to shop at Water, Paws, and Wings for their pets. Some customers said they would like to be part of the business if ever there was a chance.

Garnet and Aneka began to discuss developing the business further. Aneka wanted to begin importing luxury dog accessories from various countries. Garnet talked about carrying saltwater fish and a wider range of birds: crested cockatoos, breeding pairs of cockatiels, and some new breeds of singing canaries. However, to do this would require a significant amount of money, and both of them had exhausted their savings and the extra cash their families had offered. They wanted to continue to control the development and management of their business, but needed to find a source of funds.

One afternoon Garnet was talking with one of his regular customers about their plans for expansion and the need to find the money to finance it. The customer said that Water, Paws, and Wings was exactly the type of investment opportunity she had been looking for. She had some extra funds to invest in a growing, well-managed business, but didn't have the time to be involved because her dental practice was so busy. Garnet had a sudden, scathingly brilliant idea! He quickly guided the customer to the back of the store, where Aneka was styling a poodle's fur. He introduced the customer as the answer to their prayers—and then thought to ask her name.

Limited Partnerships

Garnet had suddenly remembered reading about limited partnerships in *Canadian Business Law Today*, the excellent textbook used in his business law course at the college. He recalled that a limited partnership was a form of partnership in which investors were only at risk for the amount of money or assets contributed to the business, and they could not take part in the control or conduct of the business. In essence, the investors were silent partners—exactly what Garnet and Aneka were looking for.

A **limited partnership** consists of at least one general partner that assumes responsibility for managing the business of the partnership and is liable for all the debts and obligations of the partnership to an unlimited degree, and at least one limited partner whose liability is limited to the amount of money contributed to the partnership business. The limited partner has an interest in the firm, but may not take part in managing the business or it will be seen as a general partner and also become personally liable for the partnership debts and obligations.

> **Limited Partnership**—consists of at least one general partner that is liable for the debts and obligations of the partnership to an unlimited degree and at least one limited partner whose liability is limited to the amount contributed to the partnership business.

The common law provinces and territories recognize the limited partnership as a form of business organization. Generally it is created by filing a declaration of partnership under the relevant statute in the jurisdiction in which it is organized and registering the name of the limited partnership. Also, an *extraprovincial limited partnership*—one that, for example, owns real property or is soliciting business within a province or territory other than the one in which it was created—may have to file a declaration or register with the government authorities in the jurisdiction in which it is operating.

© Masterofall686 | Dreamstime.com

> Link to find provincial forms for declaration of limited partnership: www.forms.ssb.gov.on.ca

DID YOU KNOW?

Limited Liability Partnerships

Several Canadian jurisdictions permit the formation of a limited liability partnership (LLP), principally for providing professional services such as accounting or legal services. Partners remain liable for their own negligence or wrongful actions, but not for the negligence or wrongful conduct of the other partners.

DID YOU KNOW?

Limited Liability Partnerships in British Columbia

In British Columbia, an LLP is not restricted to the provision of professional services and can be used for any type of business activity. Generally, the liability of a partner in an LLP in British Columbia is limited to his or her capital investment and a partner is not personally liable for the obligations of the LLP.

Generally, a record of limited partners is required to be kept by the general partner at the principal place of business in the jurisdiction. Limited partners are provided certain rights under the legislation, such as a right to inspect the books of the business of the limited partnership and to provide advice to management, provided they do not take part in the decision-making process. Profits or losses from the business of the limited partnership flow through to the limited partners according to the percentage of their contribution and are taxed in their hands at the individual's personal rate.

LEGAL SCENARIO

The Case of the Disappearing Limited Liability

Arthur had completed his Diploma in Culinary Arts and wanted to open an organic restaurant specializing in nouvelle fusion cuisine. His aunt, Tamzin, was wealthy and agreed to finance his dream. Together, they decided to create a limited partnership as a way to fund Arthur's venture. Financially this would help Tamzin because the restaurant was expected to lose money for the initial two-year period while it became established and she could write off her percentage of the losses against her income. It was anticipated that the restaurant would start making some profit by the third year and generate greater income annually after that. Tamzin, as the limited partner, would receive annual reports on finances and how business was developing.

In its third year, the restaurant was still operating at a loss and Tamzin was becoming concerned, as she no longer needed losses to reduce her income. By the fourth year she was becoming anxious, and began to turn up at the restaurant at odd times to see how things were going. In the fifth year, Tamzin began to suggest improvements to operations and had gone so far as to fire a couple of servers she thought were particularly slow at waiting on tables and to hire a new server to replace the other two. Arthur wasn't happy, but she was his aunt and a major investor. When a customer became seriously ill and almost died from tainted seafood, Arthur and Tamzin were sued for over a million dollars.

Tamzin claimed that the business was a limited partnership and, as the limited partner, she was liable only for the amount she had invested in the operation. The customer would probably succeed in claiming that Tamzin has lost her limited liability status by taking on a role in making management decisions, and now is liable as a general partner for all the debts and obligations of the partnership.

Although the general partner in a limited partnership has all the rights and duties, and exposure for liability, of a partner as previously discussed in this chapter, there are some restrictions on the general partner's ability to take certain actions without the consent of all the limited partners. Examples would be the addition of a party as a general partner or the continuation of the business of the limited partnership on the death or retirement of a general partner.

Many of the issues dealt with in the legislation are subject to any agreement made between the parties. For example, in some jurisdictions a limited partnership does not need to dissolve on the death of the general partner if the limited partnership agreement specifically states that any remaining general partners are allowed to continue the business of the partnership. It is strongly recommended that a written limited partnership agreement be drawn up to modify any matters specifically addressed in the relevant partnership legislation that the parties wish to revise, or to handle any issues not dealt with in the statute.

Garnet and Aneka created a business plan and financial forecast for their proposed limited partnership and four individuals promptly agreed to invest their money. A limited partnership agreement was drafted up, the appropriate declaration filed with the government, and the limited partnership's name was registered. The additional capital allowed Aneka and Garnet to expand the product lines carried by the business and to start selling online. Their reputation was so strong that it brought in customers from across the province and there was significant profit from operations. Garnet bought a condominium and moved out of the basement of his parents' house. Aneka bought a house with a huge backyard for her dogs to enjoy. Both of them traded in beaten up, old cars for brand-new, expensive vehicles with all the options. For the first time, Aneka owned a car that was younger than her.

The next phase in the development of the business started because Garnet was having a bad day. Garnet had slept in and arrived late to open the store that morning. At the store, he had taken his favourite blue and gold macaw parrot out of its cage and let it climb onto the eight-foot-tall parrot tree that stood beside the cash register. When the macaw reached the top it turned the food tray upside down, spilling the entire contents onto the floor. The day was not going well. Just before lunch break, a customer who had bought a canary brought it back claiming something just wasn't right with it; the bird sang beautifully, but it didn't move around the cage much and seemed to want to stay in one place. The customer repeatedly insisted that Garnet do something about it. In frustration, Garnet replied to the customer, "What did you want, a singer or a dancer?" (Garnet immediately regretted his words!)

Outraged at being spoken to in this manner, the customer started shouting at Garnet, which startled the parrot, causing it to jump off the tree onto the head of the angry customer. The customer screamed, which caused a store employee carrying a 25-kilogram bag of dog food to turn quickly to see what was happening, dropping the bag on another customer's foot, breaking three toes. (Cast your mind back to Chapter 3 on torts, where we discussed personal injury, damages, and vicarious liability—are you surprised this fact situation wasn't part of the review questions? Notice how these different areas of law begin to intersect.)

After working with their insurance company and resolving the various legal claims arising from this unhappy event, Aneka and Garnet realized they had experienced a very close call and some bad customer relations. It could have been much worse. However, it made them aware that as general partners with unlimited personal liability, their newly acquired assets—houses, cars—were at risk if something more serious occurred.

Aneka had heard that with a corporation the owners/shareholders had the protection of limited liability; so, personal assets might be protected from the debts and liabilities of the business operated by the company. She mentioned to Garnet that perhaps they should consider a corporation as a form of business organization. Garnet immediately agreed to look into it further.

LO 10.5   10.5 Corporations

A corporation is a distinct legal entity created by a government statute with the legal abilities of a natural person. A corporation may own land, borrow or lend money, carry on a business, and sue or be sued in its own right. A corporation is considered to be separate from its owners, the shareholders, who, unlike the sole proprietor or a partner, have limited liability and are not personally responsible for the debts or obligations of the corporation. It is one of the most common forms of business organization in Canada.

CASE STUDY

Rockwell Developments Ltd. v. Newtonbrook Plaza Ltd. (1972), 27 D.L.R. (3d) 651

The case of *Rockwell Developments Ltd. v. Newtonbrook Plaza Ltd.* illustrates the separation of shareholder and corporation.

Facts: K owned almost all the shares of Rockwell Developments Ltd., a real estate company he had incorporated. A contractual dispute arose between Rockwell and another company, Newtonbrook Plaza Ltd. In the course of events, Rockwell started a legal action against Newtonbrook for specific performance of the contract and lost. The court awarded costs of $4,800 to Newtonbrook. Newtonbrook tried to recover the costs from Rockwell, only to discover that Rockwell's sole asset was a bank account that held $31.85. When Newtonbrook tried to recover the costs awarded against Rockwell from its main shareholder, K, personally, they were unsuccessful.

DID YOU KNOW?

Corporation or Company?

In some Canadian jurisdictions, the incorporating statutes use the term "company" instead of corporation.

DID YOU KNOW?

Limited Liability May Be Qualified

Although a shareholder is considered to have limited liability, in certain exceptional circumstances—for example, the corporation being used to commit a fraud—the shareholder may be considered personally responsible for a corporation's liability.

There are federal and provincial/territorial statutes that govern the incorporation and regulation of corporations. These statutes are similar in most respects but each jurisdiction has specific elements that should be considered. Issues such as ease of incorporation, fees, taxes, and licensing requirements may influence the decision whether a federal or provincial/territorial corporation is used for business purposes. If a business will be subject to federal government regulations, then a federal corporation should be used. Some organizations, such as banks and insurance companies, are governed by statutes that are specific to that industry, rather than general federal or provincial/territorial corporation statutes.

Link to *Canada Business Corporations Act*, R.S.C. 1985, c. C-44: http://laws-lois.justice.gc.ca/eng/acts/C-44/

Link to *Business Corporations Act* (Ontario), R.S.O. 1990, c. B. 16: https://www.ontario.ca/laws/statute/90b16; *Business Corporations Act* (Nova Scotia) R.S., c. 101: http://www.nslegislature.ca/legc/statutes/corporations%20registration.pdf; *Business Corporations Act* (British Columbia): http://www.bclaws.ca.

A decision to incorporate provincially or territorially would be appropriate if the intention is to carry on business primarily within that specific jurisdiction. A corporation has the ability to operate outside of the jurisdiction in which it is incorporated; however, as an extraprovincial/territorial corporation it is necessary to register or be licensed in the territory or province in which it will be carrying on business prior to commencing operations. As well, there may be annual filings and notices required.

A federal corporation has the right to carry on business in any province or territory but is subject to the laws of the jurisdiction in which it operates, and may have to register with the appropriate government department if opening an office or holding assets in the province or territory.

Methods of Incorporation

There are three methods by which a corporation may be created under provincial/territorial legislation or the federal statute. In Prince Edward Island, an application is made to the provincial government, which issues Letters Patent granting a charter that creates the corporation. In Nova Scotia, documents entitled the Memorandum of Association and the Articles of Association are filed with the government, which issues a Certificate of Incorporation. Other jurisdictions require Articles of Incorporation or their equivalent to be filed and a Certificate of Incorporation is issued creating the corporation. The incorporating documents set out the corporation's purpose and such information as the number of directors and the types of shares it will have.

© Supandi Munawi Wijaya | Dreamstime.com

DID YOU KNOW?

Corporations Canada @ Industry Canada

Corporations Canada, a branch of Industry Canada, administers the *Canada Business Corporations Act*. Federal incorporation forms are available by Internet, by mail, and online.

There are several procedural steps for incorporation, including the selection and approval of a name, the selection of directors, and the completion and filing of the incorporating documents with a provincial/territorial government or the federal government.

At the time of incorporation, the director or registrar responsible for registrations will assign a number to the corporation for identification purposes. As well, every corporation must have a name that is registered with the government. If the business is to be carried on using a specific name, it must have three elements:

1. A distinctive element that is a unique identifier of the name (for example a created word such as "KODAK");
2. A descriptive element that describes the company's line of business (for example, "Manufacturing"); and
3. A legal element that indicates its legal status as a corporation (Limited, Incorporated, Corporation or their abbreviations or the French equivalent if operating in Quebec).

If the business is not concerned about the name it will be using for its operations, or it is in a hurry to incorporate and wants to save time and the cost of doing a search with a name search company to confirm the availability of a name, it can use the number assigned at the time of incorporation. In this situation, the name of the incorporating jurisdiction is added to the number, for example 123456 Canada, along with the required legal element of Ltd., Inc., or Corp. (or the full form of these abbreviations). If the numbered company intends to carry on business under a trade or business name other than its numbered name, it must complete the necessary form required by the jurisdiction in which it will be operating and register the name with the appropriate government department.

DID YOU KNOW?

Corporate Name Search

The selection and approval of a corporate name that complies with applicable provincial/territorial or federal legislation and regulations may require a name search to be completed and a report generated using a search company authorized for this purpose. The submission of a computer-generated printout confirming the availability of the name is a requirement for incorporation in most jurisdictions.

Link to Provincial Form 2 (Ontario) for registration of a business name by a corporation under the *Business Names Act*: www.forms.ssb.gov.on.ca (key in form 007-07197).

Link to Industry Canada's "Guide to Federal Incorporation": https://www.ic.gc.ca/eic/site/cd-dgc.nsf/vwapj/Guide_2011-En.pdf/$FILE/Guide_2011-En.pdf

Link to federal incorporation forms: https://www.ic.gc.ca/eic/site/cd-dgc.nsf/eng/cs03988.html

Link to a page showing an example of a completed Federal Articles of Incorporation with two classes of shares: https://www.ic.gc.ca/eic/site/cd-dgc.nsf/eng/cs04977.html

DID YOU KNOW?

Office of the Registrar for Provinces or Territories

For provincial or territorial incorporations contact the office of the registrar for the province or territory. Some provinces and territories have websites where the appropriate forms can be downloaded.

Link to a sample of blank Provincial Articles of Incorporation (key in form 007-07116): www.forms.ssb.gov.on.ca

Shares

Shares represent ownership interest in the corporation and are held by shareholders. They entitle the holder to certain rights involving the corporation. Corporations commonly have two classes of shares, common shares and preference shares, each class usually having different rights and restrictions attached to them. At least one class of shares must carry the right to vote. **Common shares** normally possess the right to vote on certain corporate matters, to share in dividends when declared by the corporation, and to participate in the breakup value of the corporation upon dissolution. **Preferred (preference) shares** are usually non-voting, and carry certain rights in priority to other classes of shares, such as the right to have dividends paid first, or to the return of capital before any capital is paid to common shareholders.

Shares—percentage interests in a corporation.

Common Shares—have the right to vote on certain corporate matters and to receive a percentage share of the residual property of the corporation on its dissolution.

Preferred (Preference) Shares—have a priority over other classes of shares in terms of certain corporate actions, such as the payment of dividends.

DID YOU KNOW?

Authorized Capital

The share structure of a corporation reflects the number and class of shares that a corporation may issue to its shareholders and is set out in the incorporating document.

DID YOU KNOW?

Equity Financing

The purchase of shares by shareholders is known as an equity financing.

DID YOU KNOW?

Dividend Payments

Dividends are a method of distributing the profits earned by a corporation from its business activities to its shareholders, with payment based on the number of shares held.

LO 10.6   10.6 Ownership and Management

Shareholders

The shareholders own the corporation, but not the business or the assets of the corporation. Depending on the class of share held and the rights attached to the share, they may possess such rights as the ability to vote in the annual election of directors, to inspect certain corporate records, to approve the financial statements and the company's annual report, and to share in the breakup value of the corporation upon its dissolution.

MaleWitch / Shutterstock.com

As a separate legal entity the corporation is responsible for the debts or obligations it incurs to run the business, and the shareholders' liability is limited to the amount invested in purchasing the shares. This limited liability on the part of the shareholder is an important feature of the corporate form of business organization and the management of business risk.

DID YOU KNOW?

Shareholder Guarantee

If a shareholder personally guarantees a company's debts, the benefit of limited liability is lost, and the guarantor's personal assets may be at risk for the obligations of the corporation.

Directors and Officers

The directors of a corporation are responsible for managing the business and affairs of the company and for supervising the management team. Management of the company is separate from the owners, and the directors must act and make decisions that are in the best interests of the corporation—not of the shareholders. Directors and officers have a **director's fiduciary duty** to act honestly and in good faith in the best interests of the corporation. This would require, for example, disclosure of any conflicts of interest, and not taking advantage of information obtained while acting as a director or an officer. They must take reasonable steps to make sure a violation of their fiduciary duty does not occur. To avoid liability for any failure in fulfilling their duty, a director or officer must demonstrate he or she exercised **due diligence** by showing their duties were performed with the care, diligence, and skill of a reasonably prudent person. If this standard of care is met, the director or officer may be able to avoid liability for a corporate action that has caused a problem or resulted in injury.

tinbee / Shutterstock.com

Director's Fiduciary Duty—an obligation to act honestly, in good faith and in the best interests of the corporation.

Due Diligence—the obligation for corporate directors to ensure proper measures have been taken to comply with legal duties.

CASE STUDY

Canada Safeway Ltd. v. Thompson, [1951] 3 D.L.R. 295

The case of *Canada Safeway Ltd. v. Thompson* illustrates a fiduciary duty owed by a director to the corporation.

Facts: The defendant was a director of a company that was looking for locations to purchase to expand its chain of grocery stores. The identification of suitable independent stores for the corporation to acquire was a major part of the defendant's duties. He arranged with a friend to buy the locations that were considered a good bargain and resell them to Canada Safeway without disclosing the defendant's ownership. Ultimately the defendant's interest in the transactions became known and the company brought a legal action against him.

Decision: The court held that the defendant was under a duty to acquire the properties for the corporation and held the properties as agent for the company. He was also in breach of his duty as a director to disclose his interest.

CASE STUDY

R v. Bata Industries Ltd. (1992), 9 O.R. (3d) 329

The case of *R v. Bata Industries Ltd.* illustrates a director's fiduciary duty and the defence of due diligence.

Facts: Bata Industries Ltd., a shoe manufacturing company, stored large containers of toxic industrial chemical waste outdoors in an unprotected location. Some of the containers became rusted and developed leaks, allowing the toxic waste to leach into the soil and the groundwater. The corporation and its three directors were charged under provincial environmental protection legislation. The directors were required under the statute to prove they were not negligent. All the defendants claimed they had demonstrated due diligence in carrying out their duties.

Decision: The court held that the corporation had not taken reasonable steps to ensure the system operated effectively to prevent the escape of toxic waste. Only one director, Mr. Bata, was able to successfully prove he was not negligent. The court found he had "responded to the matters brought to his attention promptly and appropriately. He had placed an experienced director on site and was entitled in the circumstances ... to rely upon his system ... unless he became aware the system was defective." The other two directors were found guilty and personally fined for their breach of the law.

Each province and territory, as well as the federal government, has restrictions on the minimum number of directors required and on who may act as a director of a corporation. Generally those qualifications require a director to be, among other things, at least 18 years old, of sound mind, and not bankrupt. Residency requirements for the directors exist as well. The federal *Canada Business Corporations Act* requires at least 25 percent of the directors of a federal corporation to be resident Canadians, and if the board comprises fewer than four directors at least one must be a resident Canadian. Each province/territory has different residency requirements that should be confirmed when creating a corporation within the jurisdiction. As noted, directors take on a number of responsibilities in managing the business of a corporation. In many jurisdictions, if they do not carry out their duties properly they may be personally liable for such things as employees' unpaid wages for a specified period of time, employee source deductions, and environmental pollution. In some circumstances, insurance can be purchased by the corporation to protect directors from certain liabilities.

The directors appoint officers who are responsible for the daily management of corporate activities. The responsibilities associated with each officer's appointment are set out in the bylaws of the corporation and are subject, as indicated previously, to the same fiduciary duty to act in the best interests of the corporation as the directors.

DID YOU KNOW?

Directors

Generally there is a legislative requirement for a minimum of three directors for a public company and a minimum of one director for a private company. It is not uncommon with private corporations that one individual fills the roles of shareholder, director, officer, and employee.

Shareholders' Agreements

In a company with three shareholders it could be important that, should one of them wish to sell their shares in the corporation, the other two shareholders would have the first opportunity to buy them. There may be a number of business and ownership issues that the shareholders would want to make arrangements for. A written **shareholders' agreement** can be used to restrict the transfer of shares to third parties, provide a formula for valuation of a shareholder's interest, provide provisions for the resolution of a dispute, or establish a condition that allows one shareholder to buy the other out in certain circumstances. A **unanimous shareholders' agreement** can be used to restrict some of the powers of the directors in managing the corporation, with the shareholders assuming responsibility for the rights that have been removed from the directors. It is recommended that a lawyer be consulted when drafting a shareholders' agreement.

Shareholders' Agreement—a written agreement between two or more shareholders of a corporation setting out specific terms and conditions that will govern their relationship during or after incorporation.

Unanimous Shareholders' Agreement—a written agreement among all of the shareholders of a corporation that restricts in whole or in part the powers of the directors to manage or supervise the management of the business and affairs of the corporation. (*Business Corporations Act*, R.S.O. 1990, c. B.16, s. 108(2))

Private and Public Corporations

A corporation raises capital by selling and issuing shares and is usually described as being a **private corporation** or a **public corporation**, depending on whether or not it offers to sell its shares to the general public.

Private Corporation—subject to a limit on its total number of shareholders whose shares are not offered for sale to the public.

Public Corporation—sells shares to the public through a recognized stock exchange in compliance with provincial or territorial securities regulations.

Corporations that offer to sell their shares to the public are highly regulated in Canada to ensure the public is protected from deceptive or fraudulent activity. These corporations are required to apply to a stock exchange before they are allowed to list their shares on it and sell to the public. A corporation selling through the stock market is required to register under the relevant statutes and will be subject to ongoing review by the appropriate government agencies. It is often described as an "offering corporation" in the governing legislation of the province or territory.

Link to the Toronto Stock Exchange: https://www.tmx.com.

DID YOU KNOW?

Canadian Public Company Information

Details including contact information, press releases, financial statements, and the Annual Report to Shareholders for every public company listed in Canada are available online at www.sedar.com.

Non-offering corporations are sometimes referred to as private or closely held corporations. This type of corporation does not offer to sell its shares to the general public and usually has restrictions in its incorporating documents on the transfer of shares or the total number of shareholders it may have. Private corporations are the most common corporate form used in Canada for business organization.

DID YOU KNOW?

Unlimited Liability Corporations

The unlimited liability corporation (ULC) is a type of corporation that has been structured for taxation purposes and is most often used by foreign investors expanding into Canada who are looking for advantageous tax treatment. Unlike shareholders of other corporations, shareholders of a ULC are personally liable for the debts of the corporation. Only Alberta, British Columbia, and Nova Scotia currently allow for the creation of this type of corporation as a form of business organization under their respective statutes.

Advantages and Disadvantages of Corporations

Advantages of corporations include the following:

- The greatest advantage of incorporation is the limited liability offered to shareholders, while sole proprietors and partners may be personally liable for the debts of their business operations.
- The ability to transfer shares of a corporation to other parties, for example on the sale of the corporation, makes the transfer of ownership much easier and simpler than the sale of assets required with a sole proprietorship or the transfer of an interest in a partnership.

- A corporation can easily raise funds through an equity financing by issuing shares to investors. There may be government grants and loans that are available only to corporations.

- The corporation is taxed separately on its earnings, while the shareholder is taxed only on dividends when declared. As well, various jurisdictions may apply lower tax rates to corporations.

- The separation of management and ownership in a corporation makes running a business easier if there are a large number of people involved with the company. Further, because the corporation is a separate legal entity with perpetual existence, it will continue to carry on business despite the death of a shareholder or director.

Disadvantages of corporations include the following:

- The disadvantages of incorporation are the time and costs associated with incorporation, the separate filing of taxes, the annual meetings of shareholders, and the ongoing recordkeeping obligations required for regulatory compliance.

After several discussions over copious amounts of coffee where they weighed the pros and cons of incorporating their operation, Garnet and Aneka decided that a provincial corporation would be the best form of organization for their business. They decided to offer preferred, non-voting shares with an annual dividend in the new company to their limited partners. Garnet and Aneka wanted to expand the business as well and thought this might be a good time to see if there might be other individuals interested in investing by purchasing preferred shares in the corporation. Garnet and Aneka would hold common shares with voting rights, which would allow them to determine who would be elected as directors. There would be two directors to start, Aneka and Garnet, so they could continue to direct how the business would operate. Both would be officers of the corporation. Aneka would take the offices of President and Treasurer; Garnet would hold the offices of Chair and Secretary. The corporation would be named "Water, Paws, and Wings Corp." (marketing still not being one of their strengths). The necessary incorporating documents were drafted and filed and the corporation was up and running.

Aneka's reputation on the dog show circuit continued to grow, bringing in more customers for dog grooming and orders for dog accessories from across the country. The online business became a major contributor to the corporation's income. After speaking with Garnet's friend Zander about the value of intellectual property to a business, and in particular the value of a well-designed trademark, Garnet and Aneka had a trademark designed for their company that gained immediate recognition through a multimedia publicity program. The business was growing so well that it was highlighted in several business magazines. Garnet and Aneka were profiled as young Canadian entrepreneurs to watch and requests came in for them to speak at various colleges and business conferences.

Their success caught the eye of a business consultant who approached them about taking their one of a kind operation to another level by franchising the business across the province, and possibly the country. Garnet and Aneka were aware of the success of other franchise operations, such as Canadian Tire, and eagerly agreed to meet and hear more about what would be involved.

LO 10.7   **10.7** Franchises

Franchise arrangements are governed generally by the law of contracts (for a refresher on contracts, refer to Chapters 5, 6, and 7). This type of business operation has grown so much that some provinces have enacted legislation specifically aimed at franchising.

A **franchise** is a contract by which the **franchisor** grants rights to the **franchisee** to use its business name, trademark, business methods, product lines, and advertising in connection with the supply of goods or services. The franchisee is independent from the franchisor, and is not a partner or an employee. The franchisee is required to conduct the business according to operating procedures and methods developed and controlled by the franchisor. The franchisor is compensated by the franchisee through a percentage of the profits from the business or a fee, and possibly from the sale of products of the franchisor.

Franchise—a business arrangement formed by a written agreement in which a business grants the right to use its trade name, trademark, and operating procedures to operate a similar business.

Franchisor—the person granting the rights under the franchise agreement.

Franchisee—the person receiving the rights from the franchisor under the franchise agreement.

The franchise agreement between the franchisor and franchisee is very detailed and covers all elements of the business relationship and the franchise operation. There is usually a condition that allows the franchisor to revoke the franchise agreement if the franchisee does not follow the exact terms of the contract.

A franchise arrangement can be very helpful to both parties. The franchisee has the opportunity to run his or her own business using a business model that has been proven successful. The franchisor is able to expand into new market areas without taking on the startup cost of a new operation or the risk associated with an untried location.

DID YOU KNOW?

Franchise Legislation

Alberta, Ontario, and Prince Edward Island have enacted specific franchising statutes. The legislation, among other matters, requires fair dealing in the franchise relationship and provides remedies to address any abusive conduct by the franchisor.

The consultant tabled a business proposal for Water, Paws, and Wings Corp. and left the meeting. Garnet turned to Aneka and suggested they talk about this opportunity over a Lhasa. Aneka groaned at Garnet's attempt at a joke based on their first meeting, shook her head slowly, and replied she would rather have a latte. The two entrepreneurs have a great deal to think about. (Okay, maybe not the best play on words, but....)

FOR REVIEW

Questions

1. What type of exposure to personal liability does the owner of a sole proprietorship have? (LO 10.1, 10.2)
2. Is a sole proprietorship taxed at the personal rate of the owner? (LO 10.2)
3. Do all of the partners in a limited partnership have joint and several liability for the debts of the partnership? (LO 10.4)
4. What involvement do the partners in a limited partnership have in the day-to-day business of the partnership? (LO 10.1, 10.4)
5. Can a partnership exist without the parties agreeing formally to create a partnership? (LO 10.1, 10.4)
6. What is the term used to describe the number and class of shares a corporation is authorized to issue? (LO 10.5, 10.6)

7. Which of the following are elected to their position in a corporation: (LO 10.6)
   a. Shareholders
   b. Officers
   c. Directors
8. In what situations would a corporation use a number name? (LO 10.5)
9. What is the test to determine if a business is being carried on as a partnership? (LO 10.1, 10.4)
10. Can an individual be a shareholder, director, and officer at the same time? (LO 10.6)

Activities

1. With reasons, explain which type of business operation each of the following is: (LO 10.1, 10.2, 10.3, 10.4)
   a. Collin has a landscape operation where he ploughs snow in the winter, cuts lawns in the spring and summer, and collects leaves in the fall. He has an uncle who loaned him $2,000 to buy his equipment.
   b. John and Helen own and operate a dog walking service in their neighbourhood for which they charge an hourly rate. Their main clients are the tenants of a large apartment complex.
   c. We Mine UR Business Inc. has drilling and exploration equipment for locating deposits of minerals. Trucks R Us Ltd. has transport trucks for carrying material dug out of the ground. The two corporations agree with Hector to use their respective equipment in testing Hector's field for mineral deposits that could be developed. Any income would be divided among the three of them.
2. What steps are necessary for a person to start a sole proprietorship? (LO 10.1, 10.2)
3. Briefly describe the two forms of joint venture that might be used to carry on business, and provide examples of when you might use them. (LO 10.3)
4. Briefly explain the three elements generally found in a corporate name and provide some examples of names that demonstrate those elements. (LO 10.5)
5. Compare the advantages and disadvantages of raising capital for a corporation through issuing shares. (LO 10.5)
6. Outline the advantages a private corporation would gain with a unanimous shareholders' agreement. (LO 10.5, 10.6)
7. Briefly explain a franchise as a form of doing business, and give an example. (LO 10.7)
8. Briefly explain two reasons for carrying on a business in the following form:
   a. A partnership (LO 10.4)
   b. A corporation (LO 10.5)
   c. A sole proprietorship (LO 10.2)
9. Discuss what joint and several liability in a partnership means and what steps you might take to limit the partners' exposure to risk. (LO 10.4)

CASES FOR DISCUSSION

Case #1

Cyndi wants to check with you before she says something to the general partner of the limited partnership in which she is a limited partner. At a conference, she saw some new computer systems that would help the business, and she would like to be able to tell management of the limited partnership about these systems. Because she receives information of this nature regularly, she wonders if she can provide advice to management from time to time. Advise her on this matter. (LO 10.1, 10.4)

Case #2

Janet and Jared had a partnership providing bookkeeping services to local businesses under the name of J&J Accounting. Jared had recently incurred some large gambling expenses and owed Elsie, his bookie, a considerable amount of money. Jared offered to work off his debts by providing bookkeeping services to Elsie's legitimate businesses in the evenings and on weekends. Things were working out until Jared made an error in his calculations on Elsie's accounts, which cost her $15,000 to correct.

Elsie called Janet and told her that she would bring an action against J&J Accounting to recover the money that Jared's negligent bookkeeping had cost her unless Janet paid her right away. "Talk to that jerk Jared, it has nothing to do with me!" is all Janet responded to Elsie before slamming the phone down. Elsie sued Janet and Jared as partners of J&J.

Outline and explain the legal implications of this fact situation for Janet and Jared. (LO 10.1, 10.4)

Case #3

Saldan was an employee of Organo Farm Corp. Organo owned and operated a 200-hectare farm and allowed Saldan to harvest soybeans from the fields. Saldan would pay the corporation a certain price per kilo. Hector, the president of Organo, had become unhappy with the price per kilo that Saldan was paying and the two of them got into a heated argument over the money. Hector had taken to carrying a gun to scare off rabbits from the fields and, in the heat of the argument, he took out the gun and shot Saldan, who died from his wounds (these cases are taking a rather dark turn, it seems).

The executor of Saldan's estate brought a legal action on behalf of Saldan's children against Organo Farm Corp., based on vicarious liability for the actions of its president, as well as Hector. Hector has very few assets but Organo has some very valuable equipment and the farmland. Hector has admitted his actions and his personal liability but Organo is not willing to admit liability, claiming Hector was not acting within the scope of his employment when he shot Saldan.

Outline the legal issues in this case and present arguments on behalf of the following: (LO 3.1, 3.2, 8.2, 10.1, 10.5, 10.6)

a. The executor of Saldan's estate; and
b. Organo Farm Corp.

[See *Hawes v. Ryczko*, British Columbia, 1988.]

CHAPTER 11

BANKING, CREDITORS' RIGHTS, AND BANKRUPTCY

Learning Objectives

After reading this chapter the student will:

LO 11.1   Understand the different financial institutions to which businesses have access

LO 11.2   Understand electronic commercial transactions

LO 11.3   Explain the financing of business operations

LO 11.4   Understand the remedies available to secured and unsecured creditors

LO 11.5   Describe insolvency and bankruptcy and the procedures involved

LO 11.6   Rank the creditors in a bankruptcy

HELP!

As a businessperson, you may experience any of these scenarios:

- HELP! I asked my bank for a business loan and they asked me for proof of income before they will answer. I asked first!
- HELP! A credit union loans manager is offering me a loan at a lower rate of interest than the bank where I have my accounts. Do I have to move all my business over to the credit union if I take the loan, or can I do business with more than one financial institution?
- HELP! The lender wants to use the app I designed as security for a loan. Really?! Is that possible?
- HELP! My company applied for a loan and the bank wants me to use my house as security for the loan to my business. What's up with that?
- HELP! What's a general security agreement and why is the lender insisting it's that or nothing?

- HELP! One of my creditors said she would "push me into bankruptcy." Come on … wouldn't it be better to let me keep the doors open and try to come to some arrangement with her?
- HELP! I was telling my uncle that my business couldn't pay its bills anymore. He suggested I transfer the company's main asset, the building it owns, into his name so I don't lose it because of the business debts. Is that a legitimate option?

LO 11.1   11.1 Financial Institutions

It had been a long day for Sal. Sal runs a small business providing financial advice to various organizations. He had opened his office several years ago after completing the business program at his college and receiving a business diploma. A classmate named Garnet, who was looking for money to purchase fixtures and equipment for his pet shop, had asked Sal to provide him with advice. It was this experience that taught Sal the importance of networking and contacts for the growth of a business. Garnet had referred other people to Sal, and Sal's operation had grown from there.

Today began with a startup technology company looking for funding. Next, it was a bakery having problems with creditors who wanted to repossess the ovens. It finished with Zander, a local musician referred to him by Garnet, who ran a very successful music studio. She had been asking about crowdfunding to raise money to make a CD of music for accordion and orchestra. When Sal told Zander that he had heard of her unique musical compositions but it appeared crowdfunding might be difficult, Zander muttered something about recognition being all well and good, but cash is king! It had been a long day for Sal.

After his last meeting, Sal finally had an opportunity to read and answer his emails from the day. Sal had a reputation for providing solid, innovative advice on money matters and posted a weekly blog on managing finances for small to medium sized businesses. He often received comments on his blog from businesses asking for advice. Sal opened his laptop to check the comments on his blog post from the night before. The first comment to catch his eye had the user name Confuzd in the Cty and an intriguing title: Credit Union??!

CONFUZD IN THE CTY: Hi Sal. I was introduced to a loans officer from a credit union today and she has offered my business a loan on incredibly good terms. However, I've never heard of this type of organization. Is it a form of bank or what????

SAL: Dear Confuzd. Every business has a relationship with a financial institution. A number of different organizations exist and, lucky for us, the competition among them is increasing. Federally chartered Canadian banks, foreign subsidiary banks, and branches of foreign banks offer financial services to Canadian businesses of all sizes. All are regulated under Canada's federal *Bank Act*. Other financial institutions looking to service your business needs are provincially chartered trust and loan companies, credit unions, and in some instances insurance companies. There also are caisses populaires; these exist primarily in Quebec or those provinces with large francophone communities. This results in a wide range of financing sources and options for a business to choose from for its financial services. Whichever you choose, there will be an account agreement between your business and the financial institution. This agreement should be reviewed carefully as it covers all the services offered to you by the organization, and will usually include matters such as who will be liable if a mistake is made, or how long a cheque or funds will be held before they are made available to you.

© Kevinbrine | Dreamstime.com

Sal pressed Send on his reply to Confuzd. He was ready to move on to the next comment when he heard his laptop ping, indicating a new comment had been posted. Looking at his screen, he read the title: YOU CAN EARN BIG MONEY WORKING FROM YOUR HOME!!! "Give me strength," Sal groaned as he hit the delete key.

Confuzd promptly responded with another question.

CONFUZD IN THE CTY: Hi Sal. I don't want to deal with instalment payments or cheques being returned because they bounced. I want to be as paperless as possible in my business. What is involved in order to offer my customers the options of using a credit card or debit transactions for making payments?

LO 11.2   **11.2** Electronic Commercial Transactions

SAL: Thanks for your question, Confuzd. The growth of e-banking and new forms of financial transactions involving Internet banking and electronic commercial transactions has taken business a long way toward cashless transactions becoming the basis for operations. However, we are not there quite yet! If this is the direction you want to go, you should be aware of the following information concerning credit cards and debit cards.

Credit Cards/Debit Cards

The electronic transfer of funds, where e-banking is available, has greatly reduced the use of **cheques**. The use of credit cards and debit cards in financial transactions has grown enormously in Canada. Although a business would not usually use a credit or debit card for the purchase of a major asset or large-scale inventory, they are used regularly for minor, everyday business purchases such as paper for a copier. Merchants pay a fee to a card issuer (VISA, American Express) in order to participate in a credit card or debit card network that allows their customers or clients to use this electronic payment service.

Cheques—bills of exchange drawn against a bank and payable on demand.

DID YOU KNOW?

The Federal Bills of Exchange Act

Section 16(1) of the federal *Bills of Exchange Act* (R.S.C. 1985, c. B-4) states: "a bill of exchange is an unconditional order in writing, addressed by one person to another, signed by the person giving it, requiring the person to whom it is addressed to pay, on demand or at a fixed or determinable future time, a sum certain in money to or to the order of a specified person or to bearer."

Credit cards and debit cards are not bills of exchange; consequently the federal *Bills of Exchange Act* does not govern the use of this substitute for money. The continuous growth in use of credit and debit cards in Canada resulted in the creation of the federal government's voluntary "Code of Conduct for the Credit and Debit Card Industry in Canada" (the Code). The Code's purpose is the promotion of fair business practices and increased disclosure with the goal of helping both consumers and merchants understand the costs and benefits associated with the use of credit and debit cards. The Code applies to both the issuers and the acquirers participating in payment card networks.

© Cafebeanz Company | Dreamstime.com

Link to the "Code of Conduct for the Credit and Debit Card Industry in Canada": http://www.fcac-acfc.gc.ca/Eng/forIndustry/publications/lawsReg/Pages/CodeofCo-Codedeco.aspx

DID YOU KNOW?

The Payment Card Networks Act covers electronic payments

The federal government's *Payment Card Networks Act* (s.c. 2010, c. 12, s. 1834) defines payment card networks as "an electronic payment system ... used to accept, transmit or process transactions made by payment card for money, goods or services and to transfer information and funds among issuers, acquirers, merchants and payment card users."

Link to the *Payment Card Networks Act:* http://laws-lois.justice.gc.ca/eng/acts/P-4.3/

Sal pressed Send and heard the familiar whooshing sound confirming his response to Confuzd's question had been posted. He looked down the list of comments and saw one titled "Need to Grow—Short on $$," written by someone who signed off as Crnch Time. Curious, Sal read the comment.

CRNCH TIME: Hi Sal. I own a company with great potential for growth. The problem is, I have used up all my available cash. I'm at a critical stage in developing the business and without more financing it may not manage to survive. I have borrowed money from my parents and relatives already (I'm avoiding family dinners and their questions!). What are my alternative sources for funds?

LO 11.3   **11.3** Financing Operations

SAL: Hi Crnch. What you are experiencing is not unusual for a startup company (the money crunch, not the avoiding family gatherings part). You need to determine your short-term money (capital) needs, as well as your long-term capital needs. Then you can consider whether to finance your business operations through debt or equity.

Debt or Equity

Debt financing involves borrowing the capital for a period of time and repaying the loan plus any interest charged, in accordance with the terms of the loan agreement. **Equity financing** is accomplished through the sale of shares in your corporation to investors. The investor receives an ownership interest in the company and its potential growth in exchange for the capital paid to buy the shares.

> **Debt Financing**—borrowing capital for a period of time and repaying the loan plus any interest charged in accordance with the terms of the loan agreement.

> **Equity Financing**—selling shares in a corporation to investors.

A financial institution, finance company, or an individual may be willing to lend money to a business on an unsecured basis, if it considers the loan to be a low risk. In this arrangement, the debtor promises to repay the loan in accordance with the terms of the lending agreement. If the debtor defaults on the repayment, the lender will sue for breach of the lending agreement and enforce its judgment against the debtor.

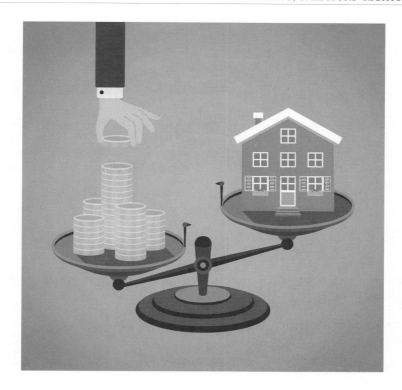

Alex Oakenman / Shutterstock.com

LO 11.4   11.4 Secured Creditors

More commonly, the financial institution will want to have its loan secured against some valuable property or asset of the borrower, as well as the debtor's promise to repay. The borrower's ability to repay is the primary interest of the lender. Financial institutions are in the business of lending money, not the business of taking property and selling it to get the capital and interest owed. However, the reassurance provided by the debtor giving the creditor the security of being able to claim and sell some valuable asset of the debtor will sometimes make the difference as to whether a loan will be made or not. The security is referred to as collateral and the creditor has the right to take and sell the collateral and use the money to pay down or eliminate the loan. A **security interest** in the collateral is created through an agreement between the lender and the borrower, referred to as a **security agreement**, setting out the rights, duties, and remedies available to both parties. It will usually take the form of a general security agreement in which the borrower offers all or specific assets as collateral for the repayment of the debt. If the collateral consists of a pool of assets that may change from time to time, for example the inventory of the business, it is referred to as a **floating charge**. This type of arrangement allows the business to continue to sell the secured assets in the normal course of business. When the loan is repaid, the interest in the secured property reverts to the borrower.

Security Interest—an interest in personal property that secures the payment of a debt.

Security Agreement—an agreement that sets out the rights and obligations of the borrower and lender and creates a security interest in the personal property of the borrower.

Floating Charge—a security interest on a class of collateral which may change, that allows the debtor to dispose of, replace, and add to assets in that class.

In the event of a default under the loan the lender can sell the secured assets. If the sale proceeds are not enough to eliminate the debt, the creditor can start a legal action for the balance owing based on breach of the lending agreement. The creditor must make a reasonable effort to obtain a fair price for the asset being sold, which may be done at public auction or possibly privately provided proper commercial procedures are followed. If the sale results in funds that exceed the debt, the excess amount is paid to the debtor.

 CASE STUDY

General Motors Acceptance Corp. of Canada Ltd. v. Snowden et al., (1990), 76 D.L.R. (4th) 519 (N.B.C.A.)

The case of *General Motors Acceptance Corp. of Canada Ltd. v. Snowden et al.* illustrates that a secured creditor selling collateral must attempt to obtain a commercially reasonable sale price.

Facts: The defendant, Snowden, had financed the purchase of a car through the plaintiff, General Motors Acceptance. When Snowden defaulted on the loan payments, the creditor repossessed the car and sold it at a car auction restricted to licensed car dealers. The sale price at auction was approximately $6,000 less than the amount owing to the plaintiff. General Motors Acceptance demanded the defendant pay the remaining amount and he refused, claiming the sale had not taken place in good faith.

Decision: The court held General Motor Acceptance's action for the outstanding debt was refused. The creditor failed to show it had obtained the best price for the car. The auction involved car dealers who purchase at a low wholesale price, to resell at a profit. A better price would have been received through a retail sale of the vehicle.

Security for a loan can be taken against real property, in the form of a mortgage or charge (an immovable hypothec in Quebec).

Security for a debt can also be taken against personal property where the collateral can take the form of such things as accounts receivable, equipment, inventory, corporate shares, and even intellectual property rights.

At this point in his response, Sal referred Crnch to Chapter 9 of an excellent business law textbook called Business Law Today, *which included a discussion of real property and personal property being used as security for debt.*

The creditor, referred to as a secured creditor, can register its interest in the personal property through a public registry system. The common law provinces and territories have each enacted somewhat similar *Personal Property Security Acts* (PPSA) governing the creation, perfection through registration, and enforcement of security transactions involving personal property. A lien is filed under the PPSA by completing a financing statement and registering it with the government. Each province and territory provides an electronic system for the registration of a security interest created under a financing agreement over personal property. The proper registration of the financing statement formalizes or "perfects" the security interest in the creditor and generally establishes the priority of interests in the personal property.

Courtesy of Australian Financial Security Authority

In considering a loan to a startup company, an early-stage business operation, or a high-risk enterprise, the financial institution may require an individual or the directors of a corporation to pledge their personal assets as collateral for the loan to the business. As a business operation matures and grows, this requirement could be negotiated with the lender.

Guarantee

Another form of security for a loan involves a third party acting as a **guarantor** for the debt. The guarantor agrees to pay the debt if the borrower defaults in making the payment. The guarantee must be in writing, and until default occurs there is no liability on the guarantor. In the event the debtor and creditor agree to change the terms of the original loan without the written permission of the guarantor, the guarantor is released from his/her obligation under the loan. If the borrower defaults and the guarantor is called on by the creditor to pay the debt, the guarantor assumes the rights of the original creditor to receive payment of the debt, or, if secured, to sell the assets and apply the money against the debt.

> **Guarantor**—an individual who agrees to pay the debt of another person if that person defaults in making payment to the lender.

DID YOU KNOW?

Alberta Is Unique

The Alberta *Guarantees Acknowledgement Act* sets out a specific process requiring guarantees to be in writing from any person other than a corporation. As well, a lawyer must certify that the guarantor is aware of the guarantee and understands the obligation.

CRNCH TIME: Wow, Sal. I would rather not go into debt! What was the other option you mentioned?

Equity Financing

SAL: The alternative to debt financing is equity financing, which involves selling shares to investors who receive an ownership interest in the corporation. Those investors participate in the potential growth or failure of the business operation in exchange for the capital paid to buy the shares. For example, investors might be offered voting common shares in the corporation or preferred shares that carry a dividend but no right to vote on who will be directors of the company. The shares that are issued and the degree to which those shares can participate in making decisions will depend on whether the company is a private corporation or a public company listed on a stock exchange, the share structure of the corporation, and the type of financing the company wants to undertake.

An initial public offering or listing a company on a stock exchange to be able to sell to the public at large is complicated, requiring compliance with a very strict program of disclosure under provincial and territory securities legislation and regulators. An offering of this nature is generally undertaken with the help of a lawyer. There are also some private issuer exemptions available, but a strict set of criteria are applied if a closely held corporation wants to use these exemptions. A lawyer should be consulted if this form of equity financing is being considered.

Dooder / Shutterstock.com

Link to National Instrument 45-106: https://www.osc.gov.on.ca

Crowdfunding

Crowdfunding is a practice that has been growing rapidly, particularly as a popular way to fund a project or venture such as a startup company by raising many small amounts of money from a large number of people using the Internet. According to the Canada Revenue Agency, depending on the circumstances of the fundraising and the facts, the money raised could be seen as a loan, a capital contribution in the form of equity, a gift, business income, or some combination of these elements. In the context of a business, if the crowdfunding is for a new product, service, or project it would likely qualify as income for tax purposes.

In Canada, both private and public companies are able to raise funds by crowdfunding to a maximum amount of $1.5 million in any 12-month period. Financial statements and other necessary documents are required for this type of corporate financing, and investors will be subject to limits on the amount of money they may invest depending on their personal financial conditions and other factors. The crowdfunding transactions are conducted through an online gatekeeper that is a funding portal, independent of the issuer raising the funds, registered with the appropriate government agency. Corporations considering this type of crowdfunding will need to assess the benefits of being able to access a large pool of investors against the drawbacks of having a much larger number of shareholders with the rights attached to their ownership interest.

Sentavio | Dreamstime.com

DID YOU KNOW?

Acceptance of Crowdfunding

Multilateral Instrument 45-108—Crowdfunding, has been adopted in Manitoba, New Brunswick, Nova Scotia, Ontario, and Quebec. It is being considered for adoption in Saskatchewan. There is a limited startup crowdfunding rule in British Columbia.

Link to Multilateral Instrument 45-108—Crowdfunding: https://www.osc.gov.on.ca

DID YOU KNOW?

Crowdfunding in Alberta and Nunavut

Alberta and Nunavut are considering a prospectus exemption allowing a startup or early-stage business to raise up to $1 million using an offering document. Check current legislation if considering using crowdfunding in Alberta or Nunavut.

Financing Assistance through Government Programs

There are government programs to provide financial assistance to qualifying businesses at the federal and provincial/territorial levels.

The following is not a complete list of the various funding programs available, but provides an example of some of them. Appropriate government sites should be checked to determine the currency of a program.

Federal government programs:

- Export Development Canada—provides risk insurance for Canadian exporters and some loans to support sales of goods.
- The Business Development Bank of Canada (BDC)—provides high-risk loans to small and medium sized Canadian businesses through various Canadian banks, especially in knowledge-based industries.
- *Canada Small Business Financing Act*—through this legislation the government guarantees repayment of 90 percent of certain equipment and fixturing loans up to $500,000 made to small businesses by Canadian chartered banks.
- Employment and Social Development Canada (ESDC)—job creation subsidies through agreements with all provinces and territories.

Link to Employment and Social Development Canada: http://www.esdc.gc.ca/

Link to Service Canada: www.servicecanada.gc.ca/

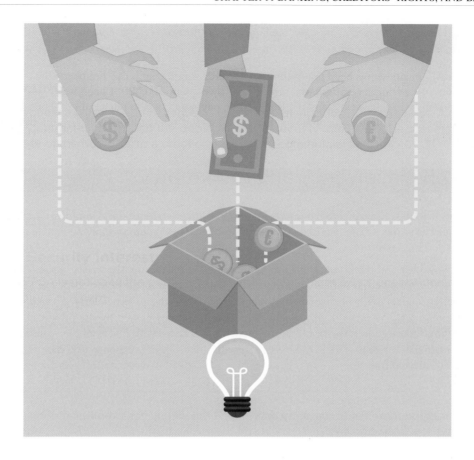

venimo / Shutterstock.com

Each province and territory has some form of government support programs. There may also be special provincial tax incentives and credits available to support local businesses.

Provincial government programs:

- Newfoundland/Labrador: www.business.gov.nl.ca
- Nova Scotia: www.gov.ns.ca/snsmr/business
- Ontario: www.ontario.ca
- Alberta: www.programs.alberta.ca/business
- Prince Edward Island: www.gov.pe.ca/infopei
- Quebec: www2.gouv.qc.ca
- Manitoba: www.gov.mb.ca/ctt
- New Brunswick: www.gnb.ca
- Saskatchewan: www.gov.sk.ca
- Yukon: www.gov.yk.ca/services
- British Columbia: www.gov.bc.ca/main_index/business_development
- Northwest Territories: www.iti.gov.nt.ca
- Nunavut: www.gov.nu.ca

Sal reviewed his message and pressed Send. He then turned his attention to a comment with the title "Besieged by Creditors—Help! (When is an asset not an asset?)," written by Goin Undr.

GOIN UNDR: Dear Sal. My business has been going through a VERY rough patch. I've not been able to pay the bills or make payments on the business loans for several months now. I now owe about $20,000. I keep receiving nasty letters from the creditors who are threatening to take next steps if I don't make payments on the outstanding debts. I know that it will all work out once a big order I'm trying to land comes in but don't know if my creditors will give me time. What choices do I have in this situation? Thanks.

LO 11.5   11.5 Insolvency and Bankruptcy

SAL: Hello, Goin Undr. It sounds like you are having a rough time right now. Let's start by taking a look at what the possible outcomes are in these circumstances. The fact that you owe more than $1,000 and have not been able to meet your payments technically means that you are insolvent.

The laws relating to insolvency and bankruptcy in Canada are aimed at preserving the assets of the debtor for the benefit of the creditors, while providing the debtor with an opportunity to restructure or let go of the burden of the debt and start again. The majority of the rules dealing with insolvency and bankruptcy are found in the federal government's *Bankruptcy and Insolvency Act* and *Companies' Creditors Arrangement Act*. Several statutes passed by the provinces and territories aimed at creating and preserving security interests for creditors impact this area as well. For example, you might look at the rights of secured creditors under the *Personal Property Security Act*, discussed in my response to Crnch (and in Chapter 9 of the excellent textbook I also referred him to).

> Link to the federal government's *Bankruptcy and Insolvency Act*, which provides a definition of insolvent person: www.laws-lois.justice.gc.ca

Bankruptcy and Insolvency Act

The federal *Bankruptcy and Insolvency Act* governs all insolvencies and bankruptcies in Canada and creates a process that can be applied to insolvency situations for almost any form of business organization—individuals, partnerships, and corporations. It details the responsibilities and rights of all the parties involved in the process, the Superintendent of Bankruptcy, the official receivers who represent the Superintendent of Bankruptcy, the court, licensed bankruptcy trustees, the debtor, and the creditor. Unlike the United States, Canada has no separate bankruptcy court. The Act gives jurisdiction to the provincial courts over which federally appointed judges preside.

Under the *Bankruptcy and Insolvency Act,* a business is insolvent if it owes its creditors $1,000 or more and is unable to meet its obligations generally as they come due. The Act allows debtors to make a proposal to their creditors to restructure their debt and try to reach a compromise. This can be done informally, through an agreement between the debtor and its creditors. The debtor's notice of intention to file a proposal creates a 30-day stay period that can be extended up to six months, against unsecured and most secured creditors. A trustee in bankruptcy is retained to work with the debtor to prepare the proposal, which is then sent to the official receiver for approval. If approved, the proposal is sent to the creditors who vote as a group to accept or reject the proposal. If accepted, the debt restructuring under the proposal is binding on the debtor and its unsecured creditors. Secured creditors still retain the right to seize and sell the secured assets. However, the debtor does not go into bankruptcy as long as it lives by the terms of the proposal.

WendellandCarolyn/Getty Images

DID YOU KNOW?

Courts for Insolvency Proceedings

Some provincial courts have established a commercial court branch to deal with insolvency proceedings. In Ontario, a specialized Commercial List branch was established for this purpose.

DID YOU KNOW?

Reciprocal Enforcement of Court Orders

The *Bankruptcy and Insolvency Act* and the *Companies' Creditors Arrangement Act* are federal statutes and contain provisions that require orders made by one provincial or territorial court to be recognized and enforced by the provincial or territorial courts in other jurisdictions.

Link to Canada's regulator of bankruptcy and insolvency, the Office of the Superintendent of Bankruptcy Canada: www.osb.ic.gc.ca

If the proposal is rejected, there are two possible actions. The debtor can make an assignment into bankruptcy voluntarily, or a creditor may apply to the court to have the debtor petitioned into bankruptcy.

If the debtor decides to act voluntarily, an assignment into bankruptcy is filed with the official receiver for that area. A trustee in bankruptcy takes control of the debtor's assets (referred to as the debtor's "estate"), meets with the creditors to confirm claims on the estate, sells the assets, and distributes the proceeds according the each creditor's percentage of interest in the estate of the bankrupt debtor.

If the debtor is petitioned into bankruptcy by its creditors, the creditors must obtain a receiving order from the court that will transfer substantially all of the debtor's assets into the hands of a court-appointed trustee in bankruptcy. A debtor will be allowed to retain some basic assets such as clothing, tools for a trade, and furniture. To get a receiving order, the creditors must prove the debtor owes at least $1,000 and has committed an act of bankruptcy as defined by the Act. The most common act of bankruptcy used for this purpose is insolvency, the debtor's inability to meet its obligations generally as they come due. Other acts of bankruptcy involve fraudulent preference by paying one creditor to the disadvantage of another creditor, or transferring ownership of an asset to another party prior to bankruptcy, a relative or friend for example, to keep the asset out of the hands of the creditors, known as a fraudulent conveyance.

DID YOU KNOW?

Acts of Bankruptcy

Certain acts of bankruptcy are in contravention of both the federal legislation and provincial/territorial statutes. A fraudulent preference contravenes both the federal *Bankruptcy and Insolvency Act* as well provincial or territorial legislation such as Ontario's *Assignments and Preferences Act.*

CASE STUDY

Viva Developments Inc. v. Icarus Properties Ltd., [2004] BCJ no. 1858 (SC)

The case of *Viva Developments Inc. v. Icarus Properties Ltd.* illustrates a fraudulent conveyance.

Facts: Viva Developments was awarded judgment against Icarus Properties in a court action. Following judgment and prior to the court attaching a dollar amount to the damages awarded, Icarus entered into a mortgage with its shareholders. Icarus claimed the mortgage was security for shareholder loans to the corporation and for management fees. The amount of the shareholder loans was found to be inflated. The resolution approving payment of management fees was passed by the board of directors after judgment was granted. Icarus claimed the main purpose for the mortgage transaction was to keep the company in business to avoid foreclosure proceedings.

Decision: The court held the granting of the mortgage was a fraudulent conveyance and therefor void. The court found it was intended to "delay, hinder, or defraud creditors...of their just and lawful remedies." The main purpose was to secure shareholder loans and management fees, not to keep the corporation in business.

LO 11.6   11.6 Creditors in a Bankruptcy

Once the assets are transferred to the trustee in bankruptcy, claims of creditors, other than secured creditors, are put on hold while the trustee reviews the claims of the creditors and evaluates the estate of the debtor. Subject to confirmation of the validity of their security and a short waiting period, secured creditors are not affected by the proceedings and are entitled to take possession and sell the secured assets. Unpaid suppliers have the right, under certain circumstances, to reclaim goods that were delivered to the debtor within the 30 days preceding the bankruptcy. Any payments or transfers of assets that took place within certain defined periods prior to bankruptcy that impact on the claims of creditors can be challenged by the trustee in bankruptcy. The trustee sells the remaining assets, establishes the priorities of creditors' claims, and distributes the proceeds.

There are three basic classes of creditors in a bankruptcy procedure. In priority, they are the secured creditors, the preferred creditors, and the unsecured creditors.

- *Secured creditors*—this class of creditor may take possession of the secured goods and sell them to pay the debt. Any surplus funds are given to the trustee, or if the proceeds are not enough to eliminate the debt, the creditor ranks as an unsecured creditor for the balance.

- *Preferred creditors*—this class of creditor includes, among others, the trustee in bankruptcy for the fees involved in the bankruptcy process, funeral expenses, landlords for up to three months' back rent on leased premises, and some employee claims for unpaid wages.

- *Unsecured creditors*—this class of creditor shares in the total remaining proceeds from the sale of the debtor's estate after payment of the preferred creditors. Each unsecured creditor receives a percentage of what was owed to it.

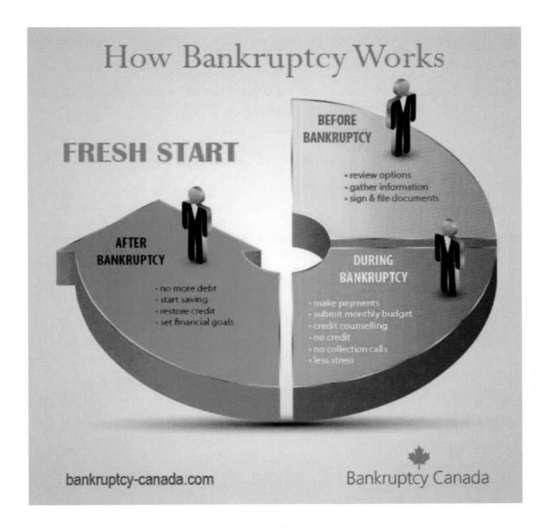

J. Douglas Hoyes, LIT, Bankruptcy-canada.com

The court usually discharges a debtor from bankruptcy without conditions within one year. However, if a creditor objects to the unconditional discharge, a hearing will be held and the debtor may receive a conditional discharge, for example subject to certain payments to be made to a creditor, or an absolute discharge. An absolute discharge remains subject to certain debts that a bankruptcy cannot extinguish, such as an order for family support or a court-assessed penalty.

A receivership involves creditors applying to the court to have a receiver appointed. The receiver assumes control of the property and operations of the debtor and continues running the business for the benefit of the creditors.

A secured creditor will usually include terms in the security agreement giving it the right to take over management of the business in the event of a default under the agreement. In this case a professional receiver will be appointed under authority of the terms in the security agreement and there is no need to proceed through a formal bankruptcy process.

Link to *Bankruptcy and Insolvency Act* and *Companies' Creditors Arrangement Act*: www.laws-lois.justice.gc.ca

Companies' Creditors Arrangement Act

The federal *Companies' Creditors Arrangement Act* governs the insolvency of corporations. It allows an insolvent company with total debts over $5 million to restructure its financial affairs. A formal plan of arrangement or compromise with the creditors is reached that allows the business to avoid bankruptcy while the creditors receive some form of debt repayment.

Link to *Companies' Creditors Arrangement Act* Records List of all companies owing creditors over $5 million: https://www.ic.gc.ca/eic/site/bsf-osb.nsf/eng/h_br02281.html

SAL: So, Goin, based on the information provided above you can see a number of possibilities exist regarding what can be done in your situation. Each set of circumstances in an insolvency or bankruptcy is unique and there are both federal and provincial/territorial laws that apply. There are organizations in each province and territory to assist businesses facing the issues that you are currently dealing with. For example, Bankruptcy Canada has a website with an enormous amount of information concerning bankruptcy and insolvency organizations, as well as applicable legislation at the federal and provincial/territorial levels. You may want to speak with a licensed bankruptcy trustee in your area to discuss your company's financial issues and get appropriate information to deal with your specific situation.

Sal tapped Send and leaned back in his chair. It had been a long day. A short clip from his favourite movie soundtrack alerted him to a text on his cell phone. It read: Where R U? Garnet and I are waiting at the restaurant to discuss next steps in franchising our business!!

Looks like Sal's evening was just about to start...

FOR REVIEW

Questions

1. How are debit cards governed? (LO 11.2)
2. What is a general security agreement? (LO 11.4)
3. What are the rights of a secured creditor under a PPSA registration? (LO 11.4, 11.5, 11.6)
4. Who are the parties to a guarantee? What rights and obligations does each party have? (LO 11.4)
5. Compare equity financing with debt financing. What are the advantages and drawbacks of both? (LO 11.3)
6. Identify the risks and benefits of crowdfunding. (LO 11.4)
7. What is the definition of insolvency? (LO 11.5)
8. Explain what constitutes an act of bankruptcy. (LO 11.5)
9. Indicate whether the following are federal or provincial/territorial chartered financial institutions: (LO 11.1)
   a. Commercial banks
   b. Caisses populaires
   c. Credit unions
   d. Branches of a foreign bank
10. Explain whether a patent may be used as collateral to secure a loan. (LO 9.6, 11.4)

Activities

1. List and briefly explain each of the three categories of creditors in an insolvency/bankruptcy. (LO 11.6)

2. What is the purpose of having a public registry for security interests in borrowers' assets? (LO 9.3, 11.4)

3. Discuss whether you think the federal government's "Code of Conduct for the Credit and Debit Card Industry in Canada" should be voluntary or mandatory for business operators. (LO 11.2)

4. How is a security interest "perfected," and why is this important? (LO 11.4)

5. What is the purpose of the *Bankruptcy and Insolvency Act*? (LO 11.5)

6. Should a secured creditor rank higher in priority than an unsecured creditor for any remaining debt after the secured asset has been sold for less than the loan amount? (LO 11.4, 11.6)

7. Explain the benefits and problems involved with debt financing for a business. (LO 11.3)

8. Discuss whether it is reasonable for a lender to a corporation to require a director to personally guarantee the corporation's loan. (LO 10.5, 10.6, 11.3, 11.4, 11.6)

9. Outline the elements that constitute an act of bankruptcy and discuss whether they are appropriate to current business operations. (LO 11.5)

CASES FOR DISCUSSION

Case #1

Jared's business has been experiencing a huge decline in sales over the past 12 months. Five months ago, Jared had to suspend payments on the two loans with his bank and a private investor in order to keep business going. The business is now $65,000 in debt and he is not sure what to do. Jared believes that the business will improve in another three months when a new bus stop in front of his store is added to the transit line. On the other hand, Jared is not sure he can take another three months of phone calls and letters from his lenders and suppliers demanding payment or else.

a. Explain to Jared the differences between insolvency and bankruptcy. (LO 11.5)

b. Explain to Jared the process of submitting a proposal to creditors under the *Bankruptcy and Insolvency Act*. (LO 11.5)

c. What are Jared's alternatives if the proposal is rejected? (LO 11.5)

Case #2

Adelaide had saved a considerable sum of money over the years. She was very proud of her niece Elandra, who had incorporated and started her own horseracing stable, which had become quite successful and quickly grown to four horses. Elandra's horses had done very well at the racetrack and she was in the process of planning the next stage in the development of her racing stable. To make her plans a reality, Elandra required financing of $100,000. She was experiencing difficulty in finding the money because of the risky nature of horse racing and the fact she had been in operation for only four years.

Adelaide believes Elandra has what it takes to be a success and wants to help her by investing in the racing stable. Adelaide also wants to make sure that the risk to her investment is minimal. Adelaide heard that you took an excellent business course at college and has come to you for advice.

Please advise Adelaide on:

a. The options available for investing in Elandra's business. (LO 11.3)

b. The process involved with each form of investment. (LO 11.3)

c. The risks and benefits associated with each form of investment. (LO 11.3)

Case #3

Kendal's 10-year-old IT security company, Security Focus First (SFF), has achieved great success. It began as a sole proprietorship that later became a corporation that moved progressively forward toward obtaining financing with selling shares in the company to friends and family. Now Kendal has been told by other successful CEOs that the time is ripe for SFF to obtain more financing by "going public."

How should Kendal take his company public? What is involved? What advice would you give to Kendal? (LO 11.3)

Glossary

Acceleration Clause Term in the mortgage agreement that permits the mortgagee to demand immediate payment of the full amount of the loan in the event of a default.

Action A litigation term where one party sues another.

Alternative Dispute Resolution (ADR) Different ways to solve a dispute that do not involve the formality of a court or civil litigation such as mediation and arbitration.

Amortization Period The length of time it takes to repay a mortgage loan in full following the schedule of payments set out in the mortgage.

Appeal When the losing party in any court case disagrees with the decision of the court, it will wish to have a higher court look at the case and come to a decision.

Arbitration (1) Parties come together in a process that is more formal than mediation but less formal than a court setting to resolve their issues with the assistance of a selected arbitrator. (2) In a union context, a final resolution where both parties agree to the decision of the arbitrator. Once decided, the decision cannot be appealed; the decision of the arbitrator is final and binding.

Arbitrator Parties come together to solve their issue(s) with the assistance of an arbitrator who is trained in the more formal arbitration process and is prepared to make a decision on the issue that is final and binding.

Arbitrator and/or Conciliator A third party who helps resolve labour disputes between a business and the union.

Assault The intention or threat of unwanted physical contact that causes harm.

Assignee A person who receives rights from an assignor under an assignment.

Assignment An arrangement under which the tenant transfers the tenancy to another person for the balance of the term of the lease.

Assignor A person who transfers rights to an assignee under an assignment.

Bailee Person in possession of the goods under a bailment.

Bailment The legal relationship that arises when the elements of ownership and possession of personal property are intentionally divided for a period of time.

Bailor Owner of the goods under a bailment.

Balance of Probabilities In a civil matter, the standard of proof requiring that something be proven to have more likely occurred than not occurred.

Battery The physical intentional and unconsented contact that causes harm; is an unlawful offence and a tort.

Binding Arbitration A decision by an arbitrator or an arbitration board that is final and cannot be appealed.

Breach The failure of a party to perform their obligations to the other party's reasonable satisfaction.

Business Ethics The way a business behaves; moral decisions made by the stakeholders of a business.

Business Exposure Actions that make a business vulnerable.

Business Law All the laws that are created in order to form and run a business.

Capacity The parties must be capable of understanding what they are getting into.

Chambers Where judge and lawyers present motions that affect the case for a decision by the judge (in some provinces, e.g., Nova Scotia).

Charter of Rights and Freedoms Included in the Canadian Constitution, 1982; protects Canadians' fundamental freedoms such as freedom of religion, our mobility, legal and democratic rights, to name a few.

Cheques Bills of exchange drawn against a bank and payable on demand.

Civil Law The area of law that deals with parties that have a dispute. The parties go through a well-defined process in order to bring the matter to a resolution. The plaintiff must prove her/his case on the balance of probabilities.

Civil Litigation Process The process that the party suing or being sued must go through from the beginning to the final disposition.

Claim The plaintiff's legal assertion or demand for a loss; the defendant can respond to this claim.

Collective Bargaining Negotiation between a union and management to reach a union contract that outlines the rules that govern the relationship.

Common Law Based on decisions handed down from case to case that is not criminal law; decisions of previous and similar cases are used as a basis for a court decision.

Common Shares Have the right to vote on certain corporate matters and to receive a percentage share of the residual property of the corporation on its dissolution.

Conciliation Used when issues between the parties require resolution by a third party in a voluntary, flexible, and results-oriented manner.

Condition An essential term of a contract.

Condition Precedent A clause that ends a contract when a certain condition necessary for the contract to be performed is not met.

Condition Subsequent An uncertain event which, if it occurs, ends the contract.

Confidential Information Information that retains its commercial value as long as the public or a competitor does not know it.

Consideration The obligations each party owes to the other under the contract.

Consignment The transfer of possession of goods from one person to another for the purpose of offering the goods for sale.

Constitution Act Constitution Act 1867 outlines the executive and legislative powers of federal and provincial governments; Constitution Act 1982 entrenches the Canadian Charter of Rights and Freedoms as well as other rights such as Aboriginal rights.

Constructive Dismissal Occurs when the employee has not been fired but believes the employer has not complied with the terms of the employment contract.

Consumer Product Means a product, including its components, parts, or accessories, that may reasonably be expected to be obtained by an individual to be used for non-commercial purposes, including for domestic, recreational, and sports purposes, and includes its packaging.

Contracts Agreements that are enforceable through the law, agreed upon by two or more parties with benefits for all parties to the contract.

Contributory Negligence (1) Plaintiff's own conduct contributed or caused the damage. (2) Where the court apportions responsibility to the injured.

Copyright Statutory protection of the intellectual property rights of the creators of musical, dramatic, literary and artistic works, and software.

Corporation A legal entity created by government legislation that has a separate existence from its owners.

Costs The judgment may include a portion of the costs (legal fees, filing fees, etc.) the successful party incurred during the course of the case and paid by the unsuccessful party.

Counter Offer A new offer that also rejects the previous or original offer.

Counter-Claim A claim made by the defendant against the plaintiff in the same matter.

Criminal Law The area of law where a defendant is charged with a crime and the lawyer who prosecutes the accused (the Crown prosecutor) brings the defendant to trial. The Crown prosecutor must prove beyond a reasonable doubt that the defendant is guilty of the crime(s).

Cross-Claim A claim against a co-defendant.

Damages A remedy that is in the form of money.

Debt Financing Borrowing capital for a period of time and repaying the loan plus any interest charged in accordance with the terms of the loan agreement.

Defamation A false statement that must harm a person's or business's reputation.

Defence The response by the defendant to the claims/demands made by the plaintiff.

Defendant A person(s) or organization that is being sued.

Director's Fiduciary Duty An obligation to act honestly, in good faith and in the best interests of the corporation.

Discovery A meeting where questions and answers are asked of the parties and their witnesses, held under oath, prior to trial to obtain further information and evidence.

Dismissal Occurs when an employer informs an employee that they are no longer employed at their business.

Due Diligence The obligation for corporate directors to ensure proper measures have been taken to comply with legal duties.

Duress Coercing a party into entering a contract through the threat or use of harm to their person, their reputation, or their finances.

Duty of Care Not to cause injury; is owed by one individual or business to another.

Employee A person who is given direction and supervision along with the resources to do the job in exchange for money for work they do below a management level.

Employer A business or organization that gives direction and supervision to a person and provides the resources to do the job in exchange for money.

Employment Contract An agreement outlining the specifics of an employer and employee's responsibilities for a period of time; can be written or verbal.

Employment Law An area of law that governs the relationship between the business and its employees.

Equity Financing Selling shares in a corporation to investors.

Exclusion Clause A term that removes liability and damages after certain specified breaches.

Expectation Damages Compensation for the loss of profit caused by a breach, calculated based on the profit a person anticipated earning from the contract.

Express Repudiation A stated intention by a party not to perform any of their obligations under a contract.

Express Terms In a written contract, the terms that actually appear in the document.

Fair Dealing Permitted use or copying of copyrighted material for specific limited purposes such as research and review.

False Imprisonment Intentionally confining an unwilling person within a specified area.

Federal Court of Canada Deals with cases between individuals or organizations and the federal government, such as income tax disputes; also deals with patents, customs, immigration, and maritime law.

Fee Simple Ownership The most absolute form of land ownership, including the right to exclusive possession and the right to transfer the land for an indefinite period of time.

Fiduciary Duty A standard by which professionals have a legal responsibility to their client to provide a service or advice in the best interest of their client without personal gain.

Filing Presenting your documents: claim, defence, or counter-claim, for example, to the court and the opposing parties.

Fixed Tenancy A tenancy that has a fixed beginning and end date that can be for any period of time, from months to years.

Fixtures Movable property/chattels that become permanently fixed to the land, such as a fence.

Floating Charge A security interest on a class of collateral which may change, that allows the debtor to dispose of, replace, and add to assets in that class.

Foreclosure A court action following which the lender obtains legal title to the real property after default by the borrower under a mortgage.

Franchise A business arrangement formed by a written agreement in which a business grants the right to use its trade name, trademark, and operating procedures to operate a similar business.

Franchisee The person receiving the rights from the franchisor under the franchise agreement.

Franchisor The person granting the rights under the franchise agreement.

Fraudulent Misrepresentation A false statement made by one party about an important term in a contract that they know was a reason why the other party agreed to the contract.

Frustration An unforeseen outside event that makes a contract impossible to perform, or changes it completely from what the parties intended.

Gratuitous Promise Doing, or agreeing to do, something for another person with no expectation of getting anything in return.

Gratuitous Waiver The release by one party of the other party from performing their obligations under the contract. It is gratuitous because the releasing party does not receive the benefit to which they are entitled.

Guarantor An individual who agrees to pay the debt of another person if that person defaults in making payment to the lender.

Human Rights Legislation Federal, provincial, and municipal legislation that is determined by the division of powers under the *Canadian Charter of Rights and Freedoms* to prohibit discrimination in all aspects of business.

Illegal Strike Occurs when there is a collective agreement and employees have no legal platform to strike.

Implied Repudiation An intention by a party not to perform any of their obligations under a contract that can be presumed by their actions or lack thereof.

Implied Terms Items occasionally added to contracts by judges in situations where the contract reaches the courts.

Indemnification A promise by one party to bear the monetary costs for losses or damages incurred by another party.

Independent Contractor Performs a service for an employer and renders an invoice or bill.

Inducing Breach of Contract An economic tort where a person or person convinces a third party to breach his/her contract with the plaintiff.

Industrial Design Unique visual elements incorporated as part of a manufactured product's design.

Injurious Falsehood When a reputation is lost because of false statements about a product or service. Also called slander of goods.

Innocent Misrepresentation A false statement, made by one party about an important term in a contract, which they in good faith believed to be true, that was a reason why the other party agreed to the contract.

Intangible Personal Property Things that can't be physically touched, e.g., reputation, goodwill, etc.; sometimes called a *chose in action*.

Intellectual Property A type of personal property resulting from an individual's creative activities.

Intentional Tort Deliberate harm.

Interference with Economic Relations Deliberate illegal interference with the interests of a third party.

Interrogatories Written questions provided by one party to the other that are answered in writing and signed under oath.

Intrusion upon Seclusion Where one intrudes upon the seclusion or privacy of another.

Invasion of Privacy Private information that is disclosed to unauthorized people.

Invitation to Treat Anything that shows a willingness to conduct a business transaction.

Invitee A person, persons, or organization that enters the land of the occupier with an invitation so that the occupier benefits from the invitee's business.

Joint Venture A business activity, usually for a specific project or time period, carried on by two or more parties according to terms and conditions set out in a contract.

Judgment The remedy given to the successful party by the court.

Judicial Sale A court-ordered and -administered sale of property after default under a mortgage.

Land Titles System A system of land registration under which the provincial government guarantees the accuracy of the title to the land.

Laws The rules of conduct that protect the rights of individuals and businesses.

Lawsuit A dispute between two or more parties brought before a civil court for a decision.

Lease A contract setting out the terms and conditions for the rental of a property.

Leave to Appeal Permission for a case to be heard in the Supreme Court of Canada.

Legal Strike Occurs when there is no collective agreement in effect.

Legality The purpose of the contract must be legal, and even if legal, must be one that a court of law believes should be enforced.

Libel Written defamation.

Licence A contractual right to use a trademark, copyright, patent, industrial design, or trade secret for a specified limited purpose and time.

Licensee (1) A person, persons, or organization that enters the land of the occupier with permission. (2) The individual receiving the right to use a copyright, trademark, patent, industrial design, or trade secret.

Licensor The individual granting the right to use a copyright, trademark, patent, industrial design, or trade secret.

Limitation of Liability Clause A term in a contract that places a limit on the amount of damages that would follow a breach of the contract.

Limited Partnership Consists of at least one general partner that is liable for the debts and obligations of the partnership to an unlimited degree and at least one limited partner whose liability is limited to the amount contributed to the partnership business.

Line of Credit A debt arrangement under which a lender agrees to make a maximum amount of money available to a borrower.

Liquidated Damages Clause A genuine negotiated estimate of the amount of damages that would follow a breach of the contract.

Litigation A complex process to resolve a legal dispute in the civil court system based on the evidence presented by those involved in the dispute.

Lockout Employers do not allow employees to enter the premises to work, usually during the bargaining process.

Mediation (1) Parties come together and solve their issue(s) with the assistance of a trained mediator. (2) In a union context, occurs when a third party helps to resolve issues between the parties and assists in developing a solution. Not used in a union–management dispute.

Mediator A trained and certified third party who will assist the parties with their dispute through negotiation.

Mistakes Wrongful beliefs about the terms of a contract that cause a person to enter into it.

Mortgage A debt using real property as security.

Mortgage Term The length of time for which the mortgage loan is available to the borrower.

Mortgagee The lender under a mortgage.

Mortgagor The borrower/owner under a mortgage.

Negligence A failure to exercise the degree of care toward another individual expected of a reasonable person in the circumstances.

Nondisclosure Agreements Contracts between two or more parties to maintain information exchanged between them confidential.

Nuisance The interference in the right to enjoy real property.

Occupier A person, persons, or organization that may be the owner, landlord, tenant, or anyone who has responsibility, dictates the activities, and decides who enters the property.

Offer A promise to enter into a contract, under complete and specific terms, once there is a communicated acceptance.

Offeree The person to whom the offer is made.

Offeror The person making an offer.

Option Agreements Contracts between a potential buyer and the seller of some item whereby in exchange for a fee the seller gives the potential buyer the first chance to buy the item, up to a certain date.

Option to Terminate A condition, for example giving notice, that allows a party to end the contract.

Partnership A legal relationship between two or more persons carrying on a business for the purpose of earning a profit.

Partnership Agreement An agreement among all the partners in which such issues as management and procedures for carrying on the business, the division of profits and contributions, and dispute resolution are addressed.

Passing Off Falsely representing to the public another company's product or service as your own.

Patents Statutory grants of an exclusive right to make, sell, and use an invention within the jurisdiction in which it is granted.

Performance The completion of a party's obligations under a contract to the reasonable satisfaction of the other party.

Periodic Tenancy A tenancy that renews automatically at the end of the relevant rental period until terminated by the landlord or the tenant.

Personal Property All property that is not real property.

Plaintiff A person(s) or organization that sues another person or organization.

Pleadings Written legal documents that start and defend a claim/allegation (e.g., statement of claim, defence, cross-claim, counter-claim, etc.).

Post Box Rule An offer is accepted when the acceptance is given to the postal service, not when it is received by the offeror.

Power of Sale A remedy available to the lender under a mortgage allowing the sale of the real property in the case of default.

Pre-trial Applications Motions made before the court and made in chambers (less formal) where the judge decides on small matters connected with the case.

Preferred (Preference) Shares Have a priority over other classes of shares in terms of certain corporate actions, such as the payment of dividends.

Privacy Plan (or Policy) A list of rules of conduct for employees relating to the creation, usage, control, and maintenance of information.

Private Corporation Subject to a limit on its total number of shareholders whose shares are not offered for sale to the public.

Private Law Sets the rules of engagement between individuals. Also called *civil law*.

Product Liability The responsibility of the manufacturer to create safe products.

Professional Liability A tort of negligence for professionals that protects them from economic loss in the event that their client suffers from injury due to the service(s) they have provided.

Property Law A field of law that includes a broad range of legal rights and duties in the areas of real property and personal property.

Public Corporation Sells shares to the public through a recognized stock exchange in compliance with provincial or territorial securities regulations.

Public Law Sets the rules for the relationship between the person(s)/organization and society.

Public Policy The purpose of the contract must not conflict with the interests of society.

Quantum Meruit A Latin phrase meaning "what one has earned"; it is how contract law determines that a reasonable price has been paid for a service.

Quiet Enjoyment The right of the lessee to occupy and use the leased premises without interference by the landlord. Also known as *quiet possession*.

Rand Formula States that regardless of an employee's union status, they must pay their labour union dues.

Real Property Land, including everything attached to it.

Reasonable Person An ordinary person, someone who would give careful thought to the probable results of their actions before taking the first step in performing them.

Registry System A system of land registration operated by provincial governments to record interests in land; generally requires title to the property to be searched back 40 years for the current owner's interest to the land to be considered clear.

Regulations Laws developed by departments and other organizations in specific areas.

Rejection A negative statement that terminates the current offer.

Reliance Damages Compensation for expenses incurred because one party relied upon the other party to perform their part of the contract, intended to put the injured party back in its precontract position.

Remedy The compensation, financial or other, when a person(s) is successful in a lawsuit. Also called damages.

Remoteness of Damage No reasonable connection exists between the actions of the defendant and the harm caused to the plaintiff.

Restrictive Covenants Items in an employment contract that outline conditions, promises, and restrictions of the employee with regard to the business.

Right of Distress The right of a commercial landlord to seize and dispose of the tenant's property following nonpayment of rent.

Right of Forfeiture The landlord's remedy of evicting the tenant for breach of an obligation under the lease.

Risk Management A positive business management practice that realizes and assesses the risks associated with the activities of the business.

Royalty A payment made to the licensor in exchange for the use of a copyright, trademark, patent, industrial design, or trade secret; the amount usually is based on a percentage of sales or the number of units produced.

Seal A mark on a contract that signifies the intention of the parties to be bound by the terms even in the absence of any consideration.

Security Agreement An agreement that sets out the rights and obligations of the borrower and lender and creates a security interest in the personal property of the borrower.

Security Interest An interest in personal property that secures the payment of a debt.

Settlement Resolution of the dispute that is acceptable to both sides bringing the matter to its final disposition.

Severance Pay Where the employee is provided termination or separation pay based on the specific duration of their employment and they lose their job. It's most common when massive layoffs occur. It is most commonly calculated by the employee's salary multiplied by the number of weeks/years worked up to a specified number of weeks/years. These calculations do vary, however, and are determined by the employer.

Shareholders' Agreement A written agreement between two or more shareholders of a corporation setting out specific terms and conditions that will govern their relationship during or after incorporation.

Shares Percentage interests in a corporation.

Slander Oral defamation.

Sole Proprietorship A business operated for a profit by one individual who is responsible for the debts and liabilities.

Stakeholders People and groups that are directly and indirectly involved in the business such as employees, shareholders, suppliers, and charitable organizations.

Stare Decisis A doctrine where lower courts, in similar matters, use the decisions of higher courts.

Statute A law enacted at the municipal, provincial, or federal level.

Statute Law A set of codes, rules, and regulations that are created by the government or an administrative body (e.g., *Criminal Code of Canada, Income Tax Act, Copyright Act, Matrimonial Property Act, Family Law Act*).

Strike Work stoppage in a unionized environment; can be a refusal to work, a slowdown of work, and various other options. A strike can be a legal or an illegal strike.

Sublet An arrangement under which the tenant leaves a leased space for a specified period of time and allows another person to occupy the leased space until the tenant returns to resume occupancy.

Substantial Performance Occurs when all except for a trivial part of the contract obligations have been performed.

Substantive Aspects of Contracts What a contract is actually going to do.

Tangible Personal Property Things that can be touched that are movable, e.g., furniture, consumer goods, etc.; sometimes called *chattels*.

Tender of Performance An attempt by one party to a contract to perform its obligations under the contract. Indicates a willingness, readiness, and ability to complete the contract.

Termination Pay Payment by the employer to the employee when an employee is fired for the time they would have been paid had they not been fired and been given notice. This happens when an employer does not give dismissal notice.

Test for Remoteness of Damages The cost and effect of a party's breach of contract must have been something that could have been predicted at the time the contract was formed.

Tort An action committed by an individual or business that causes harm, intentionally or unintentionally.

Tortfeasor The person committing a tort.

Trade Secrets Confidential information regarding a product or production process that has commercial value to the owner.

Trademarks Identifiable features used to distinguish the goods or services of a business from those offered by another.

Trespass to Chattels Causing damage, destroying, using, or removing a plaintiff's chattels.

Trespass to Land Entering and/or occupying land or property not owned and without permission or restricting the enjoyment of the property by its owners.

Trespasser A person, persons, or organization that enters the land of the occupier without legal right or permission.

Trial The formal hearing of a court case before a judge (or jury or both).

Unanimous Shareholders' Agreement A written agreement among all of the shareholders of a corporation that restricts in whole or in part the powers of the directors to manage or supervise the management of the business and affairs of the corporation.

Undue Influence Influencing a party into entering a contract through the abuse of a position of dominance.

Unintentional Tort Not deliberate harm.

Union A collection of employees in a trade or employment organization formed to protect and further their rights and interests through the negotiation with management and establishment of a signed contract that outlines every aspect of the employment relationship for a specific duration.

Union Contract A legal document between employees and management that outlines the rights, terms, conditions, and benefits that all employees of that union can expect for a specific period of time; also called a *collective agreement*.

Utmost Good Faith A duty of disclosure, arising out of a special relationship of trust between the parties.

Vicarious Liability An employer is responsible for injuries caused by an employee while acting in the course of their employment.

Void Contract A contract regarded by the courts as never having existed, with neither party able to enforce anything under it.

Voidable Contract A contract whose defect allows one of the parties to end the contract as if it had never existed.

Voluntary Assumption of Risk The plaintiff is aware of the risk associated with the activity and has consented to assume that risk.

Warranty A minor term of a contract. Any term less important than a condition is assumed to be a warranty.

Wildcat Strike An unofficial action where employees walk out of their employment with no warning to the employer or to union officials.

Wrongful Dismissal Occurs when an employer does not have the basis to dismiss an employee; there is no cause for dismissal under their contract or under a statute of law; also called *unjust dismissal*.

Index